The
Wenner-Gren
Foundation
For Anthropological Research, Inc.

Hearing Cultures

WENNER-GREN INTERNATIONAL SYMPOSIUM SERIES

Series Editor: Richard G. Fox, President, Wenner-Gren Foundation for Anthropological Research, New York.

ISSN: 1475-536X

Since its inception in 1941, the Wenner-Gren Foundation has convened more than 125 international symposia on pressing issues in anthropology. Wenner-Gren International symposia recognize no boundaries—intellectual, national, or subdisciplinary. These symposia affirm the worth of anthropology and its capacity to address the nature of humankind from a great variety of perspectives. They make new links to related disciplines, such as law, history, and ethnomusicology, and revivify old links, as between archaeology and sociocultural anthropology, for example. Each symposium brings together participants from around the world, for a week-long engagement with a specific issue, but only after intensive planning of the topic and format over the previous 18 months.

In fulfilling its mission to build a world community of anthropologists and to support basic research in anthropology, the Foundation now extends its distinctive and productive pattern of pre-symposium planning to the preparation and publication of the resulting volumes. Never before has the Foundation taken responsibility for publishing the papers from its international symposia. By initiating this series, the Foundation wishes to ensure timely publication, wide distribution, and high production standards. The President of the Foundation serves as the series editor, and the symposium organizers edit the individual volumes.

Some landmark volumes from the past are: *Man's Role in Changing the Face of the Earth* in 1956 (William L. Thomas); *Man the Hunter* in 1968 (Irven DeVore and Richard B. Lee); *Cloth and Human Experience* in 1989 (Jane Schneider and Annette Weiner); and *Tools, Language, and Cognition in Human Evolution* in 1993 (Kathleen Gibson and Tim Ingold). Reports on recent symposia can be found on the foundation's website, *www.wennergren.org*, and inquiries should be addressed to *president@wennergren.org*.

The
Wenner-Gren
Foundation

For Anthropological Research, Inc.

Hearing Cultures

Essays on Sound, Listening, and Modernity

Edited by

VEIT ERLMANN

BERG

Oxford · New York

English edition
First published in 2004 by
Berg
Editorial offices:
1st Floor, Angel Court, St Clements Street, Oxford, OX4 1AW, UK
175 Fifth Avenue, New York, NY 10010, USA

Paperback edition reprinted in 2005

Berg is the imprint of Oxford International Publishers Ltd.

Library of Congress Cataloging-in-Publication Data

A catalogue record for this book is available from the Library of
Congress.

British Library Cataloguing-in-Publication Data

A catalogue record for this book is available from the British Library.

ISBN 978-1-85973-823-8 (Cloth)
      978-1-85973-828-3 (Paper)

Typeset by JS Typesetting Ltd, Wellingborough, Northants.
Printed in Great Britain by the MPG Books Group, Bodmin and King's Lynn

www.bergpublishers.com

Contents

Acknowledgments

The essays gathered here originated in a symposium held on 24–28 April 2002 in Oaxaca, Mexico. The event was generously funded by the Wenner-Gren Foundation for Anthropological Research. I thank its president, Richard Fox, for bringing up the idea of a conference of this sort and especially for his forbearance when the symposium had to be postponed in the wake of the events of September 11, 2001. Special thanks are also due to Laurie Obbink, conference organizer at Wenner-Gren, for making travel arrangements, circulating draft papers, and delicately reminding contributors of deadlines.

Not all the papers presented at the symposium were included in this volume. A report on the event itself can be found at http://www.wennergren.org/progisp129.html#129.

Participants in the 2002 Wenner-Gren Symposium

Linda Austern, Northwestern University
Michael Bull, University of Sussex
Paul Carter, University of Melbourne
Steven Connor, University of London
Veit Erlmann, University of Texas (Austin)
Penelope Gouk, University of Manchester
Charles Hirschkind, University of California (Berkeley)
Douglas Kahn, University of California (Davis)
Janis B. Nuckolls, University of Alabama
Hillel Schwartz, independent scholar
Anthony Seeger, University of California (Los Angeles)
Bruce R. Smith, University of Southern California
Emily Thompson, Massachusetts Institute of Technology

But What of the Ethnographic Ear? Anthropology, Sound, and the Senses

Veit Erlmann

In the introduction to *Writing Culture: The Poetics and Politics of Ethnography*, one of the most influential and controversial collections of anthropological writing to have appeared in almost two decades, James Clifford asks an unexpected question: "But what of the ethnographic ear?" (Clifford 1986: 12). Given the context in which it appears, the inquiry about the ear appears to be at odds with the idea—by now enjoying a certain, albeit contested, hegemony within anthropology and the humanities more broadly—that culture is ultimately the result of acts of inscription and that anthropology, because it seeks to decipher the meanings resulting from these inscriptions, is best understood as an act of reading and interpretation. So why bother about the ear?

Clifford's answer seems plausible enough. The impact of critiques of "visualism" advanced by Walter Ong and other scholars of orality on the then emergent interpretive anthropology, he suggests, has made us aware of the need for a "cultural poetics that is an interplay of voices, of positioned utterances" (1986: 12). In such a poetics, he claims, "the dominant metaphors for ethnography shift away from the observing eye and toward expressive speech (and gesture). The writer's 'voice' pervades and situates the analysis, and objective, distancing rhetoric is renounced."

One knows what has become of this renunciation of the observing eye and distancing rhetoric, and this is not the place for prolonging a debate over the merits of an intended paradigm shift in anthropology that certainly produced more "utterances" but rather few accounts of actual listening practices. Not that anthropologists have given short shrift to the body and sensory perception. But few are those who have actually approached the senses as more than just another "text" to be read. Among the notable exceptions are David Howes (2003), Nadia Seremetakis (1994), Michael Taussig (1993), and Paul Stoller (1989).[1] In the work of the last two authors, in particular, one gains a clearer sense of the limitations and problems of the "textual" paradigm and of the ways in which attention to the senses might not only yield new and richer kinds of ethnographic data but, perhaps more importantly, also force us to rethink a broad range of theoretical and methodological issues. Thus, Stoller's long experience with Songhay cultural practice has led him to formulate the outlines of what he calls a "sensuous scholarship." Similarly, Taussig's work on the Cuna and their entanglement with the forces of Western domination prompted him to question the estranging and authoritarian uses of mimetic technologies and to mobilize mimesis for a more reflexive, mutually empowering kind of representation. The result is a kind of scholarship in which images and sounds—ours and theirs—adhere more to the skin of things and thereby erode the alterity on which so many of our disciplinary practices rest.

The scarcity of ethnographic accounts of sensory perception stands in marked contrast to a flurry of recent publications from other disciplines bearing on topics as diverse as the role of auscultation, sound in film, and twentieth-century avant-garde verbal arts—to name just a few examples of work by authors not represented in this volume and published since 2000 (Kassabian 2001; Meyer-Kalkus 2000; Sterne 2003). Even in ethnomusicology and musicology—two disciplines that might lay superior claim to sound and auditory perception as their very birthright—a new thinking seems to be taking hold, one that is increasingly drawing attention away from readings—of scores or meanings that are the result of acts of inscription—and focusing it on the materiality of musical communication, issues of sensuality, and the like. But because important work has recently appeared in these two fields (Austern 2002; Baumann and Fujie 1999; Feld 1996; Wegman 1998a), it seemed reasonable in this book to limit the number of essays devoted to music and instead to focus primarily on extramusical sound.

In light of this resurgence of the ear—musically and otherwise inclined—the present collection can offer only a small cross-section of the wide range of topics, methodologies, technologies, historical periods, and geographic areas awaiting further study. Nevertheless, these essays might contribute to an anthropology of the senses in a variety of ways. Most importantly, perhaps, they bring an interdisciplinary perspective to the debates in which anthropologists interested in overcoming the hegemony of textual analogies have been engaged. Thus, although some of the contributors are anthropologists, for the most part they represent other disciplines, including history, communications studies, literary studies, sociology, and the history of science. Despite this variety of backgrounds, all the authors share a recognition of the need for the cultural and historical contextualization of auditory perception. Generalities, as one often encounters them in the literature on the senses (see Ackerman 1990), have no place in this project of charting the cultural production of sensory perception. Hearing—be it the views of eighteenth-century European medics on sound and healing that Penelope Gouk writes about or the place of the ear within the broader framework of a theory of cross-cultural communication as proposed by Paul Carter—is seen to be culturally variable and subject to the prevailing ideologies and power relations of a given place at a given time.

But the essays in this collection do not simply alert us to the significance of one of the less studied senses or open up uncharted ethnographic terrain. Implied in the title *Hearing Cultures* is the notion that our quest for the ethnographic ear requires more than a metaphorical understanding of ethnography as being in need of more dialogue, more sensitized ears, or a third ear. "Hearing culture" suggests that it is possible to conceptualize new ways of knowing a culture and of gaining a deepened understanding of how the members of a society know each other. It is not only by accumulating a body of interrelated texts, signifiers, and symbols that we get a sense of the relationships and tensions making up a society. The ways in which people relate to each other through the sense of hearing also provide important insights into a wide range of issues confronting societies around the world as they grapple with the massive changes wrought by modernization, technologization, and globalization. In what follows, I outline some of these issues—in an order that does not always follow the sequence of the chapters—beginning with what is arguably the most fundamental: the close and contested relationship between vision and hearing in the West and the significance of this relationship for struggles over the course and direction of modernization in the postcolonial world.

Vision—A Modern Sense?

To assert that modernity is essentially a visual age (Levin 1993) or that bourgeois society rests on technologies of seeing, observation, and surveillance (Lowe 1982) is no longer of much heuristic value. By the same token, the parallel notion that colonial and postcolonial power relations hinge fundamentally on the "gaze," even though it helped spur the questioning of Western monopolies over knowledge and representation, appears to have generated only more texts and more images. The number of accounts detailing how the West's *sounds* are cast back on it is still shockingly small. Even more striking is the absence from current debates of Third World scholars interested in auditory perception.[2]

Despite this, it seems problematic to make the reverse proposition that, if we are to explore new possibilities for challenging Western hegemony, it will become necessary to map an alternative economy of the senses in which prominence perforce must be given to the neglected "second sense." Nearly all the contributors to this volume reject such a simplistic perspective. They are skeptical of a countermonopoly of the ear, not only because it makes scientific sense to conceive of the senses as an integrated and flexible network but also, and more importantly, because arguments over the hierarchy of the senses are always also arguments over cultural and political agendas. Thus, when Paul Zumthor in his *Oral Poetry* (1990) hopes for a voice that "is soon in a state to pierce the opacity around us that we take for reality" and praises Africans' verbal prowess, one is tempted to welcome this turn toward the ethnographic ear. Yet if the same author in the same breath sees a "candle that is lit somewhere"—in front of the altar of the spoken word? —we ought to examine this strange juncture of piety and primeval origins more carefully.

Similarly, one wonders about the implications of Marshall McLuhan's early call for a sensory reawakening—for what he called the "man of total awareness"—especially because it appears to have sprung from the desire to stem the return of the twentieth-century subject to what he calls "the Africa within." Do the two projects share the same basic philosophical and political underpinnings? Might it be possible that such efforts at redeeming the ear—whether from within Africa or against it—conceal a deeper-seated conservative impulse, a restorative project, metaphorically and literally Catholic? Are we dealing in these and other antiocular discourses, such as those put forward by McLuhan's fellow antivisual critic and reborn Catholic Paul Virilio, with rather belated attempts at restoring to a new Rome the supreme aural and oral authority to command and to judge? What really is meant by this new center with the presumably more benign, "evangelical" power to spread, *urbi et orbi*, the good news of more wholesome, more communicative times ahead?

Clearly, postcolonial and poststructuralist critiques of modernity at times appear to be couched in nostalgic terms, wishing for the living voice, the cry, and sonic guerilla tactics. Which is why it is crucial to emphasize that it is not enough to denounce vision and replace it with a new sensibility based on the ear. The rejection of a simplistic dichotomy between the eye as the quintessential modern sensory organ and hearing as some kind of pre- or antimodern mode of perception must be replaced by a more nuanced approach like the one adopted in the contributions to this volume. The essays gathered here go a long way toward allowing the ear "an unromanticized place alongside the eye" (Schmidt 2000: 36). Like Steven Connor in his chapter, the other contributors collectively caution against using hearing as a way of "softening the rigor mortis of a social body that we imagine has gone deaf and dumb, blind and numb." The task that the authors set themselves, then, is not to ascertain how modern auditory practices might differ from traditional ones. Rather, they ask how listening has come to play a role in the way people in modernizing societies around the globe deal with themselves as subjects in embodied, sensory, and especially auditory ways. Hearing and associated sonic practices, instead of being sequestered in their own domain, separate from the other senses and defined as some kind of historical residue, for the most part are seen to have worked in complicity with the panopticon, perspectivism, commodity aesthetics, and all the other key visual practices of the modern era we now know so much about.

If the auditory is deeply caught up in the modern project—rather than standing apart from it—and if therefore the ear joins the eye in consolidating the fragile modern self, we must nevertheless also ask the reverse question: How are these modern identities constantly being sonically haunted and—perhaps confirming McLuhan's greatest fear—troubled by a return of the repressed? What do we really know about vocal knowledges that are being forced underground, silenced, or ridiculed as superstitious? Much of recent efforts to retrieve such voices has concentrated on female forms of vocality, primarily in the realm of cinema and opera (Dunn and Jones 1994; Lawrence 1991; Smart 2000), but anthropologists have yet to seriously investigate how other acoustic practices are being drawn into the maelstrom of globalization and modernization and how they often escape, resist, or succumb to the dictates of Western visualism.

Janis Nuckolls's work on sound symbolism in this volume is a pioneering attempt to show how a specific form of sound communication produces "relational knowledge," to use Michel Serres's apt phrase, and how this type of knowledge is being marginalized as a result of modernization. Through their language, Quechua-speaking Runa living in the upper Amazonian region of Ecuador articulate a "sonically driven disposition" toward what Nuckolls calls "sound alignment." By this she means that Runa model natural processes with sound by imitating the resonant and rhythmic properties of experiential phenomena. By doing so, they foreground the animacy they share with such processes. The chief linguistic vehicles for such sound alignments are ideophones, a broad range of signifiers that do not refer to a signified but are instead related to it by simulation and semblance. These expressions are integral to a style of communication that is embedded in and provides cohesion for social and cultural practices different from those of the industrialized West. They put subjects among things, or, as Nuckolls phrases the matter, they enable Runa to "express a sentiment of common animateness."

An example that is also familiar from other contexts—such as the Renaissance views of sound and magic examined in Gouk's chapter—is a class of Runa myths about genesis. In these narratives, themes of analogy, similarity, and interrelatedness between earthly and celestial realms loom large. Similarly, sound not only figured prominently in the thinking of Renaissance theorists and early modern Englishmen but was the chief medium for enacting transitions from one realm to another.

Ideophones work in many different ways, of course, not all of which Nuckolls discusses. The ones she does examine, however, provide fascinating illustrations of the intertwining of orality and visuality in Runa culture and of how Runa society differs from what Nuckolls calls "technologically complex societies." Ideophones in Runa culture "shoulder a great deal of communicative responsibility," in that they perform many of the functions that would be allocated to visual modes of expression in the West. Their polysemiotic status allows Runa to mobilize ideophonic speech to communicate a wide range of multisensory experiences. Rather than simply restating the semantic content of a verb, for instance—something Westerners would call redundancy—ideophones add a gestural component to relatively soundless phenomena.

This dense social embedding of ideophones comes under immense pressure, however, in the wake of missionization and the intrusion of modern mass media into the fabric of Runa social life, leading to a diminished use of ideophonic speech among young, politically active, and economically ambitious Runa.

Sound, Techniques of the Body, and Technology

Nuckolls's chapter is not the only one in which issues of technological mediation of sound production and auditory perception loom large. The invention of audio technologies has always been met with a good deal of cultural pessimism, which still resonates in current debates over music, technology, global culture, and commoditization. Working toward a more nuanced assessment of the effects of modern technology on sound and auditory perception, several of the contributors interrogate from an ethnographically informed perspective commonly held assumptions about modernity and ask how Western intellectual anxieties about sound technologies play themselves out in non-Western cultural contexts.

In the past, it is true, the role of acoustic technology in the making of modern sensibilities has attracted sustained scholarly attention, with "schizophonia"—Murray Schafer's (1977) term for the separation of sound from its source—being considered the most distinguishing (and at the same time most enthralling and angst-ridden) feature of the modern world's soundscape. But although the vast literature on the telephone, phonograph, radio, and electronic media might lend credence to claims of modernity's being an auditory rather than a visual era, the real problem seems to lie in the technological determinism, scientism, or cultural pessimism in which discussions of audio technologies have bogged us down for so long.

The essays in this book that directly address questions of technological mediation—those by Michael Bull, Steven Connor, and Emily Thompson—in many ways take us beyond these paradigms by locating hitherto overtheorized practices of media consumption in specific cultural settings. For instance, on the basis of extensive interviews with users of portable radios and cassette or compact disc players (Walkmans), Michael Bull seeks to understand the complex nature of proximity, distance, and mobility in media consumption, scrutinizing the common assertion that Walkman users can be seen as postmodern flaneurs. At first sight, Bull's argument resembles that of the Frankfurt-school theorist Walter Benjamin. Bull begins his investigation in the familiar and intertwined terrain of myth and modernity: the story of Odysseus and the Sirens (drawn from Max Horkheimer and Theodor W. Adorno's interpretation of that myth), a reading of Werner Herzog's film *Fitzcarraldo*, and Sigfried Kracauer's remarks on radio listening in the 1920s. But he gives these "texts" an unexpected twist. They can be understood, he suggests, as part of the cultural "prehistory" of personal

stereos and, more broadly, as part of the Western project of the appropriation and control of space, place, and the "other" by sonic means.

One space that has come increasingly under pressure in the twentieth
century is the "home." Bull recognizes that communication technologies have played an important part in the symbolic construction of
"home," but unlike other commentators, he sees these private spaces—
and the subjects who inhabit them—as fraught with ambiguity. Thus,
Raymond Williams's notion of "mobile privatization" posits an experiencing subject unreflectively appropriating, through acts of private
consumption, everything that stands before it. What remains elusive
in this model of media-generated distance is the way feelings of
omnipotence are just the flip side of relations of dependency. Con-
versely, the sonic mediation of proximity—defined by Bull as "mediated
presence that shrinks space into something manageable and habitable"—in the past has been inadequately conceptualized. Echoing
Adorno's notion of "we-ness," he argues that it is hearing, more than
any other sense, that appears to perform a "utopian" function in the
desire for the proximity and connectedness that is sorely lacking in
capitalist society.

Much of this dynamic appears to be prefigured in myth. As Bull
characterizes the Siren episode in the story of Odysseus: "As Odysseus
listens, tied safely to the mast of his ship, the sirens' song transforms
the distance between his ship and the rocks from which they sing. Their
song colonizes him, and yet he uses this experience to fulfill his own
desire for knowledge. . . . Socially speaking, Odysseus is in his very own
soundworld." Similarly, in the more recent, industrial past, radio users
have transcended geographical space by communing not with those
next to them but with the "distant" voices transmitted though the
ether. Herzog's Fitzcarraldo, for his part, aestheticizes the Amazon jungle
by blasting Caruso from his phonograph into the forest.

Such historical continuities between gramophone, radio, and Walkman and the way they are embedded in or, in Fitzcarraldo's case, origin-
ate from the ecology of urban life have been remarked upon often.
Echoing Benjamin, Bull acknowledges that Walkman users share with
the flaneur the desire to aestheticize the alienating urban space by
"colonizing" it sonically, but at the same time he is aware that Walkman
listeners get "more out of the environment, not by interacting with it,
but precisely by not interacting with it." Bull reaches this conclusion
on the basis of extensive interviews with Walkman users—definitely a
novelty in the otherwise highly speculative domain of cultural studies.

Other essays offer a different kind of thinking about sound and technology in which it is not technology that makes music more inhuman but rather music that rubs off on technology in unexpected ways, until technology itself becomes a little more like sound or even music. Thus, Steven Connor's wide-ranging reflections on intersensory perception in the broader dialectics of (Western) culture and (Western) bodies—and the growing sense of unease with the dominance of spectacular modes of consumption and the perceived sensory impoverishment and downright anesthesia within this dialectic—could be read as an attempt to map an unusual landscape of flesh and metal, the human and the inhuman, anatomy and technology. Exploring the linkages between hearing and touch, Connor recovers interconnections that for Western moderns have largely become unconscious but that were much more present to people in previous phases of European history—and, to a certain extent, have always been to some other cultures as well. As the chapters by Bruce Smith and Penelope Gouk also illustrate, early modern Western subjects conceived of the place of the senses within the larger framework of the human body in more connected, networked terms. Little wonder, then, that sounds not only possessed a strange sort of agency of their own but also seemed to form a different kind of aggregate. As they course through the cosmos and the body, sounds maintain a tactile relationship with their source, an "umbilical continuity," as Connor calls it.

Much of this sonic tactility is still embedded in modern audio technology. Key technologies such as the telephone do not so much insert themselves as quasi-neutral interceptors between the perceiving subject and its object but are deeply imbricated within the subject's very fibers. (Another example Connor discusses in this respect is the microphone and the peculiar eroticism it occasions.) Our discourses and popular practices often register this osmosis with a lingering sense of eeriness, a mixture of fear and fascination. Instead of the presumed rationality of such technologies, which is founded on the belief that the isolation and manipulation of each individual sense somehow naturally corresponds to the social compartmentalization in industrial capitalism, there are seemingly unruly intersections between the sense of hearing and a motley array of skin textures, body fluids, and body organs. The juxtaposition of the rational, the disembodied, and the fleshy, organic aspects of audio technology is the reason we attribute a whole string of almost magical effects to the telephone, for instance. For, as Connor points out, despite the telephone's reliance upon the new, clean, dry power of electricity, its tactile nature made it a moist and dirty medium, and thus we still associate it with sexuality and disease. At the same time, such technologies generate an almost utopian desire and fear of the unified body, subverting the very rationality of a subject thus constituted. There appears not to have materialized, then, even under conditions of modern media of mass communication such as the telephone and the gramophone, the kind of epistemic break Michel Foucault famously saw as occurring in the early seventeenth century, in which "the eye was thenceforth destined to see and only to see, the ear to hear and only to hear" (Foucault 1994: 43). Rather, from the angle of magically condensed and commingled body parts adopted by Connor, one might rephrase Foucault by saying, "Teeth are for eating, but not for eating only."

Another fascinating facet of the hearing-touch linkage explored in Connor's chapter is the often-made association—presumably going back to Aristotle—of hearing with passivity and affect. Although this was certainly a powerful trope, which over the centuries served a variety of political and cultural projects, from Augustinian piety to Romanticism, Connor astutely sees hearing as operating on both sides of the active-passive, productive-receptive dichotomy. "The one who barks a demand or screams an insult," says Connor, "is using sound as a weapon to effect his will, but the means whereby this is effected is through an assault on sound itself." In this, of course, sound is imagined in the same two-sided way as skin: as both that which touches and that which is touched; as both a medium through which we feel and something that is itself subject to touching and assault.

As the preceding discussion shows, it would be naïve to assume that projects such as those represented by the essays in this volume can in any way bypass technology. But auditizing reason without othering it, as Steven Connor calls it in another context (1997: 162), also means that a theory of modern sound technologies as media for modern self-fashioning of necessity will have to illuminate how such "rational" and "primitive" forms of listening are situated in and contingent upon the mirrored and fluctuating power relationships between the metropolis and the colonial frontier, how an acoustic imaginary is never just the product of only one place and time. A good example of this is R. Anderson Sutton's pioneering study of the soundscape of Indonesia (Sutton 1996), in which he argues that inferior or malfunctioning Western sound technology does not automatically lead to a deterioration of "Third World" musical practices. Rather, overmodulation and distortion may be a premeditated effect meant to reinforce traditional aesthetic norms. All it takes from there is to ask—perhaps a little less naïvely trusting the "native" capacity for almost naturally upholding difference—how such auditory hijacking techniques might not also mimic Western sound technology at higher decibel levels, as it were, thereby wresting from it some of the power that so much of our media and loudspeakers are all about.

The Sonic Contestation of Identity

The global impact of sound technology and the way in which it became a site for the contestation of cultural meaning attached to sound is also the focus of Emily Thompson's essay. Thompson examines the practices and universalist ideologies of early Hollywood sound engineers, who perceived themselves to be on a technological mission, trying to get the world "in sync" with modern America through synchronous sound technology. By wiring the world for sound, 1920s sound engineers believed that they were installing a conduit to modernization, as Thompson calls it, creating a universal ecumene of viewers/listeners who would enthusiastically abandon their heritage and traditions in favor of some new form of global citizenship centered on uniformity of taste and, above all, appreciation of technological progress.

But early film sound technology also left a complicated legacy in its wake. Through its association with progress and rationality and by constructing (in theory at least) a citizenry of technical experts and technically savvy consumers of audio-visual technologies, the "talkie" played a role in shaping notions of governance far more effective than the imposition of Western standards through discursive reasoning.[3] But as Thompson succinctly illustrates, in many places the same technology also became one of the principle means by which this very form of colonial governance was contested.

Charles Hirschkind advances a parallel argument in his chapter. By attending to seemingly marginal cultural phenomena such as regimes of aural sensibility and specific forms of "ethical" listening, Hirschkind proposes to arrive at a better understanding of the complex and often contradictory dynamic of the modern public sphere and new notions of agency, authority, and responsibility in Third World countries. As key components of Islamic practice in Egypt, sermons have undergone significant changes as a result of two major forces shaping modern Egypt: the ideology and structures of the nation-state and mass media. Yet contrary to the assumptions underlying nationalist politics and many reformist and modernization agendas, older practices, languages, and techniques of ethical listening persist that often go against the grain of nationalist ideology and at other times overlap with the modern state's attempts to construct a modern public sphere. Instead of producing a citizenry of willing listeners ever attuned to the codes and messages emanating from the state, Egypt's political, cultural, and religious landscape is witnessing the tenacious survival of what Hirschkind calls the "embodied listener."

Listening in Islamic dogma has played a different role from listening in the Christian tradition, and these differences are crucial for an understanding of the current debate over pious listening in the modern nation-state. For Muslim theologians and philosophers, the act of listening takes precedence over oration and rhetorical skill, because the beauty and perfection of the divine message—the Qur'an—do not require persuasion. If this message falls on deaf ears, it is because sinful acts have corrupted the Muslim's heart. In other words, correct hearing is not submission to a convincing speaker but a more active disposition required to open human hearts to God's word.

With the rise of Egyptian nationalism in the late nineteenth century, and as a result of the new nation-state's attempt to align religion more closely with the secular-liberal and technocratic discourses central to the state's legitimacy, the religious sermon became redefined as an instrument of state propaganda. Henceforth, such sermons were to imbue Muslim listeners with modern virtues of discipline, individual initiative, cooperation, and obedience to state authority. In this way, the two sides in the preacher-audience equation changed positions. Now the *khatib*, or preacher, assumed a more active role while the audience was stripped of its agency.

Yet as the state increasingly failed to meet the expectations engendered by its own rhetoric, a variety of Islamist counterforces and their dissatisfied constituencies appropriated sermons as a key medium for contestation. Ironically, the models for this counterhegemonic role of listening lay in the realm of nationalist politics and popular culture. Radio broadcasts of Gamel Abd al-Nasser's speeches and weekly concerts by the singer Umm Kulthum provided Egyptian audiences with a lasting legacy of vocal prowess and an ideal template for experiencing aural pleasure and cathartic release. But, says Hirschkind, because the successors of neither Nasser nor Umm Kulthum could match their popular impact, hearing and the human voice were rapidly recuperated by an opposition movement grounded in Islamic institutions.

There is also something deeper at stake in the resurgence of pious listening. The debate over the role of sermons and ethical listening in the modern Egyptian nation-state pits against each other two contrasting

ways of understanding agency and authority. In the first, more tradi-
tionalist position, the sonic components of the corpus of sacred and
liturgical texts take precedence over their meaning. The opposing—
more secular, as it is—view posits that a contemporary reading of the
Qur'an "must take as its goal the uncovering of symbolic meanings
through an interpretive approach founded upon the same notions of
language, history, and context that are applied to contemporary literary
texts."

Reenchantment in Sobering Times

Clearly, then, sound, listening practices, and various forms of audio
technology have massively intervened in processes of modernization,
often complicating simplistic notions of modern selfhood in surprising
ways. Instead of just positing a modern sonic self, the essays by Connor,
Thompson, Hirschkind, and others sketch the outlines of a somewhat
more dialectical process, insecurely poised between the modern and the
"primitive," between the rational and the affective, the discursive and
the embodied. The tenacity of culture to shape and sometimes even
revert the trajectories of modernization that we see at work among
Egyptian listeners of religious sermons is of course not something that
is embedded in sound or auditory perception alone. Similar processes
have been observed in the appropriation and subsequent subversion
of Western visual technologies and modes of consumption (e.g., Poole
1997). Thus, hearing and vision might in fact both partake in a vastly
reconfigured sensory order in which demands for rational, focused, and
goal-oriented forms of apperception are dialectically juxtaposed with
allegedly irrational and yet more authentic modes. Following Jonathan
Crary's latest work (1999), for instance, we might ask what the auditory
parallels are, if any, of a situation in which individuals increasingly have
to adjust their perception in paradoxical ways—a situation that demands
attentive behavior while at the same time stimulating a more "regressive," distracted, trancelike state. Similarly, what do we make of the
strange continuities between supposedly "archaic" and "occult" forms
of knowledge and modern constructions of scientific method or
modernist understandings of art?

Both of these questions are addressed in Penelope Gouk's and Douglas
Kahn's essays. Comparing Renaissance notions of music's effects on the
soul with eighteenth-century medical uses of music, Gouk finds a
number of unusual linkages between cosmology, music, and the
production of knowledge and the ways in which they are socially

mediated. This is all the more remarkable in light of the fact that until about 1800, Europe's enlightened elites saw nothing mysterious in music's supposed potential for curing sick bodies. As Gouk puts it: "Contrary to popular belief that the soul ceased to be important to science after Descartes, medical theorists continued to invoke this entity as a necessary part of understanding the body's workings into the eighteenth century and beyond."

But for Gouk these continuities are far from given. Rather, they were embedded in a specific aural environment that shaped people's inner sense of themselves as well as their relationship to the outer world. Thus, the concept of music's emotional powers, although widespread during antiquity, reemerged only during the late seventeenth century and, according to Gouk, gave rise to a soundscape that eighteenth-century doctors could draw on in explaining music's effects on the human body. At the same time, this soundscape was also constitutive of physiological models, in turn naturalizing as modern, objective, and apparently culturally neutral representations of music and human nature that in reality were the result of specific historical conjunctures. Thus, the flurry of works appearing in the early eighteenth century on medical uses of music—titles such as Richard Browne's *Medicina Musica, or a Mechanical Essay on the Effects of Singing, Musick and Dancing* (1729)—purported to be articulations of scientific truth, because they claimed the effects of music on the body's interior to be explainable in the terms of Newtonian physics.

By adding music to the mix and by extending her earlier work on the scientific revolution of the seventeenth century, Gouk enriches our understanding of the deeply fraught period of Western history we call the Enlightenment. The mid-eighteenth-century cultural environment she describes and traces back to Renaissance pursuits is not only generally more diffuse than conventional occularcentric interpretations of the Enlightenment suggest, but music itself, in its articulation with science and medicine, was just one element in a much larger landscape in which sentiment and scientific discovery were consciously fused (Riskin 2002).

Douglas Kahn, in his chapter, brings the story up to the early part of the twentieth century. He is interested in the music of Dane Rudhyar, a relatively forgotten composer of twentieth-century modernism, and its linkages to Eastern forms of spirituality. Rudhyar's peculiar brand of exoticism sprang from a variety of sources and was an attempt to respond to a wide range of pressures under which turn-of-the-twentieth-century Western society and culture had fallen. Foremost among

Rudhyar's intellectual sources was theosophism, with its attempt to reconcile science and religion in times of all-out disenchantment. As for the pressures, advances in acoustical research, musical acoustics, and audiophonic and musical technologies—and rampant commercialization, one might add—were beginning to threaten the very metaphysical foundations of absolute music that avant-garde composers, with few exceptions, sought vigorously to defend. In most cases, it appears, this attempt involved a radical formalism that survived even where the idea of form and of the work of art itself came to be demolished. But there is also ample evidence suggesting that encounters with non-Western musics, while often tearing at the fabric of Western functional harmony, were in reality achieving what Edward Said (1993) has called a "new inclusiveness," providing a sense of closure and revitalization to otherwise exhausted forms. What has been less appreciated in this overall picture is the discourses and compositional practices centering on sound and its physical materiality coming out of a variety of occultist and esoteric movements current in early twentieth-century Europe and existing alongside—and sometimes against—an aesthetics more narrowly focused on musical sound.

Rudhyar's philosophy, as Kahn makes clear, hinged on a fundamental distinction between the "note" and something Rudhyar called the "Single Tone." The former term denoted what he saw as being at the core of the "discontinued" music of the West: its scales, harmonic progressions, and abrupt changes. As for the latter concept, Rudhyar ostensibly borrowed it from the East—or rather, what he took to be the essence of Asian music. Meaning in Asian music, he believed, traditionally resided within one single tone and not, as in the West, in the relations between tones that are in principle interchangeable because of the emphasis on polyphony and equal temperament.

Paradoxically, though, and through a series of convoluted arguments, Rudhyar equated the Single Tone with the fundamental in a series of harmonics, a move that strongly resonates with Rameau and his theory of the *corps sonore*. But it also ties in closely with the fervent debates of the 1920s over the rational foundations and hence the legitimacy of atonal music. (Even Arnold Schoenberg referred to the series of harmonics, claiming that listeners would eventually become accustomed to the higher partials as the basis for his more dissonant strains.) The result of this mapping of the notion of the Single Tone onto the series of harmonics is a strange conundrum. What was initially thought of as a bulwark against Western musical relationality "becomes a conduit through which [such relationality] is asserted with renewed vigor, preserving the harmonic basis of Western art music, returning it to an intrinsic spirituality. What was at first rationalized through an implicit 'Eastern' critique of the contemporary 'West' becomes a means through which 'the West' is fortified."

Embodied Knowledge and the Methodology of Sound Research

How, then, does all this translate into viable empirical method? What would an ethnographic ear be like, and what would it hear? At the risk of veering toward some sort of neo-Keplerian belief in universal harmony, I elaborate here briefly on an age-old idea: the idea of the "frozen" speech. This was a common metaphor in the European Middle Ages—with deep roots in antiquity—that organized conceptions of the relationship between speech and text around such opposites as fluid and frozen, liquid and crystal, and soft and hard. The era abounded in fables in which words that had been uttered at one time and then frozen were being thawed out and thus made comprehensible long after their producers had departed from the scene. Although clearly already the product of literacy, the metaphor of the frozen speech perhaps quite unintentionally raises the possibility that sounds might, if not represent life, have a life. What this idea might induce us to reconsider is the impoverishing effect the reification of sound has since had on our ways of thinking about sound. It might behoove us to think about it as an ongoing, free-wheeling flow rather than a finite object—as a reverberation in the "wild blue yonder," to use Smith's evocative image, rather than a score, a record, a page.

In more concrete terms, are there ways of documenting, analyzing, and interpreting sounds as they arise, fade away, and rebound like echoes in a canyon? Are all sounds, once they become encapsulated in some mechanical form, really just strings of 0s and 1s, grooves, traces? What about print-through—that strange phenomenon of the reel-to-reel era when one could hear a taped sound several seconds before the tape segment it was on had passed the recording heads—a thawing before the freezing, as it were? What life cycles can a sound go through? Does it have a biography? What role does the body play as a storage device for sounds? Again, literary theorists, historians, and art historians can teach us a great deal about the sometimes messy relationship between sound and image in a variety of ages and cultures. To the medievalist Horst Wenzel (1995), for instance, we owe a radical revision of the so-called oral Middle Ages in which hearing and seeing were inseparably linked elements of sensory perception, bound together in and through the human body. Scholars of early modern Europe, in particular, have been unrelenting in reexamining the divide between vision and hearing, orality and literacy, that informed scholarship until the 1960s and is associated overwhelmingly with the work of Marshall McLuhan. It is now becoming increasingly clear not only that the boundaries between the spoken and written word were much more fluid than McLuhan imagined but also that they were blurred by a host of factors such as class position, ethnicity, and geographic location.

Some of these issues are the focus of Bruce Smith's chapter. Expanding on an old medieval notion that sounds never fade away but instead reverberate endlessly through space, he analyzes the role of what he calls an acoustical archaeology of early modern England in "un-airing" sounds of the past by means of a careful extrapolation of sounds from a variety of textual genres and practices popular during the sixteenth and seventeenth centuries. Printed play scripts are one such genre, broadside ballads another. Printed broadside ballads were composed, performed, enjoyed, and remembered, but upon closer examination, it turns out, these written records reveal a "sense of aural immediacy." They carry what Smith calls the "bodily force" of the spoken word. Just as Renaissance thinkers saw a world made of contiguities, sympathies, and antipathies, there existed until well into the seventeenth century a palpable connection between written words and the things they signified. Renaissance culture and even the classical age had not yet developed a full theory of representation in the sense that Michel Foucault ascribed to the term. Save a few exceptions influenced by Cartesian thought, signification in many domains of everyday culture— in either written or oral form—did not yet involve the representation of unrelated things in an act of mediation guaranteed by nothing but an autonomous, knowing subject. Consequently, Smith argues, writing functioned more like an index, implying bodily experience rather than signifying it.

Of course all these sonic microworlds did not exist in a vacuum. They were part of a broader soundscape structured, roughly, along three axes: the country, the court, and the city. The countryside, for instance, differed from the court not only in that it contained many more nonverbal sounds but also in that these sounds themselves often carried very different meanings, more intimately connected as they were to agricultural production. The court, by contrast, was a logocentric soundscape, and the city, harboring specific sounds associated with the crafts, stood somewhere in the middle. To reconstruct these acoustic ecological systems required a recombing of the archival record. Maps, site plans, legal documents, travelers' accounts, surviving structures, and landscape features all provided clues about the sonic environments that different sets of people inhabited and constructed for themselves.

In line with this, Smith argues, an acoustic archaeology of early modern England also requires a rethinking of our modern concepts of hearing. But even as he recognizes the danger of romanticizing the protocols of listening prevalent in 1600—protocols that were essentially based on a "whole-body experience"—Smith argues for a "historical phenomenology," a methodology that "insists on the embodiedness of all knowledge and yet recognizes the cultural differences that shape that knowledge." An early modern example of this kind of knowledge is the use of middle voice, now completely absent from modern-day English. It is in phrases such as "methinks" that the object, although seen as different, exists not quite apart from the subject.

What kinds of ears do we need, then, to pick up all these sounds adrift, these echoes, reverberations, hums, and murmurs outside or in between the carefully bounded precincts of orderly verbal communication and music? Do we hear past music, as Douglas Kahn urges us in his *Water, Noise, Meat* (1999), past the historical insignificance assigned to noise that is? And what about the completely different kind of hearing advocated by the French-Hungarian researcher Peter Szendy (2001)? Having grown up with the experience of listening as an obligation, a submission to the work, the Law, he feels a desire to escape from this auditory one-way street by opening it up to a twofold process of hearing another person listen. One area where this seems to be possible, surprisingly, is in musical arrangements. Arrangers, Szendy says, sign their listening into the work of another. Arrangements then are no longer second-class citizens in a world of original musical works but rather key elements in Szendy's concept of ears that hear each other hear.

Szendy's approach resonates strongly with Paul Carter's reflections, in his chapter for this volume, on sound as knowledge and interaction in three interrelated domains: cross-cultural encounters, communicational strategies in contemporary migrant communities, and the theory and practice of performance. Noting that sound knowledge is antiperspectival, immersive, and looped in the feedback between listening and speaking, Carter seeks to home in on the ambiguity inherent in communicative events. Cross-cultural encounters and the discourses of migrancy, for instance, are performances in which people attempt to create shared auditory spaces in which sounds constantly reanimate themselves in a potentially never-ending feedback loop. The same goes for acting and actors, for whom an essential ambiguity of communication obtains in which, in a sense, the one who speaks is already spoken for.

Carter's call for a cross-cultural auditory practice foregrounding ambiguity and doubling-up also resonates with a long-standing interest among anthropologists in social action as performance. Associated with the work of Victor Turner, Clifford Geertz, James Fernandez, Don Handelman, Andrew Apter, Johannes Fabian, Margaret Drewal, and many others, this tradition has been important in shifting attention away from societies as closed systems and toward more fluid notions of process, negotiation, and improvisation underlying social interaction. Fabian's *Power and Performance: Ethnographic Explorations through Proverbial Wisdom and Theater in Shaba, Zaire* (1990) is an excellent example of how, in a performative ethnography, the ethnographer ceases to be a mere questioner and instead becomes a provider of occasions for acting. In Fabian's opinion, the emphasis on the performative makes it possible to interrogate the notions that sociality predates concrete enactment and that social actors are guided by a common script of shared values. Thus it allows for a theory of ethnographic knowledge production in which such knowledge is not contingent upon the transfer of (somehow preexisting) messages via signs, symbols, or codes (Fabian 1990: 11). In this sense, such a performative approach is especially useful for studying situations without equilibrium or without a homogeneous, shared culture embodying undisputed values and norms.

The similarities of Fabian's views to what Carter, quoting Roy Wagner, calls "echolocation" are striking. Like Fabian's performative ethnography, echolocation refuses to submit to the Western concept of communication as an instrument or a goal-directed technique. As a communicative scene that defers the moment of final semiosis for the sole purpose of keeping the lines of communication open, echolocation—or perhaps "echolocution"—might be best understood as a way of creating contexts not by naming or denoting them but by filling a vacuum with sound. In this sense, echolocation/echolocution is not so much presemiotic as perisemiotic.

The lack of perfect semiosis makes the unscriptedness of such ambiguous moments valuable for anthropologists and other researchers interested in a world cultural situation in which constantly shifting contact zones are not the exception but the rule. But to be able to fully immerse themselves in such situations, Carter warns in critiquing both the title of this book and some of anthropology's colonial (and, more often than not, also postcolonial) legacies, anthropologists must reconsider the detached registration that marks so many of anthropology's core practices. What they need to rehearse more vigorously is new forms of listening. Rather than simply "hearing cultures," Carter envisages forms of auditory engagement in which "the ground rules are not established."

Ultimately, then, it is the kind of dialogic and participatory knowledge advocated by Paul Carter, Bruce Smith, and other students of the senses such as Michael Taussig and Paul Stoller that an ethnographic ear seeks to capture. Technology, modernization, and commercialization, as the essays presented here argue forcefully, are not necessarily to be taken as either anathema to or the end of such knowledge. By the same token, audio-centered forms of social practice cannot in themselves be construed as alternatives to relations of power thought to be anchored in vision, surveillance, and mass-mediated forms of visual production and consumption.

Notes

1. See also Seeger 1981, Geurts 2002, Classen 1993, and Keifenheim 2000. For an excellent overview of the literature on the senses, see Classen 1997.

2. See, however, for the Japanese context, Inoue 2003.

3. For another example, see Mrazek 2002. The author discusses, among other things, the role of cinema and radio in Indonesia.

Listening to the Wild Blue Yonder: The Challenges of Acoustic Ecology

Bruce R. Smith

Down is the direction in the archaeology of physical objects; up is the direction in the archaeology of sound. Images of the earth transmitted from space present a ball, faintly glowing blue in the penumbra of the earth's atmosphere. To an observer stationed on the earth's surface, the space upward likewise presents itself as blue—an effect of refracted light waves in the molecules of air, water, and other substances that blanket the earth's surface to an altitude of about a hundred kilometers. That blanket of molecules constitutes the medium of sound. A vibrating object sets the molecules into motion in waves of greater or lesser magnitude, at intervals of greater of lesser frequency. The vast majority of the mobile organisms that humankind knows as animals possess receptors sensitive to those waves of air molecules. Unlike the infinite reaches of space across which light energy can travel, the medium of sound is finite. Air exemplifies the indestructibility of matter. It is always there, in the same volume. It is also constantly moving, not only because of changes in temperature (effects that humans experience as wind) but also because of the so-called Brownian movement whereby all substances maintain and lose their integrity as masses of molecules. The periodic waves of molecules of air that humans perceive as sound emerge out of this random motion—and dissipate into it.

But perhaps not entirely. It was the thought (I can no longer recall where I first encountered it) that all the sounds that have ever occurred still reverberate, however faintly, somewhere in the wild blue yonder that originally set me onto the project of historical recovery that became my book *The Acoustic World of Early Modern England* (1999). However dubious as a scientifically demonstrable proposition, the findableness of sounds that occurred in the historical past excited my imagination—and challenged my skills as a scholar trained to deal with tangible physical objects in the form of literary texts. In this chapter I would like to detail some of the specific challenges that acoustic archaeology presents and outline some of the strategies I have used in meeting those challenges.

Cataloguing Sounds

Just as a more conventional archaeologist first unearths the objects to be studied and then ranges them into categories, so an acoustical archaeologist must "un-air" sounds that have faded into the air's atmosphere and catalogue them. What kinds of sounds did Shakespeare and his contemporaries hear? What kinds of sounds occurred in the world around them? What kinds of sounds did they make themselves? Where were those sounds located? In a few cases we have direct physical evidence. For example, musical instruments from the period survive and can still be played (Munrow 1976). Some of the same church bells still hang in some of the same belfries and can still be rung. Some of the same interior spaces still exist, and their acoustic properties can still be experienced. Although put to other uses today, Westminster Hall was one of the largest interior public spaces in early modern London. The law courts and merchants' stalls that occupied the vast space under the hammer-beam roof made Westminster Hall one of the loudest places in London—something that more than one contemporary Londoner noted (Smith 1999: 60–62).

The best source of information turned out to be, not the inhabitants of England themselves, but foreign visitors such as Paul Hentzner (1598), Thomas Platter (1599), Philip Gerschow (1602), and Orazio Busino (1617–1618). About sound, as about everything else, they often noticed things that natives took for granted. Gerschow, for example, recorded among his first impressions of London the fact that church bells were loudly bonging as he arrived in the city. When he inquired what was going on, he was told that the youths of London rang the bells every afternoon, competing with one another over who could ring the loudest and longest. Hentzner, who noted the same custom, commented that English people were "vastly fond of great noises that fill the ear, such as the firing of cannon and the ringing of bells" (quoted in Smith 1999: 52–53).

Another place in which the sounds of early modern England lie embedded is imaginative fiction. Ben Jonson's play *Epicene, or The Silent Woman* is among the richest of these texts in its representations of sound. The play's protagonist, Morose, is so hypersensitive to noise that he lives at the bottom of a cul-de-sac too narrow for carts and coaches, and he never comes out on Sundays and holidays, when the ringing of church bells fills the air. In the course of his complaints about noise, Morose provides the acoustic archaeologist with a list of London's loudest places. If he were to marry, Morose worries, his wife might turn out not to be the model of silence that women are supposed to be. To get rid of such a wife, he would be willing to do penance "in a belfry, at Westminster Hall, in the cock pit at the fall of a stag, the Tower Wharf —what place is there else?—London Bridge, Paris Garden, Billingsgate, when the noises are at the height and loudest. Nay, I would sit out a play that were nothing but fights at sea, drum, trumpet, and target!" (quoted in Smith 1999: 60).

More allusive are the physical sounds implied by fictional texts if not represented in them directly. Play scripts, after all, were designed to be performed, not read. A chapter in *The Acoustic World of Early Modern England* is devoted to acoustic reconstructions of the 1599 Globe Theater and the indoor Blackfriars Theater, where Shakespeare's company also performed after 1609. My method in reconstructing the Globe involved correlating several different kinds of evidence: the resonance of building materials such as oak beams and plaster over lathing; the disposition of the building's main features as specified in the builder's contract for the Fortune Theater, set up to be closely modeled on the Globe; the dimensions implied by archaeological remains of the Globe uncovered in the early 1990s in Southwark; indications of special sound effects in scripts; and the calculations of modern acoustical engineering with respect to the reflectivity of the Globe's building materials, the directional properties of the building's shape, and the reverberation delays to be expected in its volume. Also important to the project were the findings of modern linguistic research with respect to the mathematical modes of pitches of adult male voices reading aloud, as compared with the pitches of women and adolescent boys. By comparing these linguistic data on pitch with psychoacoustic research on the perceived loudness and locatablity of sounds at various pitches, I was able to place men's voices in the space of the Globe vis-à-vis boys' voices.

Putting together all these pieces of information from architectural acoustics, linguistics, and psychoacoustics, I concluded that scripts written by Shakespeare and other writers for the outdoor amphitheaters were designed to capitalize on those spaces' distinctive sound qualities: a broad, side-to-side sound in which percussion and brass instruments provided the predominant keynotes in a matrix of sound that featured mostly adult male voices. Scripts for these outdoor theaters contrast with scripts for the indoor Blackfriars Theater, which offered a more rounded sound and featured a wider range of musical instruments in a matrix that gave some prominence to boys' voices. In the 1590s the Blackfriars Theater had been home to several all-boy troupes of actors, and interludes provided by musical consorts had been a regular feature of performances in that space. Play scripts provide the most obvious instances of sound as implied by written texts, but early modern culture offers plenty of other examples: ballads, sermons, even letters and poems written out by hand.

Decoding Sound in Graphic Evidence

The second challenge I faced in writing *The Acoustic World of Early Modern England* was teaching myself to hear, and not just see, the evidence encoded on pieces of paper. Even in the vision-dominated culture of contemporary Europe and North America today we understand that musical notation exists primarily to cue the reader of those notations in making sounds. My research in the written records of early modern England indicated that other graphic signs might similarly be telling readers how to listen to their memories and how to use their voices to bring those memories into sounded presence. Printed play scripts, for example, often carry on their title pages a tag that says the play is printed "as it hath been performed sundry times at London." For readers who had actually heard one of those performances, the printed text could serve as a mnemonic device. The connection between print and sound is made even more explicit in the title-page illustrations that accompany some of these printed scripts. For example, the woodcut in the 1615 edition of Thomas Kyd's *The Spanish Tragedy* (first acted in the mid-1580s and often revived) includes speech banners placed next to the mouths of three of the play's protagonists (fig. 2.1). Sound takes precedence over vision in the organization of the illustration: rather than representing a single visual moment in the play, the woodcut conflates three separate episodes as it offers tags of three of the protagonists' most notable speeches.

That this illustration was reused five to ten years later to accompany a ballad version of the same story demonstrates the even stronger mnemonic function of graphic cues in printed broadsides. Printed

The Spanish Tragedie:

OR,

Hieronimo is mad againe.

Containing the lamentable end of *Don Horatio*, and
Belimperia; with the pittifull death of *Hieronimo*.

Newly corrected, amended, and enlarged with new
Additions of the *Painters* part, and others, as
it hath of late been diuers times acted.

LONDON,

Printed by W. White, for I. White and T. Langley,
and are to be fold at their Shop ouer againft the
Sarazens head without New-gate. 1615.

Figure 2.1. Title page to Thomas Kyd, *The Spanish Tragedy* (1615). Reproduced by permission of the Folger Shakespeare Library, Washington.

ballads almost never carried musical notations of the tune to which the words were to be sung. Instead, a printed tag declared that the text was "To be sung to the tune of 'Queen Dido'" (in the case of *The Spanish Tragedy*) or some other well-known song. There is plenty of testimony that people bought printed ballads, not to read them, but to learn to perform them. More than one writer described country milkmaids as a major clientele for ballad-mongers. If a printed ballad was about love, Wye Saltonstall declared, "the country wenches buy it, to get by heart at home and after sing it over the milk pales" (quoted in Smith 1999: 177).

A particularly striking instance of the commerce between print and sound is the broadside ballad "The Fox Chase, or The Huntsman's Harmony, by the Noble Duke of Buckingham's Hounds" (c. 1690; fig. 2.2). In this rousing celebration of riding to hounds, the singer becomes a huntsman who joins the Duke of Buckingham and his gentlemen as they pursue a particularly wily fox up hill and down dale in Wreckledale Scrogs, near Helmsley Castle, Yorkshire. In the course of the chase, fifteen of the hunting party's dogs enjoy moments of glory as they are invoked by name: "That's our Lilly, whore! / Heark to Caperman! now Slaughterman's near him!" Hunting cries—"Halloo, halloo, halloo! Heark away all together!"—punctuate the story of the chase. The three woodcuts that grace part one illustrate three key visual elements in the story: a hunter, the whole pack of hounds, and a hound singled out from the rest. They also serve as mnemonic devices with respect to sound, as visual cues that the singer learning the ballad can invest with the sounds of particular stanzas. Indeed, the hunter with his horn provides the singer of the ballad with a subject position that he or she can use throughout the ballad as he or she intones the "excellent tune much in request" noted after the title. Other, more incidental sounds figure in the woodcuts. The horn in the huntsman's left hand is called for in the next-to-last stanza. In the space above the pack of hounds there is even a transcription of the hounds' yelping: "ööö—ööö—ööö—ööö—ööö." In the case of specimens like "The Fox Chase," print clearly exists to serve the ends of oral performance. It is orality, not literacy, that dominates the cultural field in which the broadside ballads of early modern England were composed, performed, enjoyed, and remembered.

Even in the absence of a tune, even in the absence of illustrations, printed broadsides in the sixteenth and early seventeenth centuries might still carry the imprint of sound. Take, for example, "The Unfeigned Retractation of Fraunces Cox, Which He Uttered at the Pillory in Cheapside and Elsewhere," printed in 1561 (fig. 2.3). The key word here is "utter," which in early modern English meant not only "to speak,

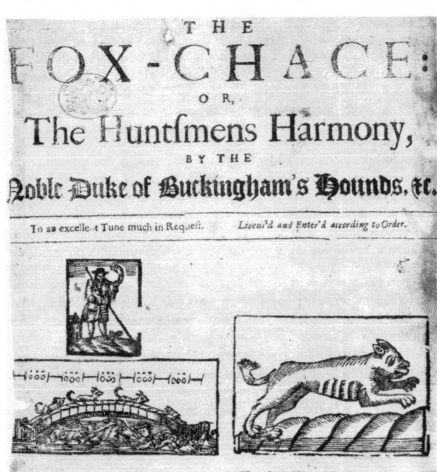

Figure 2.2. Broadside, "The Fox Chase" (about 1690). Reproduced by permission of the British Library, London.

say, or pronounce" (*Oxford English Dictionary*, "utter," II.6) but "to issue by way of publication" (I.2c). Public confessions, from a pillory fixed in the marketplace or from the back of a cart in which the malefactor was paraded through the streets, were a standard form of punishment for lesser crimes. Punishment for capital offenses entailed speeches of contrition from the gallows or the chopping block—speeches that often found their way into printed broadside ballads, sometimes within a matter of hours.

The occasion for the 1561 broadside was the public punishment of Cox and several other people for practicing necromancy, astrology, sorcery, and witchcraft. Printed at Cox's command as part of his penance, the sheet presents itself as a first-person-plural address to witnesses standing around the pillory in Cheapside, sixteenth-century London's major commercial thoroughfare: "Good people, we here whom ye see after this sort to receive worthy and condign punishment, amongst whom I myself not being the least of the offenders, led by the greedy desire of wilfulness, have most wickedly offended God, transgressed His most holy commandments, after these such like sundry sorts." There follows a list of the crimes committed by Cox and his fellow penitents—crimes that are described as fundamentally oral in nature, involving "invocations of spirits," "sciences wherein the name of God is most horribly abused and society or pact with wicked spirits most detestably practiced," prophecies, and fortune-telling. These forms of interdicted speech are in effect cancelled by the printed confession, a regimen of licensed speech that ends with expressions of gratitude to Queen Elizabeth and her counselors for sparing the offenders' lives and with a prayer for God's mercy.

All these intimations of sounded speech take on visual form in the arabesques of the illuminated *G* that begins the text and visually dominates the broadside sheet. The profiles of two grimacing faces stare out from each side of the *G*'s curved body. An open cavity on the upper right suggests, from one direction, a plucked leaf and, from the other, the mouth of a horn or pipe, perhaps even the windpipe that connects a speaker's lungs to his mouth. The sense of aural immediacy is further heightened by the resemblance of the sheet's black-letter typeface to the commonest form of writing in the mid-sixteenth century, secretary hand. The illuminated *G* likewise suits the look of a manuscript written out by the first-person speaker.

Erasmus, one of the great letter-writers of the Renaissance, testified to the intimacy between handwriting and sound. In a person's handwriting, Erasmus claimed, he could hear that person's very voice.

¶The vnfained retractation of Fraunces Cox/ which he vttered at the Pillery in Chepesyde, and els where, accordyng to the Counsels commaundement. Anno.1561. The.25. of June. Beyng accused for the vse of certayne siniftral and diuelysh Artes.

Ood people/we here who ye se after thys fort to receyue woorthye & condigne punifhment, amongft whom I my felfe not beyng the leaft of the offenders, led by the greedy delyre of wilfulnes, haue moft wickedly offended god, tranfgreffed hys mofte holye commaundementes, after thefe and fuch lyke fondrye fortes. Firft, when I was but a chylde, hauing a defire to vnderftande of newes, I began to practife the moft diuelifh & fuperfticious knowledge of Necromancie and inuocations of Spirites, in whych thyng longe trauelyng, I feafed not to fyll vp the full meafure of myne iniquities, both in that & curious Aftrologie, butyll by the prouidence of God I was called to a better mynde. Wherefore I now vtterly renounce and forfake al fuche kinde of fuperfticious, curious, wycked, & diuelyfh fciences, wherein the name of God is moft horribly abufed, and focietie or pact wyth wycked Spirites moft deteftablye practifed, as Necromancie, Geomancie, and that curious part of Aftrologie, wherein is contayned the Calculatyng of Natiuities, or as it is commonly faid, the caftyng of Natiuities, wyth all other the Magikes. Knowe ye furthermore that thefe who here ye behold, are for no leffe offences thus fharpely punifhed, fome beyng Magicians and Aftrologians, fome Necromantians, fome Wytches and Sorcerers, fome blynde Propheciers, fome Fortune tellers, a moft peftilent infection of a common wealth. Whych doth deferue the extreme wrath of God, as no les vnto vs is threatened in the moft facred Scriptures, yea death was appoynted to all fuch, as appeareth in the.xx. of Leuiticus. Notwithftandyng that both by the lawes of God, and the Realme, we haue deferued death, yet the Queenes Maieftie(whom Jefus preferue, with her moft honourable Counfell) haue extended the benefite of mercy towardes vs, wyfhing the healthe of our foules, haue thus mofte worthely punifhed vs. We therefore moft thankfully embrace it, wyllingly and gladlye we doo it, beyng fully and certainly affured, that thus vnfainedlye repentyng, as well thefe our forefayd crimes, as all others: we fhal obtaine the mercies of God, whych God of mercy, comfort, and confolacion, graunt vs al here in thys worlde fo to lyue, that in the worlde to come we may haue the fruition of his eternall Deitie. To whom bee laude, empire and glory, for euer and euer. Amen.

¶Thus as a true declaracion of my vnfayned repentaunce in thefe euyl and diuelifh practifes, I haue caufed this my Retractacion to be put in print, to haue it openlye publifhed to all fortes of people. Purpofyng (by Gods helpe) wythin thefe fewe dayes to fet foorth a fmall peece of woorke, to the vtter defafing of thofe diuelifh fciences, wyth the declaration of the horrible practifes and deathes of fuch as haue vfed thofe diabolical Artes, whych (as I truft)fhall feare al other to practife the lyke.

God faue the Queene.

¶Imprinted at London by John Awdely/ dwellyng by great S. Bartelmewes. Anno.1561. The.7. of July.

Figure 2.3. Broadside, "The Unfeigned Retractation of Fraunces Cox" (1651). Reproduced by permission of the Society of Antiquaries, London.

Erasmus's remarks come in the course of his pedagogical treatise "On Correct Pronunciation": "recognition of the handwriting can add a note of conviction, or at any rate an element of pleasure, to a letter. . . . Just as individual voices differ, so does every handwriting have something unique about it" (quoted in Smith 1999: 116–117). How-to-teach books by other authorities confirm that students were encouraged to sound out phonemes as they wrote them down. One late-sixteenth-century teacher of handwriting, Peter Bales, distinguished among three different sorts of hand, each bearing a different relationship to the human voice. "Swift writing," or "brachygraphy," is what we would call shorthand: it moves at the same speed as speaking and encodes the presence of the speaker's voice in abbreviations and symbols that do not follow the rules of conventional orthography. "True writing," though respectful of those rules, still bears the imprint of sound. "Fair writing," finally, is what we would call calligraphy. The writing calls attention to itself as a medium, quite apart from voiced sounds (Smith 1999: 118–119). Printing in lead type would, according to this scheme, stand at an even further remove from the immediacy of speaking. But not in another category altogether, as Cox's confession makes clear.

Particularly striking examples of the direct connection heard between hand and voice can be found in the bound manuscript books into which early modern men and women transcribed poems, speeches, gossip, jokes, recipes, and anything else that happened to strike their fancy. The largest surviving group of such books, more than a hundred, was put together by students in certain Oxford colleges in the 1620s and 1630s. In several respects, most of these books are group endeavors: more than likely the blank book was given to the owner by someone else, just as most of the texts inscribed in the book came from someone else by way of gift or exchange. This situation is often registered in the physical fact of several hands having a part in a single book. George Morley's manuscript book from the 1620s or early 1630s (now Westminster Abbey MS Dean and Chapter 41) even shows a change of hands within a single poem, a series of high-spirited verses on drinking and seduction under the guise of "hunting the hare" (fig. 2.4.). A stanza near the middle of the poem gives a good sense of the whole affair as a reeling *bibe mecum* ("Come drink with me"):

These broad bowls to the Olympical rector
The Troy-born eagle presents on his knee
[A copy of the same poem in Bodleian MS Rawl. poet. 147 says "ingle,"
an allusion to Jupiter's cup-bearer and sexual plaything Ganymede.]

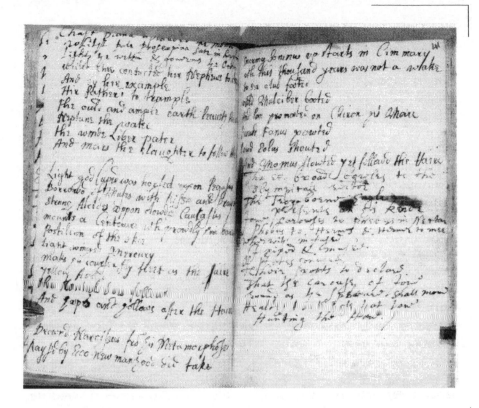

Figure 2.4. Manuscript leaf, MS Westminster Abbey Dean and Chapter 41 (about 1625). Reproduced by permission of the Westminster Abbey Library.

Now carouses to Phoebus and Hermes to me,
Wherewith infused
    I piped and mused
Of states unused
    Choice sports to declare
That the carouse of Jove
    Round as the sphere shall move
Health to all those that love
    Hunting the hare.

Each verse in this tipsy mock-epic invokes a different god or goddess, and in Morley's manuscript the hand that is doing the writing appears to shift from verse to verse. What we seem to be witnessing are the hands of two different writers, each taking a turn at writing verses—which is just what the Olympian catalogue invites. If so, the two writers were playing out an act of "associative composition"—a kind of poetry contest in which each extempore poet tries to outdo the other, perhaps drinking all the while. Certainly the same verses as they appear in Bodleian manuscript Rawl. poet. 147 are fuller and rhythmically more regular, not to mention neater on the page. George Morley may have turned out to be a bishop of Winchester, but in his youth he, like other men of his social rank, educational status, and royalist political persuasions, was eminently clubbable. Timothy Raylor (1993: 69–110) has described the twin pursuits of drinking and burlesque poetry that occupied these updatings of Plato's Symposium in the 1620s and 1630s. "Hunting the Hare" in Morley's manuscript book shapes up as a hastily scribbled record of live improvisation.

In woodcut illustrations, in handwriting, and in print, early modern readers would, therefore, have heard traces of sound where twenty-first-century students are likely to see only marks imprinted on paper—or, ignoring the imprintedness entirely, the concepts that those marks encode. Literacy, or "lettered-ness," meant something different in sixteenth- and early-seventeenth-century England than it does today. Considering the rapid changes that have overtaken human cultures all over the world over the past hundred years, we should not be surprised that orality and literacy would present themselves to many observers as a natural binary. Several social historians, however, have called attention to how misleading that binary is when applied to the culture of early modern England. In Walter Ong's formulation (1965: 145–146), England in the sixteenth and early seventeenth centuries was a "mixed" culture, "literate but with a strong oral residue." Literacy in early modern England was not a monolithic entity. Keith Thomas (1986: 98) distinguished various kinds of literacy in the period: the ability to read Latin as well as English, the ability to read only black-letter type, the ability to read only secretary hand, the ability to read but not write, the ability to write and decipher only mathematical sums. As David Howes (1991: 12) insists, "an orality/literacy divide" is radically modernist and Eurocentric in assuming an inevitable historical evolution from ear to eye.

In the sixteenth and early seventeenth centuries, as in the Middle Ages, writing was not so much a challenge to oral authority as a guarantee of oral authority (Stock 1983). Adam Fox's (2000) exhaustive examination of the documentary evidence supports that conclusion. "If anything," Fox observes, "the written word tended to augment the spoken, reinventing it and making it anew, propagating its contents, heightening its exposure, and ensuring its continued vitality" (2000:

5). The written word in early modern England still carried the bodily force of the spoken word. For us, written words are symbols, arbitrary signs of the things being signified. For Shakespeare's contemporaries, I would argue, written words functioned as indices, as signs carrying a bodily, metonymic connection with the things being signified.

Finding a Syntax

Once I had found and catalogued the sounds of early modern England, I faced an even greater challenge: that of finding a "syntax" for making sense of the sounds. How did Shakespeare and his contemporaries order the sounds they heard and made? How did they use those sounds to position themselves in the world? In my bafflement I found myself in the position of Geoffrey Streamer, a fictional character in William Baldwin's satire *Beware the Cat* (1584). Sitting in a friend's house near Aldersgate in London, Streamer cooked up a magic potion that, when applied to his ears, allowed him to hear all the sounds within a hundred miles: "barking of dogs, grunting of hogs, wailing of cats, rambling of rats, gaggling of geese, humming of bees, . . . flittering of fowls, routing of knaves, snorting of slaves, farting of churls, fizzling of girls . . . ringing of bells, counting of coins, mounting of groins, whispering of lovers"— and a great deal more (quoted in Smith 1999: 30–31). As an English professor, I knew all about the function of syntax in ordering the sounds of speech. But how could I make sense of all that Geoffrey Streamer heard?

It was at this confused juncture that I turned to the discipline of acoustic ecology, in particular to the work of Murray Schafer (1993) and Barry Truax. In *Acoustic Communication* (1984), Truax challenges listeners to free themselves from the narrow confines of speech and to listen to all the sounds around them. He orders these sounds along a continuum of syntax that is temporally more and more extended:

primal cries → speech → music → ambient sound

Discussing this model in the course of a seminar I convened at the Folger Shakespeare Library in Washington, D.C., in 1996, a professional voice coach suggested that what we had in this scheme was not a linear continuum but a circle that began and ended in primal cries. Human exclamations of "oh," "ah," "mmm," and the like take their place in the ambient world of animal sounds, wind, and rushing water. The resulting model inscribes an *O*, which is, in two dimensions at least, a representation of the shape of sound.

Most historians of early modern England have focused their attention on a very narrow range of sounds, those involved in speech. My goal in *The Acoustic World* was to attend to the full range of sounds that made England in the late sixteenth and early seventeenth centuries a place distinct from other places. That project occupied me particularly in a chapter on three representative soundscapes: city, country, and court. In each case, I singled out one specific place—the Aldersgate quarter where Geoffrey Streamer lodged in the City of London, Kenilworth in Warwickshire, Whitehall Palace in Westminster—and attempted to provide what anthropologists would call "thick description." Maps, site plans, legal documents, travelers' accounts, literary allusions, and surviving structures and landscape features gave me the evidence I sought. I turned also to the findings of modern acoustics with respect to decibel measurements, the effects of wind direction, the effects of greater and lesser degrees of humidity according to the seasons of the year, and so forth.

The soundscape of Kenilworth can stand as an example of my project. An estate map of 1628, housed in the Public Record Office, and an engraved view of Kenilworth Castle by Wenceslas Hollar (1656) allowed me to locate just which parts of the land had been forested, which had been used as open meadows for grazing, which had been farmed under the open field system, and which had been farmed or grazed as enclosed lands. Accounts of Queen Elizabeth's visit to the site in 1575 filled the woods with the sounds of hunting: horn blasts, halloing humans, yelping hounds. Agricultural historians such as Joan Thirsk (1984) described the communal conditions under which work was carried out in open fields, suggesting that continuous talk and perhaps singing accompanied the rasps, swishes, cuts, and thumps of the workers' tools as they labored close by one another, all focused on the same tasks at the same time. Travelers' accounts added barking dogs to the soundscape. Gerschow observed that as a relatively underpopulated country in 1602, England provided enough food for even the humblest farmer to keep dogs as pets and for farm use. Packing up all this evidence, I paid a visit to the site and was able to overlay the soundscape of today's Kenilworth with the sounds heard there four hundred years ago. My findings in the chapter on the soundscapes of early modern England became the basis for a series of four programs broadcast in spring and autumn 2000 over BBC Radio 4.

For all that, I have become increasingly skeptical about the idea of a universal syntax of sound, even one so inclusive as a circle of sound beginning and ending in [o:]. The witnesses whose written accounts I consulted suggested, at the minimum, three distinct syntaxes for country, court, and city. At least as these literate witnesses heard it, the countryside not only contained many more nonverbal sounds than the court and the city but also recognized more ways in which those nonverbal sounds were meaningful. Take, for example, sounds made by birds. Temporary refugees from urban life such as Thomas Dekker, in his pamphlet "The Bellman of London" (1616), were apt to hear bird sounds as abstract music: "The melody which the birds made . . . put me in mind of that garden whereof our great grandsire [Adam] was the keeper" (quoted in Smith 1999: 75). To a full-time denizen of the country, however, bird sounds took on meaning in a seasonal syntax, as Thomas Tusser, in his versified farming manual, *A Hundred Good Points of Husbandry* (1557), explained with respect to the plowman in spring: "A whole flight of crows follow him for their food, and when they fly away they give him ill language" (quoted in Smith 1999: 75).

By contrast, the court, attendant on the monarch's every word, employed a syntax of sound that was extremely logocentric. The city's syntax lay somewhere in between. Certainly there were places in the city—the Royal Exchange, the law courts, St. Paul's Cathedral—where words held sway. But the varieties of trade, still associated with specific London wards, ordered sounds in their own distinctive ways. Tailors, blacksmiths, weavers, and tinkers were associated not only with the specific sounds of their crafts (snipping, pounding, thrustling, banging) but also with specific catches or rounds that they sang while they worked (Fox 2000: 29). Street vendors, too, had their distinctive quasi-musical cries (Smith 1999: 64–70).

If geography was one determinant of the syntax of sound, social class was another. Adam Fox (2000) has studied the pressures toward standardization in diction and pronunciation that rapid economic development brought to England's speech communities in the late sixteenth and early seventeenth centuries, particularly along lines of social hierarchy (2000: 100–110). Over the course of this time period, "hey nonny nonny" and "hey troly loly" increasingly became the preserve of the lower orders (2000: 27). The most significant factor of all seems to have been book-based education. Among educated listeners in early modern England there was a pronounced distrust of nonverbal sounds. The whoops and hollers of countryfolk and lower-class crafts-men might be amusing in a pageant or a masque, but such sounds marked the boundary between civility and barbarity. That became ever more apparent as colonial expansion and voyages of conquest placed the strategic boundary between civility and barbarity ever farther away in geographical space—and made the people on the other side of the boundary ever more remote. The Irish "hubbub" in times of mourning, argument, or celebration struck horror and contempt in English ears (Smith 1999: 305–306). So, too, did the music and speeches of Native Americans. John Smith, in *A Map of Virginia* (1612), described the chanting of the Powhatan Indians as "a terrible noise as would rather affright than delight any man" (quoted in Smith 1999: 324). (One notes here the unquestioned universal criterion of judgment implied by "any man.")

The distrust of nonverbal sound extended even to music. The musical contest between Apollo and Marsyas, recounted in Ovid's Metamorphoses, Book 6, and elsewhere, provides the paradigmatic myth for understanding this distrust. Marsyas, man from the waist up, goat from the waist down, chanced to find a pipe that had been cast off by Pallas. The satyr became so proud of his playing that he challenged Apollo, whose instrument was the lyre. Apollo's victory, according to Renaissance commentators, had to do not only with cosmic resonance between the lengths of the lyre's strings and the distances between the planets but also with Apollo's ability to sing words while he played. As the Greek statesman Alcibiades is quoted to have said, "Let the Thebans play on the flute, who know not how to speak: but for us Athenians, we have Pallas and Apollo for the patrons of our country" (Sandys 1632: 225). The ultimate authority for such a prejudice is Plato, who refers sound, like all other sensible experience, to the jurisdiction of Ideas. Sound without logos is, to Plato's mind, noise. For sound without logos there can be no syntax. Our own culture's anxiety in the presence of nonverbal sounds has a very long history.

Relating Past to Present

When I stood at Kenilworth Castle at the exact spot where Wenceslas Hollar had stood drafting his view in the 1650s, it seemed all too easy to imagine what the place sounded like to Hollar. Immediately, however, I checked myself. My experience as a student of the history of sexuality caught me up short. What I was feeling was the palpable presence of the past, but the theories of interpretation dominant in my own time and place taught me to resist both the illusion of presence and my attachment to that illusion. New historicism would insist that, even if the sounds were the same, the protocols of listening to those sounds in 1600 were socially constructed and thus very different from mine. My desire to listen was nostalgic and hence unprofessional. Deconstruction would remind me that the sensation of presence I was feeling was mediated by language—and that language, at bottom, is a series of signifiers that never coincide with the things they purport to signify. In effect, both methodologies asked me to forget the sounds of 1650 and listen to the traffic noises along the A46 just over the hill. And yet . . .

The fourth challenge facing me in writing *The Acoustic World of Early Modern England* was perhaps the most formidable of all: to find a way of relating past to present that preserves the differences between them. With respect to bodily experience in the past, two extreme positions present themselves: biological essentialism and social constructionism. On the one hand, it is patently clear that Shakespeare and his contemporaries shared with us the same physiological apparatus for speaking and hearing. On the other hand, it is just as patently clear that they spoke and listened according to different ideas about how a person hears sounds and responds to them.

For early modern men and women, hearing was a whole-body experience. By the first decades of the seventeenth century, scientific anatomy was demonstrating the apparatus and functions of the inner ear, but textbook writers such as Helkiah Crooke, in his *Microcosmographia: A Description of the Body of Man* (1616), attempted to reconcile this information with received ideas about the body as a hydraulic system of four basic fluids or humors (Siraisi 1990: 97–114). With respect to hearing, the result was a compromise between ancient ideas and modern ones. The sixteenth century inherited a model of hearing that derived ultimately from Aristotle's *De Anima*, expanded and worked out in detail to accord with the medical writings of Galen and to incorporate recent anatomical investigations. According to this model, oscillations of air impinge on the eardrum, which transmits the impulses to spiritus, the aerated fluid that courses through the entire body and communicates among all its parts. Spiritus then conveys the impulses to common sense, where they are fused with other sensations of the external event (such as vision) and are thence conveyed to imagination or "phantasy." Imagination converts the sensations into a species (or internal image), which spiritus then disperses through the entire body. Anatomical studies and the philosophical criterion of efficiency led sixteenth- and seventeenth-century thinkers increasingly to question the existence of species, but authorities such as Crooke and even Descartes could not give up the idea of the body as a hydraulic system in which spiritus did the work of intercommunication among the body's parts. In his description of the physiology of hearing in *Microcosmographia*, Crooke demonstrates that he knows all about the nerves as a network of specialized tissue; what he does not know is the workings of electrical impulses (1616: 606–610).

The notion of spiritus means that every sense experience, and every making of meaning, is an experience that involves the entire body. Sound, like other forms of sensation, activates the listener's passions. As Thomas Wright explained in *The Passions of the Mind in General* (1604: 123):

> First, then, to our imagination cometh by sense or memory some object to be known, convenient or disconvenient to Nature; the which being known . . . in the imagination . . . , presently the purer spirits flock from the brain by certain secret channels to the heart, where they pitch at the door, signifying what an object was presented, convenient or disconvenient for it. The heart immediately bendeth either to prosecute it or to eschew it, and the better to effect that affection draweth other humors to help him.

The listener experiences this visceral bodily response as passion, as a chemical phenomenon rather than as an electrical phenomenon. In this model, passion stands in an uneasy relationship to reason. Reason ought to monitor and control all the sensations that heart registers, but, as Wright concedes, the passions have a friendlier working relationship with the senses than they do with reason. Indeed, the passions can prevent reason from knowing the truth about objects that the body, through the senses, sees and hears. Say, for example, a person's senses take particular pleasure in the color green. "You may well see," Wright declares, "how the imagination putteth green spectacles before the eyes of our wit to make it see nothing but green, that is, serving for the consideration of the passion" (1604: 128). It is possible, I would argue, to *hear* green as well as to see green if the listener attends to sounds other than those of rational speech.

To claim that making meaning through sound is altogether a cultural construct is, however, just as partial as to assume physiological determinism. My solution has been a compromise in which I accept the "hardwiring" of the human body with respect to speaking and listening but understand that each culture provides its own "software" for programming those capacities. The hardwiring may determine the range of possibilities, but no one set of cultural software ever exploits them all. Constance Classen (1993) has called attention to the ways in which different cultures weight the senses differently vis-à-vis one another. In some cultures, sound is more important than in others.

Steven Feld (1996), for example, has demonstrated that sound operates as the dominant means of orientation among the Kaluli people of Papua New Guinea, who live in dense rainforests.

A methodology that insists on the embodiedness of all knowledge and yet recognizes the cultural differences that shape that knowledge might be called "historical phenomenology." Let us consider the two parts of that coinage separately. The basic premise of phenomenology is simple enough: no one—in the sixteenth century or now, in Europe or in Papua New Guinea, in a library or in a rainforest—can know anything apart from the way in which he or she comes to know it. Knowledge is always embodied knowledge. The qualifier "historical" affirms that bodily ways of knowing are not universal, as perceptual psychologists are apt to assume, but are shaped by cultural differences. In effect, "historical phenomenology" combines the phenomenology of perception as practiced by Maurice Merleau-Ponty and his successors in the 1950s and 1960s (see Merleau-Ponty 1962) with new historicism as practiced by Michel Foucault and his successors since the 1970s (see Foucault 1972 [1969]).

From its first appearance in the English language in the early seventeenth century, the word *phenomenon* has been academically suspect. According to the *Oxford English Dictionary*, the earliest instance of the word in English occurred in Francis Bacon's English version of *The Advancement of Learning* (2000 [1605]). While discussing that branch of knowledge "which is the knowledge of our selves," Bacon advises that "all partitions of knowledges be accepted rather for lines and veins than for sections and separations"; as a negative example he cites the distinction between astronomy and "natural philosophy." Because of this arbitrary distinction, Copernicus's proposal that the earth revolves around the sun, and not the sun around the earth, can be demonstrated only by natural philosophy, not by astronomy, "because it is not repugnant to any of the phainomena" (2000: 93). That is to say, astronomy is concerned only with how things appear to be; natural philosophy is concerned with how things are. The implicit contrast between deceptive sensation and real knowledge—a distinction made by Plato—is deeply ingrained in Western consciousness. Kant fixed this contrast in terms that make immediate sense to us: *phenomenon* versus *noumenon:* "appearing" or "passing" versus *das Ding-an-sich*, the thing-in-itself.

All current critical models for reading texts, I would argue, take as their object—or rather they purport to take as their object—the thing-in-itself. The situation is registered in the visual bias of current critical jargon: "site," "boundary," "binary." In ancient Greek, *phenomenon* and *noumenon* are both present participles, but the emphasis in *noumenon* falls on the past tense: a *noumenon* is an "object perceived." The emphasis in *phenomenon* falls, by contrast, on the present tense. And although *phenomenon* is a present participle, it is neither active ("appearing") or passive ("being shown") but in the middle voice. The distinction between active voice ("I speak") and passive voice ("I am spoken to") strikes speakers of modern English as absolutely natural. Yet Emile Benveniste (1971) has demonstrated that passive voice is a relatively new development in Indo-European languages. Before passive voice there was middle voice. Anyone who has struggled to learn ancient Greek has had to come to terms with this concept. Middle voice covers situations in which, as Benveniste puts it, "the subject is the center as well as the agent of the process; he achieves something which is being achieved in him. . . . He is indeed inside the process of which he is the agent" (1971: 149).

Surveying a number of Indo-European languages, Benveniste finds several verbs that occur only in middle voice: to be born, to die, to follow, to be master, to lie, to sit, to come back to a familiar state, to enjoy, to suffer, to experience mental disturbance, to take measures, and—most significantly—to speak. In Latin, the middle voice survives in so-called deponent verbs, which exist only in the passive voice but carry active meanings: *polliceri* (to promise), *sequi* (to follow), *potiri* (to gain possession), *arbitrari* (to think), *loqui* (to speak). In early modern English, certain reflexive idioms may carry the force of middle voice. When Bottom in *A Midsummer Night's Dream* tries to tell the audience about his dream of making love to the fairy queen, he presents it, not as something he thought, nor yet again as something that "thought" him, but as something in between: "Methought I was—there is no man can tell what. Methought I was, and methought I had—but man is but a patched fool if he will offer to say what methought I had" (4.1.205–208 in Shakespeare 1988). In "methought," Bottom assumes middle voice. The effect is even more marked in the so-called ethical dative, when the first-person speaker gets so caught up in his third-person story that he introduces himself as the indirect object of the action, as Shylock does in *The Merchant of Venice* when he begins his story of Laban's sheep: "The skillful shepherd pealed me certain wands" (1.3.83 in Shakespeare 1988).

In middle voice the object does not exist apart from the subject. That is exactly the position I have attempted to take as an archaeologist of sound. The syntactical unit that best captures the situation of the knowing subject, Michel Serres claims (1997: 146), is not nouns, not adjectives, not even verbs, but prepositions: "before and after construct their viscous fluidity; with and without, the hesitating divisions; over and under, the false and true subject; for and against, the violent passions; behind and before, the cowardly hypocrisies and courageous loyalties; in and outside of, the corporeal and theoretical," and so on with *between* and *beyond, from* and *via* and *toward*. What Serres describes is relational knowledge. The basic premise of phenomenology—you can know nothing apart from the way in which you come to know it— applies not only to the men and women of early modern England but to contemporary investigators of early modern culture. Such a way of knowing recognizes the embodiedness of historical subjects and attends to the materiality of the evidence they have left behind at the same time it acknowledges the embodiedness of the investigator in the face of that evidence. In all three respects, the methodology I am describing here is a historical phenomenology. Texts not only represent bodily experience; they imply it in the ways they ask to be touched, seen, heard, even smelled and tasted. New historicism/cultural materialism and deconstruction, if not Lacanian psychoanalytical theory, are not really able to assume that position: they require a stance of "opposite" or "against." The operative word in acoustical archaeology is "among."

Ambiguous Traces, Mishearing, and Auditory Space

Paul Carter

Anthropologists and historians are *hearing* cultures. The result, as this volume amply attests, is a greatly expanded understanding of the ways in which cultures produce and reproduce themselves symbolically. Substituting hearing for looking has theoretical implications: the Athenians dispatched *theoroi* to observe and report their neighbors' customs. Suppose that, instead of seeing those places, these proto-anthropologists had heard them: how would they have theorized their encounters with the other?

Hearing *can* be conceptualized (like looking) as a detached registration and classification of external phenomena. In this case the epiphany of the hearing cultures project occurred over a century ago, with the invention of electro-acoustic sound-recording technology. I suspect, though, that the mobilization of audition as a mode of knowing would have had a different outcome. It would have meant *listening*. Listening is engaged hearing. Its social equivalent in the visual sphere is the experience of eyes meeting and the sense that this produces of being involved in a communicational contract. Indeed, in an environment attuned to listening, the idea of *hearing* cultures might never have arisen. Empirical support for this surmise might be found in the bilingualism that characterizes societies such as that of the Bororo of Brazil, who are divided into two exogamic moieties. For the Bororo, "it is literally through the *other* (someone of the opposite moiety) that an individual exists socially" (Novaes 1997: 143). For them, to be "heard" socially depends upon mastering a feedback loop between listening and speaking. That anthropologists have been so slow to recognize this suggests that, even when hearing cultures, they may not listen to them.

Remaining detached from the communicational contract that listening implies, they may still hear cultures as if looking at them with their ears.

To identify listening cultures not only expands the project of hearing cultures but also brings into question its premise, that hearing can be detached from listening. As a precondition of communication with another, listening is intentional. In contrast to the detached auditor, whose prosthetic ear is the microphone, the listener is after traces of significance. Listeners listen with both ears, monitoring their own mimetic responses to what is said and heard. Usually listening is unconscious. Where the ground rules of communication are established, those communicating hear and speak without listening closely to the other and without consciously hearing themselves.

Listening becomes *cultural work* where the ground rules are not established. There, vocalizations may or may not signify. They produce ambiguous auditory traces. Listening, unlike hearing, values ambiguity, recognizing it as a communicational mechanism for creating new symbols and word senses that might eventually become widely adopted. In this sense, the discourse of listening recapitulates in the cultural sphere the "inner speech" that Lev Vygotsky found characterized the speech development of children between the ages of three and five (Kozulin 1986: xxxviii). In this context of *intentional* hearing, mishearing is certainly a drawback to clear, straightforward communication. On the other hand, it may preserve "the expression of intimate thoughts [not least the thought of what cannot be communicated] in linguistic form, thus making them communicative" (Kozulin 1986: xxxviii). In this way mishearing can be creative: in situations of cross-cultural encounter, where power is distributed unevenly, echoic mimicry can be a means by which the relatively weak resist silencing, preserving instead a degree of historical agency.

Listening is intentional hearing. If the notion of intentionality "'comes by metaphor' from the Latin *intendere arcum in*, which means to aim a bow and arrow at (something)" (Anscombe, quoted in Carter 1996: 329), then listening also differs from hearing in taking account of the situation of audition. Listeners are like hunters following up ambiguous traces. Hunters never aim directly. They take account of the arrow's arcing flight. If the quarry is in motion, their aim anticipates its further flight. Listeners construct auditory space similarly. To be communicative depends upon anticipating the other's moves. The aim is not to end the communication but to keep it going. Whereas hearing remains monological, listening is always dialogical. Ideally, a conversation evolving out of ambiguity and mishearing retains these signs of what cannot be fully communicated. Then it is like the conversation that, Hans-Georg Gadamer says, is characteristic of tradition: "One breaks it off because it seems that enough has been said or that there is nothing more to say. But every such break has an intrinsic relation to the resumption of the dialogue" (quoted in Linge 1977: xxxiii). Auditory space, then, gives back to discourse its old physical sense of running hither and thither. Such a space is like the field of play in a ball game. *Hearing* its discourse is like defining the rules of the game solely in terms of the white lines governing the moves. Only by becoming a player and following the ever-uncertain flight of the ball can one begin to listen.

Active listening is not simply psychological jargon. In the context of "hearing cultures," it conjures up historical, cultural, or social situations in which listening surfaces as a device for creating new symbols and word senses. As these arise dialogically, in the back-and-forth of mutual (mis-)understanding, they have the capacity to ground communication differently, the ambiguity out of which they evolve establishing a new tradition. The cultural work done on such occasions is far from trivial. Usually precipitated in circumstances of an imminent loss of personal and collective identity, its echoic poetics is both tactical and profoundly political. The pleasure principle to which Vygotsky's inner speech is tied need not be regressive or antisocial (Kozulin 1986: xxxvi). Refusing to submit to a reality principle whose communicational goal is mutual intelligibility, those who act on what they hear insist on the erotic basis of communication. Instead of a monologue *à deux*, from which ambiguity is removed, on the principle that "meeting is for strangers" (Eliot 1969: 337), they enact a dialogue in which differences make a difference.

To illustrate listening as a cultural practice, I consider three situations: cross-cultural encounters and collisions resulting from European imperialism; experiences of misunderstanding and associated communicational strategies in contemporary multicultural migrant communities; and the construction of the persona in dramatic practice. The heterogeneity of these situations betrays a non-anthropologist's intellectual dilettantism. Yet the choice is not entirely accidental. Its object is to suggest that listening has theoretical as well as practical utility. The interpretive crisis that overtook Columbus and the Taino people of Hispaniola in 1492 is historically and geographically unrelated to the communicational difficulties faced by an Italo-Australian working on a mass-production line in 1960s Melbourne. Dramatic works *about* that interpretive crisis or those communicational difficulties are further removed again, in both space and time.

Currently, the three situations are inscribed in different disciplinary narratives. Indigenous responses to European imperialism belong to historical anthropology. Sociologists identify the plight of the migrant worker. Evaluating the *representation* of these situations is a matter for performance studies. Interdisciplinary bridgeheads are breaking down this intellectual separation of powers, but the new commonalities discovered tend to be metaphorical. In this chapter, the nexus between listening and cultural production assumes theoretical significance, for it suggests that the commonality is not metaphorical but structural. If this is true, then these apparently heterogeneous situations may be different manifestations of an acoustic ecology whose existence, maintenance, and renewal listening secures.

Echoic Mimicry

The historical, cultural, and social role listening plays emerges in the phenomenon of echoic mimicry. In its most radical form, echoic mimicry is communication in the absence of anything to say. In René Girard's anthropology, mimetic desire triangulates when one desire imitates another in seeking its object (Girard 1976: passim). Echoic mimicry precedes this, embodying a desire to create the conditions of communication from which an object of desire might emerge. What is "desired" is a common place that, through the act of imitating each other, the parties contract to share. The third term in this process of imitating the other is not an "object" beyond but the articulation of a space in-between, which can provide the ground of future discourse. If "culture is communication" (Dahl 1999: 8), then echoic mimicry recapitulates the origins of culture. What signifies at this point is not a shared language but the desire or necessity to communicate. The means of articulating this desire is the manipulation of ambiguous "sounds in-between" (Carter 1992: 11–14). Because no echo in this mimetic exchange is disinterested, but reflects the speaker's own lexical, phonological, and intonational heritage, the result is an agreement to recognize certain shared word-sounds as significant. The first *topic*, or commonplace, of this echoically performed listening is the *place* of mutual recognition.

The triangulation that echoic mimicry brings about, between the participants and the place of orientation toward each other, is suggested by the anthropologist Roy Wagner, who, meditating on the significance of bats in so-called totemic thought, posits a "genuine semiotics" in which humans would listen for themselves in conversation, by this echolocation learning about the limits of communication: "It is because sound is not meaning but the meaningfulness of direction that . . . the bat [can] listen to itself as a navigational vector." He continues:

> It is in sound's inability to merge with or directly encode the meanings attributed to language that it similarly becomes meaningful for human beings, allows them to listen to themselves as vectors of meaning through a medium that is not meaning. Those who wish to ground meaning in language are disposed to imagine the "sign" through a magical precision bridging sound and sense, but such a coding, to the degree it were precise and exhaustive, would render impossible the "play" or ambiguity, the irony of sound and meaning—would nullify sound's echolocative possibilities. (Wagner 2001: 137)

The three situations nominated earlier furnish plentiful evidence of echoic mimicry. The *locus classicus* of cross-cultural collision resulting from European imperialism, Columbus's encounter with Taino people in October 1492, largely revolved *discursively* around an ambiguously signifying word-sound, *ca*. Echoically generated from this core were such apparently significant words as *Guanahani*, *canibe*, and *caribe*, and their variants, *canoa*, *Canarias*, and *canna*. How is this consonantal concentration to be explained? Any reconstruction is of course largely speculative. However, what can be said with some certainty is that it will need to factor in the phenomenon of echoic mimicry. To speculate, for example, that *canona*, reported on 22 December, is "an error for *canoa* (canoe), probably resulting from confusion with *canoa*, Arawakan for 'gold'" (Columbus 1989: 263 n. 1), may indicate a laudable intention to *hear* culture. But its notion of a "confusion" is fanciful. Columbus and the Taino men were not ethnolinguists collaborating on a bilingual dictionary. Their efforts at dialogue were not predicated on fixed meanings—which, once established, would render further conversation superfluous. The effort was *not* to fall silent: as the sign of discourse, made fertile by ambiguity, confusion was desirable. My guess is that *ca* emerged echoically as a key word-sound because of Columbus's concern to prove that he had made landfall in China (ruled over by the Grand Khan, whose name Columbus pidginized as *Cane Grane*; see Carter 1996: 188–189). But in any case, the *ca-ca* dialogue that resulted eloquently demonstrates that echoic mimicry is not inhibited by an absence of anything to say.

A colorful instance of the echoic mimicry in which migrants find themselves immersed is supplied by R. A. Baggio, the Australian author of a self-published memoir. In *The Shoe in My Cheese*, Baggio records the distortions to which his Italian names were subjected when non-Italo-Australians attempted to pronounce them:

> They named me, Rino, pronounced ideally Rino, and locally as Reen-oh; Rhine-oh; Renault; Reo; Reen, by the over sixties; Ringo by the Beatle-maniacs; and sometimes Ringe or Roscig, out of the junkmailers' computers. Our surname, Baggio, is similarly well-suited for invention, improvisation, innovation, and fantastication: Badgee-oh; Baggy-oh; Badge-EE-oh; Bag-Eye-oh; Bug-Eye-oh; Barge-ee-oh; Buggy-oh; Bar-Joe; and the Danaean, Baggos, favoured by our dairyman on his invoices for thirty years or so." (Baggio 1989: 15)

On the face of it, Baggio laments that loss of "a magical precision bridging sound and sense" referred to by Wagner. But the echoic mimicry in which Baggio himself indulges suggests an equally strong nostalgia for the future. Imitating his mimics, Baggio cultivates some "invention, improvisation, innovation, and fantastication" of his own. The result is that he extracts from the confusion of mishearing a new identity for himself, one constructed echoically and mimetically. His baroque flourish suggests a frustrated desire of community, a sense that the communication that would enable him to be "heard" has somehow passed him by.

The structural identity of Baggio's situation with that of the actor called upon to perform a script is neatly encapsulated in John Berger's reflection on the modern migrant's condition: "His migration is like an event in a dream dreamt by another. As a figure in a dream dreamt by an unknown sleeper, he appears to act autonomously, at times unexpectedly; but everything he does—unless he revolts—is determined by the needs of the dreamer's mind" (Berger 1975: 43). The text that determines the migrant's actions is historical, economic, and social. Otherwise, Berger might be describing the situation that Antonin Artaud applauded in his essay on the Balinese shadow-puppet theater, where everything is "in effect calculated with an adorable and mathematical precision. Nothing in it is left to chance or personal initiative. It is a superior form of dance in which every dancer aims first and foremost to be an actor" (Artaud 1993: 88).

The point is that this manipulation by another does not necessarily represent a loss of agency or a diminution of identity. The dramaturgist's adorable calculations produce "a double body, doubly membered" (Artaud 1993: 89). As in Bororo society, so in Balinese shadow puppetry: it is literally through the other that one comes to exist—only the "one" is always doubled, that is, an echo constructed mimetically. Further, the cultural value of the meaning thus produced resides in the fact that it does *not* mimic the clear, straightforward communication preferred in our modern, rationalistic society. Instead, it shows the limits of communication. And it achieves this by insisting upon the truth-value of ambiguity: its "perpetual game of mirrors, in which a colour passes into a gesture and a cry into a movement, leads us without rest along rough paths we find hard to follow, plunging us into a state of uncertainty and unspeakable distress which is truly poetic" (Artaud 1993: 96; my translations).

Listening Devices

Artaud's identification of the poetic with uncertainty and unspeakable distress is worth pondering. In the context of "hearing cultures," I am making the case for listening to cultures. But what is the value of attending to the "inner speech" of history or culture? As the revival of experiences of distress—the terror of the about-to-be colonized, the repeated humiliations of the migrant or the refugee, the ethical conundrums of the impersonator—it does not seem to be therapeutic. It reinforces a skepticism about clear, straightforward, grand narratives of any kind. Would it not be wiser to let sleeping dogs lie? The model of cultural production informing the human sciences is emancipatory: individuals and cultures are imagined gaining greater control over their identities and destinies. To argue that ambiguity, mishearing, and self-doubling are integral to a true semiotics of communication undermines this project. Compare, in this regard, the different connotations of the terms "hearing device" and "listening device." The former is unequivocally associated with a simultaneous enlargement of the senses and the mind. The latter is authority's agent, a surveillance technique designed to ensure that no revolt is possible, that even our secret communications are determined by the needs of the state listener's mind. To listen into cultures or, throwing off the guise of detachment, to be a performer participating in the echolocative rituals associated with becoming in relation to another, suggests a loss of agency—a condition the modern Westerner finds unspeakably distressing.

Distressing but, if Artaud is believed, "truly poetic": the ironic stance to reality implicit in listening not only has a critical value. Recognizing that we are heard, as well as hear, and acknowledging that our speech originates, not in a disembodied silence, but in a tumultuous incorporation of the other's voice and that discourse is the process of giving meaning to echoic mimicry, active listeners can claim to transcend the dualism implicit in most hermeneutical enterprises. The mimicry that characterized cross-cultural encounters along the Caribbean littoral rarely brought indigenous people any lasting benefit. Hence, as Stephen Greenblatt argues, "improvisation on the part of either Europeans or natives should not be construed as the equivalent of sympathetic understanding; it is rather what we can call appropriative mimesis, imitation in the interest of acquisition" (Greenblatt 1991: 98). He adds: "A process of mimetic doubling and projection . . . does not lead to identification with the other but to a ruthless will to dominate" (Greenblatt 1991: 99).

Generalization in this area is difficult. I question, though, the emancipatory model of communication implicit in Greenblatt's judgment. To invoke "sympathetic understanding" is still tacitly to measure the success of communication in terms of its capacity to preserve the integrity of the individual ego (and its speaking position). Plunging the ego into uncertainty, dialogue is, from this point of view, always threatening. In cultures in which one exists literally through the other, "identification with the other" may be an unnecessary hypothesis. Equally, appropriation and acquisition need not be synonyms of domination but simply the badges of growing up.

Besides, the existential lot of *Homo imperiosus* has never been a deeply happy one: "much less unhappy when he is absolutely alone than when he is afraid he may not be," he fears nothing more than attachment to another (Mannoni 1956: 100). In this context, the value of listening's discourse becomes apparent. Refusing to submit to a reality principle— ideologically identified with clear, straightforward communication— those who plunge into the uncertain realm of echoic mimicry make pleasure their principle. They acknowledge that in the absence of anything to say, there is still a desire for communication. The myth figure who presides over this desire is that "incomplete form in motion" representable only as "a process and project of execution, deepening, retreating and recovering, searching out new moulds, and rising above and beyond every determination" (Burch 2000: 187–188), which we know as Eros. In other words, echoic mimicry may not deliver us from care, but it creates in those who yield to its power a feeling of historical agency, a capacity to rise above and beyond every determination, that, while associated with uncertainty and distress, is "truly poetic."

Consider two further Australian instances of migrant nostalgia. The first is the fable; Antigone Kefala's character Alexia learns to explain the lack of affect that typifies ordinary Australian English speech: "Many many years before, everyone on the Island had been forced to swear an Oath of Silence, and to speak only when absolutely forced, and even then to use the minimum of sounds, and if possible only a few, such as 'mg,' or 'ag,' which were forever repeated in sorrow, regret, surprise, admiration, entreaty, contempt, mockery" (Kefala 1984, unnumbered). Listening to these meaningless vocalizations, Alexia "imagined that there must be a great and subtle complexity in these sounds and that her ear was not attuned to them, so she kept listening, listening, as one would to the cry of birds, hoping to discover the key to their language" (Kefala 1984, unnumbered).

The second instance is the recollection of a postwar migrant upon arriving at Bonegilla, a migrant "processing" camp located in a kind of nowhere place on the border between Victoria and New South Wales. Like Alexia, the memorialist finds that his incapacity to communicate in a straightforward way enlarges his conception of what communication might be. He spent the day given him "to settle down," he writes, going for a walk: "My ears were getting used to the sounds about, and smiled [sic]. Cattle mooing, dogs barking, sheep, bees, birds, well THEY were 'talking' as in Europa. It lifted my morale" (Sluga 1985: 253).

Alexia's sounds may be intended to silence her (to prevent her from speaking the language of the island). Instead, driven by her desire to communicate, Alexia hears in them another language. This other language is not governed by the reality principle. Expressing emotions directly, as the cries of the birds do, it mimics the inner speech true to the pleasure principle. As the echo of her own listening, it transforms her communicational situation. No longer isolated and muted, she envisages the possibility of a universal communication, a language rising above and beyond every determination. The Bonegilla detainee finds more: detecting in the environmental sounds a language that spoke to him, echoing his desire to communicate, he is delivered into an auditory space that "grounds" him in the nonplace of the detention camp. In his case, the archetypal triangulation mentioned before has the sonorous landscape as its other. But the result is the same: the creation of a commonplace where he can hear himself think. And again, the precondition of this gain in historical agency, deeply distressing as it may be, depends on a mishearing that is truly poetic. Like Balinese shadow puppets, Alexia and the migrant at the Bonegilla camp take some control of their situations by refusing the criterion of successful self-representation—the ideological fiction of clear, straightforward language. By taking ambiguity out of the realm of representation and insisting on it as a generative principle of communication, they revolt against their role as actors in another's place. For whether that place is language or the film set of the detention center, it is a place, like the proscenium-arch theater, in which everything is justified by the fiction of representation.

What is the consequence of this? The Polish theater director Tadeusz Kantor is clear. These "sterilized and immunized places (it is difficult to call a museum or auditorium a real place)," dedicated to the presentation of "ambiguous acts of representation," prevent ambiguity from being embraced as a manifestation of reality (Kantor 1993: 99). If, as I suggest, the communicational dilemma of the migrant directly parallels the actor's difficulty, then the striking relevance of Kantor's remarks to the understanding of Kefala's character or the Bonegilla detainee is less surprising. Kantor elaborates Artaud's insight that, in order to solve "the dilemma of autonomy and representation, with ease," the new actors (but they might be new historical subjects) do not retreat into a Cartesian ego-consciousness. Without nostalgia for selfhood, they embrace their professional personae, with characteristically ambiguous results: "They do not imitate anything, they do not represent anybody, they do not express anything but themselves, human shells, exhibitionists, con artists" (Kantor 1993: 101). They are no longer actors reproducing the ambiguities of reality. They are players whose own performance is ambiguous. By this device, like echoic mimics, they bring into being a new, in-between place: "Playing is identified in the theater with the concept of performance. One says, 'To play a part.' 'Playing,' however, means neither reproduction nor reality itself. It means something 'inbetween' illusion and reality" (Kantor 1993: 100). And as Kantor stresses, redefining the poetics of performance also alters the "situation" of the audience member, who is no longer someone passively in "a state of hearing" but "a potential player" (Kantor 1993: 101).

In light of this, we can return to our first situation, that of colonial encounter. Mimetic behavior *may* have been associated with genocidal policies, as Greenblatt suggests. But even in that catastrophic scenario, it may have had a retarding role. The playful business of exploiting phonic ambiguities with a view to tracing possibly shared conceptual points of reference might not bring mutual enlightenment. It could, though, condense communicational hybrids that were sufficiently stable to engender new societies and traditions at that place. In a discussion of Lower Mississippi Indian pidgin, Emanuel Drechsel wondered "whether—with different first languages—speakers of a pidgin really understood each other in conversing in it, especially in its initial and highly variable stage." Could such a linguistic compromise, he asked, "reveal non-utilitarian purposes such as those of a linguistic game?" (Drechsel 1987: 434). If it did, the success of the "game" could not have been measured by its semantic yield. It must have been assessed phonically, *onomato-poetically*, in the echoic free variation of "players" mimicking one another in the absence of agreed terms of reference.

Even communication that is clear, straightforward, and mutually intelligible may retain traces of this "background radiation" of ambiguity. This at least is the implication of D. H. Whalen's recognition of "indeterminacy as a linguistic phenomenon" (Whalen 1981: 274). Indeterminacy arises because no two speakers speak or hear what is spoken identically. This obvious fact, although grammarians ignore it, means that every speaker stands a chance of being misunderstood (Whalen 1981: 272). A "semantic noise" backgrounds every attempt at communication. But what is its origin? Whalen speculates about divergent syntactical and lexical judgments, but not before making a significant admission: "There is a great deal of room for personal variation and divergent determinations on the phonetic scale [but] since the phonetic data does not lend itself to structural analysis, I will leave the phonetic level as an untried case" (Whalen 1981: 266). Nevertheless, in stabilizing potentially murderous situations, phonetic free variation might have played an important historical role.

Instances of mutual misunderstanding becoming institutionalized have been described by James Lockhart and Wyatt MacGaffey. Pointing out the ambiguous similarities between the cultural systems of the Europeans and the Nahuas in Mexico, Lockhart argues that they allowed a workable truce to emerge under the aegis of a "double mistaken identity:" "Each side was able to operate for centuries after first contact on an ultimately false but in practice workable assumption that analogous concepts of the other side were essentially identical with its own, thus avoiding close examination of the unfamiliar and maintaining its own principles" (Lockhart 1994: 219). In illustration of the operational value of this misconception in another colonial setting, MacGaffey cites the Portuguese promulgation of the term *fetish:* "This phantasm originated in the intercultural spaces of the Guinea coast, inhabited symbiotically by Europeans and by Africans alienated from their own societies. . . . As such it persists into modern times, where it has been cited as evidence of a continuing 'dialogue of the deaf'" (MacGaffey 1994: 219). In the context of our discussion, this last phrase might be glossed differently. Those inhabiting the in-between spaces of colonialism might not have been "hearing" each other's "cultures"; they did, though, *listen* to each other. They may have been deaf to conceptual differences, but they cultivated a good ear for phonological coincidences that drew them together. If they mistook what the other represented, this was because they were not trading in representations. Their profit, both commercial and emotional, depended upon doubling-up, being heard literally through the other.

According to David Tomas, the kinds of transactions I am describing characterize "transcultural spaces." His studies of cross-cultural encounters around the margins of the Indian Ocean prove to him "the existence and dynamics of a transient, sometimes humorous, often dangerous, and periodically cruel intercultural space—generated in situations governed by misrepresentation or representational excess" (Tomas 1996: 1). Such transcultural spaces are "predicated on chance events, unforeseen and fleeting meetings, or confrontations that randomly direct activity originating from either side of geographic or territorial, natural or artificially perceived divides that separate and distinguish peoples with different constellations of customs, manners, and language" (Tomas 1996: 1). This sounds suspiciously like the wish fulfillment of a poststructuralist ethnography, and it curiously underplays the coercive context of these meetings and the communication they generated. But I agree with Tomas's two main points: communication in such situations is characterized by "representational excess," and the form discourse assumes depends to some extent on chance (at least in the phonic realm). And as is now becoming clear, the character of communication in the other situations I have nominated is similar. Baggio's fantasia on the theme of his own names, for example, is a study in representational excess. Similarly, Kantor's emancipated actor embraces a playing that "suggests commitment, coincidence, and the 'unknown'" (Kantor 1993: 100).

His(s)tories

At the symposium in 2002 where a draft of this chapter was presented, I played my radiophonic composition "The Native Informant" (1993). The "native informant" of this thirty-minute radio work is not the (often imaginary) person the ethnolinguist quizzes to penetrate the structure of an unknown language but a remastered recording of my voice dating from 1965, when I was fourteen. In the symposium context, to play it was to reflect critically on the project of hearing culture. First, it broached the question of the hearer's own projections. Second, it questioned whether hearing could be detached from the technologies of sound recording—and, if so, in what way? Some attending the symposium attributed a third significance to it: at an occasion dominated by talk *about* the cultural and historical importance of sound, "The Native Informant" stood out because it communicated its ideas performatively in the form of a sound composition.

I return to the work here, partly to tease out the critical implications just listed, but also for two further reasons. In the comparison between hearing devices and listening devices, the latter came off rather badly. But perhaps the terms of the comparison were deceptive—as the meditation on listening in "The Native Informant" exposes. Last, the echoic mimicry that dominates parts of the work, in which a "dialogue" between environmental sounds and human voices is staged, brings into focus the topic of acoustic ecology. If, in the different situations I have discussed, the feedback loop between listening and speaking can harmonize differences, then an overarching intuition of auditory order is implied. It is to this intuition that Murray Schafer influentially appealed in his book *The Tuning of the World* (1977). But is this thesis sustainable? And except in a performance, which is not a reproduction but a self-consciously mimetic event occurring somewhere in between illusion and reality, how could it be tested?

The projections that can interfere with our efforts to hear the other are richly explored in "The Native Informant." When I rediscovered the old tape recordings, I decided to remaster them because I anticipated an autobiographical insight. However, when I was able to listen to them again, I was surprised to find that the recovered recordings consisted of a sequence of French conversational phrases, the conjugation of the ancient Greek verb *luo*, and two outdoor recordings, one of a farmyard, the other of a woodland. As I observed then,

> it might have been expected that my younger voice would have provided me with a "sound photograph," an autobiographical insight into my former self. But instead of revelations, I found myself listening to a voice that, like the [anthropologist's] native informant, spoke in a voice not its own, a voice which, as if for no other reason than to conceal its own identity, adopted a French pidgin or mechanically recited the verb forms of a dead language. If the native informant mimics the leading questions of the Western scientist, my voice seemed to mimic the expectations of the tape recorder. It was not my disorderly, mobile self my voice evoked but the orderly silence of the technology recording it. (Carter 1993: 3–4)

The first point I extrapolate from this is that the apparently neutral project of hearing cultures may carry an expectation that the sound world and its vocalizing inhabitants authentically represent nothing but themselves. This expectation might, however, preemptively encode the contents of that world semiotically, as if they already belonged to a familiar cultural grammar, one that assumes "a magical precision bridging sound and sense," in this way remaining curiously deaf to the auditory space their sonorities display. Such an expectation also overlooks Kantor's point, that the representation of nothing but oneself always means playing a part between reality and illusion. That is, the culture heard is always a complex of orientations toward others, echoic of the other's expectations. And in trying to hear what is going on, the detached hearer has to take account of the performative poetics informing what he hears, a poetics that implicates not only the participants but also the audience—who, in this case, must be regarded as a potential player. A failure to do this leaves the cultural auditor in the same position as the Merchant in Rumi's famous tale *The Merchant and the Parrot*. The Merchant craves some other self, but, as his captive pet explains, "I am an echo of yourself which you have caged. I have no other song to sing but songs of being caged to sing you songs of your own tired self" (Mason 1986: 66–67).

The issue of recording technology in hearing culture, a second matter that "The Native Informant" staged, is more diffuse. Like taking studio photographs (appropriately called in French *photo de pose*), making sound recordings involves a poetics of performance reflecting the character and limitations of the technology. Hence, when the Australian anthropologist T. G. H. Strehlow recorded Arrernte songs, he instructed the men not to keep the beat with boomerangs, because the noise rendered the vocal line less intelligible (Ellis 1964: 35–36; Catherine Ellis, personal communication). A physical stance also accompanies this auditory censorship: in what might be called the recording pose, the one speaking into the microphone characteristically leans forward (as the photographic archive of any radio station will illustrate). It is no accident that this pose mimics that of the electro-acoustic hearkener (recall HMV's famous dog). The occasion of making a recording freezes the sound maker. It also dumbs down or silences the auditory environment. In a de-noised laboratory, the speaker is asked to listen to his own voice production. Such an auto-exposure is naturally distressing. It is no accident that the "radio voice" is coeval with the emergence of electro-acoustic sound production. This voice is breathless, not from respect for the microphone's sensitivity to lisping but to avoid giving away the self. The (correct) intuition is: *only* the voice stripped of personal variations and divergent determinations on the phonetic scale creates the illusion of a precise fit between sound and sense. This, of course, is another illusion.

Then, as I suggested, "The Native Informant" usefully blurred the antithesis proposed earlier between hearing and listening. As the existence of an intermediate term like *overhearing* indicates, that opposition is considerably overdrawn. Between the disembodied ear of the spy and the embodied tongue of the lover, the relative roles played by hearing and listening undergo a hundred variations. Only one auditory step separates unintentionally overhearing from intentionally *listening in.* And so on. The interest of the radio work from this point of view was that it showed that hearing might be most intrusive when it was least akin to listening. This is the case when the anthropologist or the biologist makes recordings of "natural," or at least machine-free, environments. Virginia Madsen succinctly captures the paradox in her discussion of Murray Schafer's proposal to locate microphones in remote wilderness zones and to transmit their sounds "without editing into the hearts of the cities": "Schafer, through this 'radical radio' where no editing occurs (no cuts, no wounds), is present in nature as never before. The microphone does not open a window of transparency onto nature. Rather, the microphone and the whole machine attached to it, amplifies and heightens the sounds of nature (as well as those cultural intrusions), creating a hyperspace" (Madsen 1999: 32).

Tomas makes a related point about Steven Feld's CD *Voices of the Rainforest* (1991). Leaving aside the exploitation of digital sound recording and mixing techniques to simulate the auditory world of the Kaluli, Tomas feels that the very presence of Feld's technology tends to make disappear what it would preserve. Its semiotic inscription "is the product of the movement of Western technology through a foreign space." The Kaluli "can sing to us (to me) from track number 6 . . . [but] I can never reply" (Tomas 1996: 120). In the end, Tomas thinks, writing in his Montreal apartment, "the sounds of the Kaluli resurrect a history of colonial relations rooted in *this* as opposed to *that* space, because the compact disk has promoted a strange intermingling between a Kaluli world and a Canadian world in which the latter world serves as defining context for the former world" (Tomas 1996: 121).

These are critical reflections on the project of hearing culture that "The Native Informant" stimulated. But although a work in this genre is suggestive, it is not intended as a sustained (clear, straightforward) argument. One of its merits may be to cultivate an ambiguous attitude toward its own hearing. In "The Native Informant" this took the form of listening to the sound of the sound technology itself. The surface "hiss" of the old recordings was taken into account. Instead of being consciously filtered out, it was treated as an historical actor in its own right. Indeed, the hiss of technology's history was treated as the device that forced the listener to reflect on the hearing project itself. For what could it mean to recover noise? Noise was the signifier of technology's historical presence, the signature of its mediation between the ear and the sound world. And what that mediation revealed was the historical, culture-specific character of the desire to hear the other *in silence*. In this sense, the technology resisted the completion of the project it set in train. Listening to this resistance, one heard something else. As the script expresses it, "I hear the ear / of an ancient technology / . . . It is the hiss / of listening— / I did not hear then / that I hear now" (Carter 1993: 7). Insofar as "history" cannot be dissociated from the materials that constitute it, it is also the *hiss* of history.

This is the first implication of listening to the surface noise, the sound of what cannot be heard. The second, more "poetic," implication that "The Native Informant" took up followed from this. Once noise is readmitted to the project of hearing culture, its character changes. It ceases to be an impediment to communication. Instead, it can be recognized as representing a desire to communicate differently. The artist working with these sound materials is like one party in those cross-cultural colonial encounters discussed earlier: in order to "make sense" of the other's sounds, an echoic mimicry has to be devised. The character of that imitation will be an unstably evolving discourse associatively retracing and reinventing the listener-speaker's own phonic history and preoccupations (hence, in the Columbus-Taino case, the predominance of *ca*). In my case, stimulated by hearing the song of the nightingale scarcely able to break through the thunderous roar of the old recording's hiss, I heard in the noisy surface the repressed desire of the environment to make its own violent colonial history audible at last. To reduce this "confusion" to the order of signs in which sound and sense magically fuse would be to repress its difference again. An analogous noisy discourse had to be composed, one that, in echoic dialogue with the surface hiss, renders the environmental sound trace eloquent.

In "The Native Informant," I approached this task in three ways: linguistically, performatively, and musically. The intention to create a noisy human echo of the environment's repressed history is indicated in the script, where the "birdsongs" discernible in the old recordings are onomatopoeically transcribed. Directing the performance of these transcriptions, I asked the actors to undertake a series of improvisations. Playing commercial recordings of the bird species in question through their headphones, I asked them to imitate what they could hear. Their "fantastications" were part of the final "confusion." The musical component of the composition occurred in postproduction, when the various sound materials were edited to produce the desired noisy dialogue. An important sound element introduced at this stage was the sound of the original remastering process, which, by making it possible to listen to the old tapes, had made the whole project possible. This had involved dubbing the originals at a speed faster than the one at which they were originally recorded. At four times its original speed, my youthful voice sounded like the jargon of a small, slightly hysterical songbird.[1]

Acoustic Ecology

The project of hearing cultures begs the question of what is worth hearing. Although it is rarely admitted, a variety of aural discriminations informs what social scientists, cultural historians, and anthropologists define as sounds. Implicit in that definition is a quality whose equivalent in the visual domain of images is focus. Sounds that furnish useful cultural data are those that stand out from the background noise. Bells, birds, and other clearly differentiated sound types, the rhythmic grouping of these into events, and the repetition and counterpoint of these events, suggesting a pattern indicative of a larger collective auditory consciousness—these are the kinds of sound that speak to the researcher. They resemble (mimic?) signals; it is a reasonable guess that, within any particular situation, they will enjoy a symbolic function. From here the research program becomes clear. Assuming a bridgehead between sound and sense, it is to use them to greatly enlarge, and reinforce, the proposition that culture is communication. Evidently, this hearing bias leaves out a great deal. Auditory space is durational, but it lacks music's (and writing's) commitment to linear development. Without a sense of ending, it is not located between silences. Very few of the sounds composing it can be named, analyzed accurately, or experimentally reproduced.

As Albert Bregman has pointed out, most of the sounds we encounter every day do not correspond to the two classes of sound favored by laboratory (and, I might add, "hearing culture") research: they are neither pure sinusoidal tones nor sudden noise bursts. Such familiar sounds as a car passing, a jar falling and breaking, the clatter of knives and forks, and the sound of paper rustling are neither periodic nor random. Are they therefore culturally insignificant? Bregman states, "We have no knowledge of how to characterize these sounds or of how they are classified and organized by the auditory system" (Bregman 1990: 108). Yet such sounds punctuate and shape our sound world. They represent a kind of auditory environmental unconscious orchestrating our communications.

In this context it is worth asking not only *what are we hearing?* but *what are we listening for?* What implicit organizational principle makes sense of *what* we are hearing and *for* which we are listening? When, for example, Anthony Seeger proposes to find relationships between "ways that people conceive of their universe (cosmology), organize themselves into groups (social organization) and organize sounds (music and some of the sonic features of language)" (Seeger 2002), he implies that the principle is structural. In other societies the principle appears to be quite different. Meaning is derived not from the place of the sound sign in relation to other sound signs within the communicational system. It originates from outside the system, from the association of the sound with a sound in the environment that it mimics. In Steven Feld's account, the Kaluli, in imitating the sounds of the rainforest, hear themselves by literally *hearing the other*. One reason this scenario is so attractive to non-anthropologists is that it furnishes a real-world example of the project Schafer envisaged in *The Tuning of the World*. In Kaluli consciousness, at least in Feld's auditory representation of it, a direct relation exists between the total sound environment and the healthy functioning of society. All living (all sounding) things are implicated in each other's lives. Individual and collective well-being depends on maintaining this acoustic ecology.

In the West, as Tomas's dissatisfaction with Feld's CD illustrates, we feel cut off from this organic harmony. Recognizing this, the electronic composer Barry Truax anticipates my argument. In his communicational model of a well-tuned environment, listening is privileged over hearing and is itself recognized as involving both attentive and "background" listening. Acoustic information derived from the environment is the information that provides the "environmental context of our awareness, the ongoing and usually highly redundant 'ground' to our consciousness" (Truax 1992: 376). Agreeing, Hildegaard Westerkamp stresses, "The information we take in as listeners is balanced by our own sound-making activities, which, in turn, shape the environment" (quoted in Truax 1992: 377). At the same time, the soundscape model is incomplete. It presumes that listening is always listening *for something.* It forms part of a communicational chain, and even if it is a sophisticated way of monitoring the environment and tuning it, it assumes that its function is to process and transfer information between individual and environment. In a historical sense it presupposes loss and silence: as Truax says of the traditional soundscape, "we are only able to conceptualize that balanced relationship as an ecological one because we have since lost it" (Truax 1992: 375).

Nostalgia for a communicational plenitude informs both these ways of hearing the other. Whether the focused sound finds its cultural value as a proto-linguistic signifier (see Bruce Smith's notion of finding a "syntax" for "making sense of the sounds [of Elizabethan England]," this volume) or whether it is regarded as a proto-musical unit contributing to the harmonization of the total soundscape, it is treated as a symbol of richer social relations and communication and as a sign of loss. That is, hearing what we have lost, we listen out for what might be regained. Explicating a distinction made by Paul Ricoeur in *The Symbolism of Evil* (1969), David Rasmussen writes that "signs find their primary identification in their one-dimensional conceptually clear identity, being transparencies which strive for univocal meaning with singular intention. In contrast to the sign, the symbol is composed of polar dimensions to be identified not by univocity but by double intentionality" (Rasmussen 1971: 43). This definition accords with our earlier understanding: if hearing retains a visualist prejudice for clear, univocal signs, then listening, by responding to the communicational contract implied (a symbol is something divided and shared), respects the erotic power of ambiguity, the generative potential of a representation that exceeds every determination. Yet the nostalgia for a lost plenitude remains. Ricoeur's "symbol" is richer than his "sign." The sound worlds conjured up under the aegis of acoustic ecology are usually imagined as richer than the one the researcher inhabits.

To combat this romanticism, an altogether more radical *mislistening* is needed. Attending to the breakdowns in communication, and to the echoic, mimetic sound hybrids incubated in the gaps, it will not monitor what people say in secret. It will reconstruct the other's subjectivity from what lies secreted and unnoticed within the signifying chain, an effect Samuel Beckett sought in his drama: "The experience of my reader shall be between the phrases, in the silence, communicated by the intervals, not the terms, of the statement" (Beckett 1983: 49). In active mislistening that silence turns out to be the auditory equivalent of the conceptual white page (or tabula rasa) of clear, straightforward, univocal linear reasoning. It is a silence that deafens, of unimaginable noise. It is the sound of progress that assailed the English writer Alfred Williams in the Swindon rail factory in southern England at the end of the nineteenth century. Among the pneumatic machines cutting out rivets, "Do you hear anything? You hear nothing. Sound is swallowed up in sound. You are a hundred times deaf. You are transfixed; your every sense is paralyzed. In a moment you seem to be encompassed with an unspeakable silence—a deathlike vacuity of sound altogether" (Williams 1984: 75). The same state of paralysis overcame Caribbean people when they first heard the Spanish cannon. It is the sound which, through the sensation of being a hundred times deaf, makes audible the terror—that "unspeakable distress" which Artaud also sought to diagnose.

Reviewing a BBC record, *Vanishing Sounds of Britain*, a selection of sounds associated with the Industrial Revolution (steam engines, paddle steamers, locomotives, etc.), David Tomas reflects, "If we have not yet learned to turn our ear toward those worlds and their alien 'semio-logics,' to listen with the necessary freedom, to appreciate the extent of those other sensory revolutions that we have inherited, that is our collective unconscious, then it is time we attend to the sensuousness and erotic 'corporality' of the *'shimmering'* acoustic 'signifiers' that drift continuously in and out of our range of hearing, and heed the terror that lies at their origin, a terror that roams anonymously throughout our contemporary atmospheres" (Tomas 1990: 136). Roland Barthes compared this free listening to the project of listening psychoanalytic-ally between the phrases in order to pick up that inner speech of the unconscious (Barthes 1985: 255, 259, cited by Tomas 1990: 136). The noise secreted in those intervals may be distressing, but it is also the other of a different communication. The difference of my listening model is that it does not allow the analyst to pretend to be silent or detached. Ambiguous phonetic traces, recovered in the fantastication of echoic mimicry, signify because a "transference" occurs between the listener-speakers in which both exist socially (and historically) literally through the other. A detached hearing theorizes sounds arising out of silence and aspiring toward harmonization. The attached hearing advocated here considers that sounds begin and end in noise.

Note

1. Besides its application to the hybrid dialects characteristic of communications along the historical and geographical littoral of imperialism, *jargon* can refer to the warbling of birds.

Language and Nature in Sound Alignment

Janis B. Nuckolls

In this chapter I explore sound as a cross-cultural construct and as a medium for defining one's alignments with the nonhuman environment. A fundamental premise is that people frame their interactions with the nonhuman world just as they frame their alignments with other humans. Whereas interactional analyses of discourse have taken as their main subject people interacting with other people, I assume a perspective that allows that human discourse also comments on one's alignments with the nonhuman world. The term *alignment* is intended in the spirit of Erving Goffman's term *footing* (1981), which he uses to describe a framework for interaction, such as boss-employee or teacher-student. Through their language, Quechua-speaking Runa living in the upper Amazonian region of Ecuador articulate a sonically driven disposition that I call a *sound alignment.* By way of background, their traditional way of life combines subsistence-based swidden horticulture with fishing, hunting, and gathering of wild fruits and nuts. As their territories become increasingly enmeshed in the global economy, they are becoming more dependent on commodity goods and on opportunities for engaging in wage labor.

Of central concern for my argument is Runa's production of utterances called *ideophones*. Ideophones are a class of expression that is integral to a culturally sensitive performance style. Runa communicate by imitating a variety of subjective impressions spanning a range of sensory domains. Ideophones are functionally specialized for expressivity that is often attributed to sound symbolism (Nuckolls 1999). I consider them here as a type of cultural discourse. My claim is that they provide Runa with a linguistic medium for modeling and constructing nonlinguistic natural processes. Runa model natural processes with sound by imitating the resonant, rhythmic properties of experiential phenomena: ongoingness in time, distribution in space, instantaneousness, disruption, rearrangement, and completion. I want to claim, further, that in the act of constructing natural processes with ideophonic sound, Runa are at the same time foregrounding their shared animacy with such processes. I refer to this stance as a *sound alignment* because it is evident through performative utterances featuring imitative sound.

I articulate the concept of sound alignment by outlining the underlying assumptions about language and nature that are congenial with it. I do this by contrasting two models of language and nature, one of which is congenial with linguists' mainstream understandings of language and the other of which is more appropriate for Runa's understandings of language in relation to the nonhuman life-world. I then present data that clarify and support the concept of sound alignment through examples of affective, imitative sound and performative, ideophonic sound. The polysemiotic nature of ideophonic expression is explored because it provides a source of evidence for Runa alignments with the world by means of sound. The chapter concludes with a description of ongoing changes in Runa's use of ideophones. Ideophone use becomes increasingly restricted as young Runa become active participants in political debates and market-economy activities. Yet there is visual evidence for the continued vigor of the sound alignment concept among Runa.

Finally, the study of ideophones points to an ambitious research program that would investigate how the death of a word class can be linked to cultural ideologies of sound. There is an urgent need for investigating why ideophones continue to be a robust class of expression in some linguistic and cultural traditions but not in others. Material conditions such as literacy, market-economy activities, and urbanism can go only so far as explanations. The expression of these material conditions within a culture's religious and philosophical constructions of nature and the world is of critical importance as well. Aspects of Judeo-Christian constructions of humans in relation to their environment may constrain the development of a sound alignment and thereby inhibit a linguistic culture's use of ideophones. Animistic belief complexes, by contrast, provide the most congenial climate for the sonically driven disposition that I outline here.

Ideophones are a class of expression found in most language families throughout the world.[1] Onomatopoeic expressions such as *wuf wuf, ka-ching*, and *thwack* are a subtype of ideophone found even in languages such as English that are said to be ideophonically impoverished.[2] Although ideophones are functionally restricted in mainstream middle-class American culture, they are a significant form of expression, constituting a culturally sensitive performance style in a number of linguistic traditions.[3] Daniel Kunene (2001: 190), writing about Southern Sotho, a Bantu language, says the following about ideophones' performativity:

> The ideophone stands aloof from the connecting tissues, the sinews, and ligaments that flesh out the basic components of speech into a morphological, grammatical, and syntactic system. By thus isolating itself, it, so to speak, climbs the stage to become an act, thus removing itself from the ordinary run-of-the-mill narrative surrounding it. By its very nature, it imposes on the subject the function of an actor or performer whose surrogate is the narrator. The closest analogy is that of an oral narrative performer who from time to time "becomes" the characters he/she is narrating about and acts out their parts.

Through ideophones' performativity, speakers enact their alignments with the world by means of sound. In saying that ideophones enact a sound alignment, I do not claim that they are uniquely responsible for perpetuating the alignment, which is part of a deeply ramifying set of dispositions that are transmitted imperceptibly in the enculturation of individuals. To explain what this sound alignment is, it is necessary first to explain what it is not. There is in the culture of linguistic science a hidden cosmology that views language as an expression of universal ideal forms originating in the mind and having no motivated correspondence with nature or the world. This cosmology is evident in axiomatic principles of linguistic science such as that of the arbitrariness of the sign. It trickles into everyday awareness through aphorisms such as "talk is cheap" and "actions speak louder than words." It is congenial with cultural principles that we in the United States embrace, such as the First Amendment guarantee of freedom of speech, a freedom that entails a view of language as a tool for reasoned, rational discourse. These interrelated assumptions about language are congenial with a view of ourselves as autonomous individuals inhabiting a stochastic universe of partly understood forces and energies. Language is a tool for symbolizing our world but is distinct from that world and thus relatively unaligned with respect to it. For convenience, I refer to this set of interrelated assumptions about language as the "talk is cheap" perspective.

When catastrophic events take place, however, another language cosmology emerges from the background and asserts itself. According to this second cosmology, language is intimately connected with the greater social order and disorder. This view of language is evident in attempts to regulate and legislate language usage, attempts that bespeak a view of language as dangerous and disruptive. Recent examples of this second perspective arose as a result of the attacks on the World Trade Center and the Pentagon in 2001. With the United States in a heightened state of vulnerability, freedom of speech was often willingly suspended. A well-worn cliché about language from the naval world resurfaced in the words of the U.S. secretary of defense, who put off a journalist's question as he quipped, "Loose lips sink ships." Criticisms of the president and his administration were withheld or at least muted. The major network news organizations voluntarily restrained themselves from broadcasting videotapes made by terrorists because of their potential to incite more attacks. For convenience, I refer to this second set of interrelated assumptions about language as the "loose lips" perspective.

The sound alignment that I outline here is related to the loose lips perspective, though distinctive in a number of respects. Runa do not view language as intimately related to the world only during volatile social episodes. They make constant use of their language to express an attitude of alignment with nature. In traditional Runa culture this is their unmarked perspective. Let us turn to a couple of examples taken from my early fieldwork in 1987. In this context I was doing a lot of basic information-gathering, particularly of Quechua terminology. The following exchanges illustrate one of the ways in which Runa express their alignments with the nonhuman life-world. A group of Runa women who had gathered to visit were trying to coax a woman named Jacinta into singing for my tape recorder. She resisted their proddings, and to distract attention from herself, she picked up my dictionary, which contained simple line drawings, and identified those she recognized. She pointed to the drawing of what was labeled a star sloth. Wanting to test the dictionary's accuracy, I asked her, "Is this a star sloth?" She replied by pronouncing the name of the sloth in an intonational profile of affective recognition. Her affective intonation occurs in line 5 below:[4]

Example 1
1. Nuckolls: Is this an *estrella indillama* (i.e., a star sloth)?
2. Jacinta: Wha . . .

3. Faviola: Is that an *estrella indillama?* (she's asking).
4. Nuckolls: This one.
5. Jacinta: Oh! An *indillama*! (i.e., a sloth) (affectively)
6. Nuckolls: (So it's just an ordinary) *indillama.*
7. Jacinta: Yes, Look!

What I am calling affective intonation is a prosodic pattern that accents a word's melodic contour with a higher and then a lower pitch. In this example the higher pitch occurs on the first two syllables. The contour can be diagrammed in the following way:

In-di-
    lla- ma

The set of exchanges constituting example 2 contains an even clearer example of an affective recognition intonation. In these utterances there are two contrastive pronunciations by Jacinta. In line 3 she asks Ana María if the image she sees is that of a large rodent called *lomocha*. In this utterance she uses an affectless, neutral pronunciation, which is appropriate given that she is referring to it. After confirming with Ana María that the image is of what she thought, she uses an intonation of affective recognition when she repeats its name in line 5 as if she is hugging a long-lost friend or relative:[5]

Example 2
1. Jacinta: Look at what I'm seeing.
2. Ana María: Yes, I see.
3. Jacinta: Is this a *lomocha?* (i.e., large rodent)
4. Ana María: Yes.
5. Jacinta: It's a *lomocha*! (affectively)
6. Nuckolls: Is that a *lomocha?*
7. Jacinta: Yes! Look at that *lomocha* and notice its little beard there.
8. Nuckolls: Ah ha.

The affectivity of Jacinta's pronunciation of the word for rodent is the result of a higher-pitched first syllable followed by two lower-pitched penultimate and final syllables:

Lo-
    mo-cha

With intonational sound, Jacinta expresses an alignment of affective recognition with two nonhuman life-forms. These affect displays are indistinguishable in their intonational profiles from what we would typically reserve for another person. The difference is that whereas we would use such profiles to express a bond of common familiality or common humanity, Runa use them to express a sentiment of common animateness that foregrounds their sharing of a similar life force. It is a sentiment that has some kinship with the view of the Greek philosopher Thales, expounded by R. G. Collingwood (1976: 31), of the world as a living organism that is *ensouled*.

Going beyond alignments expressed with intonational sound, Runa alignments with the nonhuman life-world can be detected in the content of what people say. One of my main consultants, Luisa Cadena, enjoyed recounting extremely short anecdotes from her personal experiences that served to characterize the behavior of nonhuman life-forms. Two of these vignettes are presented in what follows. Both feature ideophonic performances of imitative sound that foreground a mode of thought marked by special terminology in English. Runa *anthropomorphize* nonhuman forms of life by attributing human characteristics to them. They also engage in *anthropopathism* when they attribute human feelings and sentiments to nonhuman life-forms. Such thought modes are often facilitated with the help of ideophones. When I asked Luisa to free-associate about the verb *kantana*, "to sing," her first thought was to describe the way a toucan sings sadly when it cannot find water gathered in the flowers that grow in the moss clinging to trees:[6]

Example 3
Wanting to drink flower water, if there isn't any,
He cries, singing so sadly if there is no water.
He goes *kiyaow kang kang kiyaow kang kang*,
Checking each green place, onto each branch he goes,
jump jump jump jump jump.
He sings at each branch, at each tree branch,
And after he's sung, he goes off sadly.

Another bird, the *wakamaya*, is said to sing sadly upon the death of his wife:[7]

Example 4
The wakamaya goes *garaannng garaannng garang garang*.
Crying he goes, feeling sad that his wife has been killed.
The wakamaya is such a feeler of sadness.

The existence in English of terms such as anthropomorphism and anthropopathism imposes a critical framework upon a mode of thought that Runa engage in freely and unselfconsciously, with no worries about oversentimentalization. The ideophonic representation of these birds' sounds, invested as they are with emotional motivation, serves as a vehicle for connecting and aligning with the birds.

A good deal of the affective alignment generated by the foregoing examples is derived from their contextual frames. In example 3, the toucan is sad because it cannot find water. In example 4, the *wakamaya's* sadness is attributed to the loss of its mate. The ideophones representing their cries add another dimension to the pathos that is reinforced by the intonational qualities of the speaker's voice. I want to make the point that, aside from intonation and contextual framing, ideophones all by themselves create alignment between a speaker and the world. Ideophones do not simply refer to, point to, or reinforce the social milieu. Speakers use ideophones to simulate it. If ideophones can be said to refer at all, it is a very different kind of reference that is effected by a speaker's imitation of what is felt to be naturally salient. When a speaker chooses a facet of experience to imitate, that facet becomes a construction of what is regarded as naturally apparent. Speakers engaging in an ideophonic performance become agents immersed in the process, event, or action they are bringing about with sound. Christa Kilian-Hatz (2001: 155) states that ideophones collapse the difference between the "extra-linguistic event level and the speech level" and adopts the term *Referenzverschiebung*, or reference shift, to describe this phenomenon. Speakers can at times become so involved in their performance that they allow the ideophone to substitute for an entire predication. Example 5 describes how a big tree crashes down in a storm. Although this utterance does contain the finite verb "goes and falls," the speaker could have omitted the verb without any loss of clarity.[8]

Example 5

gyauuuuuuuunng	*blhuuuuuu*	*puthunnng!*	*urma-gri-n*
(creaking sound)	(breaking off)	(impact with ground)	fall-TRSLC-3

This example illustrates how a speaker can become immersed in a natural process that is brought about by sound. The tree's falling is modeled with linguistic sounds representing the salient properties of creaking, rupturing, and falling with impact, particularly through their contrast between vocalic sounds, which allow a continuous airstream through the vocal tract, and consonantal sounds, which restrict the airflow. The performative extension of vocalic sounds in *gyaung* imitates the prolongation of the creaking sound. The force of the tree's breaking off from its base is symbolized by the aspiration of *blhu*. The lack of consonantal obstruction in this ideophone's word-final position simulates the unrestricted falling of the tree trunk toward the ground. Finally, the restriction of the airstream with the word-final velar nasal *-ng* in the second syllable of *putung* imitates the idea of contact and impact with the ground. The speaker's drawing out of these final sounds simulates the reverberative qualities of the sound of impact.

When Ideophones Express What Would Never Be "Put into Words"

Quechua speakers' use of ideophones is linked with a cosmology that sonically defines their alignments with the nonhuman world. In the foregoing discussion I have explained how, through their use of imitative sound, ideophones contribute to this attitude of alignment , even though they are not solely responsible for expressing and perpetuating it. I now discuss some of the interesting implications for the idea of alignment that arise out of ideophones' polysemiotic status. Ideophones may be considered imageic as long as we remember that images are not always visual. Paul Friedrich, in his theory of tropes (1991), outlines five tropic devices or figures that may be understood as universal schematic designs for all poetic language. The image is one of five master tropes and is defined broadly enough to include single words, extended descriptions, and even whole poems, such as William Carlos Williams's "The Red Wheelbarrow." The essence of the image trope is that it communicates ideas of firstness and of primary perceptions and qualities, no matter what their sensory modality. A train whistle, the smell of tar, and qualities of feelings that are particularly acute are all examples of image tropes.

As image tropes, ideophones communicate sound images of sounds, as in the onomatopoeic description of the two birds in examples 3 and 4 or of the tree crashing to the ground in example 5.[9] Ideophones may also make use of the intensities and rhythms of linguistic sound to communicate events, actions, and processes, many of which are only peripherally tied to sound making. Subsequent examples will reveal the wide range of ideophones' multisensorial imagery. Their synesthetic qualities make them amenable to analysis from a number of perspectives. I have argued (Nuckolls 1999, 2001) that ideophones may be usefully considered hybrid forms combining properties from what are traditionally circumscribed as verbal and gestural domains. My argument, based on the fact that ideophones tend to be highly foregrounded through intonational elaboration, gains support from the work of Dwight Bolinger (1986). His position is that intonation is part of language's gestural complex, and that gestural expression occurs along a continuum, manifested in rudimentary form by the up and down movements in voice pitch that grade into actual physical movements of the hand and body.

Further support for ideophones' links with gesture can be found in the videotaped experiments conducted by Kita Sotaro (1997), who discovered that speakers of Japanese used hand and arm gestures along with their ideophones in a large percentage of cases. The Quechua language provides syntactic evidence for ideophones' gestural status. There are many examples of ideophones in verb-adverb constructions in which the ideophone simply restates the meaning of its verb. Such seemingly redundant collocations make sense if we consider the ideophone to be semiotically rather than semantically distinctive. An example will help to clarify this point. The ideophone *illung* is repeated in example 6 to describe the repetitive gesture of a jaguar's licking itself. Here the ideophone simply restates the meaning of its verb, which suggests that it is communicating in a different semiotic mode from that of its verb. The verb "to lick" refers to the action, and the ideophone gestures that action with sound:[10]

Example 6
Licking his whole body *illung illung illung* he sits there calmly.

Ideophones, then, may function as sound images of sound or sound images of relatively soundless gestures, forces, and visual phenomena. Ideophones' functions have even been compared to visual techniques used by film artists, such as juxtaposition, close-up shots, and wide-angle shots (Nuckolls 1995). As if to reinforce the imageic status of ideophones, Quechua speakers engaging in ideophonic performances often preface them with imperative statements to "Look!" or "Look here!" One interesting consequence of ideophones' hybrid semiotic status is that in Quechua at least, they shoulder a great deal of communicative responsibility. Ideophones' functions encompass what in technologically complex societies would be allocated to visual modes of expression. For example, many Quechua ideophones map perceptual schemas that have analog representations in visual media such as film or television. There are ideophones for the pouring of liquids, the sprinkling and scattering of particles of matter, for cutting, for chopping, and for dozens of other schemas that can easily be viewed in short television commercials designed to communicate with succinct imagery.

There are also ideophones for images that, to use the conduit metaphor discussed by George Lakoff and Mark Johnson (1980), would never be "put into words." Runa use ideophonic sound to describe graphically violent, traumatic, or sexual events that would constitute sensational visual imagery in our own culture. One consequence of taking such images out of our mouths and communicating their power with visuals is that we achieve a certain distance from them. We can choose not to look at them, because the burden of perception has been shifted onto a recording device. Runa leading traditional subsistence-based lives have not had such an option. They must slaughter animals for food. They are at times directly confronted with tragic and violent events. Yet they do not seem compelled to turn their gaze from the pulsating, the dismembered, or the otherwise exposed. The tendency for people living in our own society to view such phenomena with revulsion or queasiness reflects, in part, the distance we feel between ourselves and any reminders of our own mortality. This is why we have a term such as "gawking," which implies that certain images should not be viewed. The prolific film artist Stan Brakhage, who sees his work as motivated by fundamental questions about birth and death, has written eloquently about his attempts to come to terms with images from coroners' autopsies, doctors' surgical procedures, and the victims of violent crimes investigated by police in Pittsburgh, Pennsylvania:

> Actually I was driven, for my own desperate reasons, to go down that Sunday morning, early, and suddenly walk into a room where there are several murder victims, some suicides, people who died by violent accident; I walked into this room where the day before I had only photographed . . . and everywhere I turned . . . suddenly I was surrounded by . . . slaughter! And so I just began photographing desperately. I really overshot because I was so desperate to keep always the camera going; every moment I stopped photographing I really felt like I might faint, or burst into tears, or come apart, or something like that. (Brakhage 1982: 195)

Runa perceive phenomena that make us uncomfortable not as voyeuristic gawkers. Their ability to view what we would be inclined to turn away from reflects their particular moral view of perception. They approach even the most violent images with just enough equanimity to be able to talk about them. Describing and sharing such perceptions with others takes away, I believe, some of the power of their horror, making the most traumatic events somewhat less unmanageable. Ideophones are prominent in such descriptions because they rivet our attention onto the details that we are most likely to want to bleach from our consciousness. In this way they contribute to another kind of alignment with the world. It is an alignment based on the belief that nothing is too awful to be excluded from one's field of perception or world of discourse. To adequately grasp these points, it will, unfortunately, be necessary to confront the reader with excerpts from narratives that relate horrific happenings. I focus on two events: an airplane crash and a suicide. Both are related from Luisa Cadena's perspective, which is based on her detailed discussions with others as well as her witnessing of the aftermath of both events.

A Plane Crush

This story recounts a particularly agonizing tragedy. Small military planes fly in and out of the base in Montalvo, a forty-minute walk from the village of Puka yaku, several times a day. Because there are no roads leading into Montalvo or Puka yaku, Runa are accustomed to hitching rides on these planes, usually paying only a nominal fee and often riding free all the way to the bustling town of Puyo, about thirty minutes away on a small prop plane. Luisa was working in her garden when she noticed a small military cargo plane flying very low, its tail almost touching the ground. She learned later that it had been seriously overloaded with cargo, including tanks of gasoline that exploded when the plane crash-landed into a stand of palm trees. Four passengers and one pilot were on board. Two passengers immediately jumped out and eventually recovered from their burns and injuries. Another jumped out but landed in deep, swampy mud and could not free himself without help, which did not arrive before he became severely burned. He died shortly afterward. Another man died in the plane from burns. The pilot died at the controls, so severely burned that it was only by the remaining bits of his flight jacket that he was positively identified.

Some of Luisa's accounts rely upon reports from others. She also managed to see quite a bit herself. The difference between what she herself experienced and what someone else saw and reported back to her is marked by evidential suffixes, a detailed discussion of which is found in Nuckolls 1993. For the purposes of my argument I regard the reports of secondhand witnesses as strengthening my overall point about the tendency for Runa to talk about images to which we would never give voice. The verbalization of such descriptions cannot be attributed to some personal quirk of Luisa's. It is obvious that Runa go over and discuss these images among themselves in excruciating detail. Her account emphasizes a number of details about the burned bodies. One man's death receives many angst-filled details; he was Luisa's *kumpagri*, a term designating a ritual co-parent relationship. His final wishes that his watch be given to his wife and that his children be educated are recounted. The agonizing fact that he kept asking for water but was not given any, so that he would die more quickly and suffer less, is also told. She describes how this man's shirt was removed, his burned skin sticking to the shirt in little pieces. She uses the ideophone *lok*, which describes a peeling away—for example, the way bark peels off of a tree—and also *tai*, which describes how his skin stuck tightly to his shirt:[11]

> Example 7
> Well, they washed him and removed his burned shirt and his skin just remained on that shirt *lok;* it got caught on that shirt *lok tai*, tightly, like this, now all of his flesh remained on that shirt in bits and bits and bits and bits.

Finally, using the ideophone *tsidzin*, she describes how the man's body became stiff and drawn up after he died:[12]

> Example 8
> Then my kumpagri Ostavo had become just drawn together *tsidzin* from burning.

The pilot's fate is given considerable descriptive detail as well. His body is said to have been turned into pitch by the heat. A fragment of his yellow jacket is the only piece of his clothing left. One of his shoes is found at the crash site with his foot still inside it. Luisa uses several ideophones to describe the complete severing of his foot from its leg. The ideophone *pullung* describes something with a stubby or stumplike appearance. The ideophone *chyu* describes a complete severing. The ideophone *mutyun* is synonymous with *chyu*:[13]

> Example 9
> Then his fingers had burned off, now all of them. His feet also had burned off *pullung*. His shoes had been scattered way over there, as the ones gathering [at the crash site] hadn't gathered things well. Now inside of

one of those shoes, his entire foot was there. Now it had burned
cutting itself off like that. Burning off *mutyun*, it remained inside the sh

A Suicide

The next story concerns a soldier's suicide with his own rifle. Luisa and
her husband were present at a military outpost in Chiriboga when it
happened. Her husband was an acquaintance of this man, who came
to visit them early one morning to tell them that the woman he had
planned to marry had thrown her rings at him and broken off the
engagement. The man sobbed and suddenly got up to go, saying,
"Adios," which implies a permanent departure. A short time later they
heard a rifle go off and immediately went to look. Luisa describes what
she saw in relentless detail. Apparently the man had shot himself in
the head. Because he was still alive when they arrived, his body was
trembling and he gasped quick short breaths, which are described with
repetitions of the ideophonic *ling* [14] Repetitions of *ti* describe the
trembling and shaking of his body:[15]

> Example 10
> Now the man [was going] *ling ling ling ling titititititititi ling ling ling;* he
> was actually still alive.

Luisa then explains that parts of his brain tissue had become scattered
all over, using the sound image *ta:*[16]

> Example 11
> As for his brain tissue, it was [splattered] *ta ta*, just scattered all over.

The final descriptive detail she presents has to do with the man's blood.
She describes it as flowing out like water from a faucet, using *tsala:*[17]

> Example 12
> And his blood, well, how like some kind of an animal it [bled] from this,
> from this wound! Like water flowing out, look! That's how it went, just
> *tsalalalalalalala*, like water gushing out it flowed.

It is clear from these examples that Runa are willing to confront awful
moments with the full power of their perceptual abilities, which are
put into focus through ideophonic sounds. In doing so, they take it
upon themselves to experience in a direct way what we try to relegate

...which playback mechanisms simulate recorded
...submit to such perceptions usually by our own
...mous darkness of public spaces or in our own
...regulate the imagery with a remote control but-
...are our perceptual taboos.[18] They talk of things that
...n allow ourselves to see because their world of dis-
...sses their wide-ranging alignments, enacted through
...e diverse animate processes they feel themselves to be
part o...

Sound Alignments in Myth

I turn now to examples of ideophonic sound use in myths. Runa have a large corpus of myths called *kallari timpu*, or "beginning times" myths, that concern themes of analogy, similarity, and the interrelatedness of all entities, whether earthly or celestial. Prominent in these stories are cycles of transformation from one life-form to another. In this section I offer excerpts that feature sound alignments being constructed by Runa in mythic texts. Each excerpt illustrates a pivotal moment in the text when a human becomes nonhuman, and each transformative moment features an ideophonic representation that constructs the transformed being into a ratified, natural token of its type. By their performative simulation of these transformations, Runa forge a link between the human and the nonhuman.

The Sound of Becoming a Dolphin

The first excerpt is taken from the story of a hawk who helps little children. The *bullukuku* hawk notices that two orphans are being cruelly starved by their guardians. The bird helps the children by coming at night and pecking out the guardians' eyes, to punish them for their cruelty. When the guardians wake up and discover what has happened to them, they decide to become freshwater dolphins, called *bugyu*. The *bugyu*'s sound emblems are *bhux*, which describes its forceful bursting out of water, and *kar*, which describes its arc-like path of movement through the air. Because the freshwater dolphin can breathe only out of the water, it frequently emerges from below the surface with a dramatic burst.[19]

Example 13
So then they stood there just listening with only their ears.
And then just a little bit later there was a *bhuuuu karrrrr.*

And then more of them *bhuuuuuuu karrrrrr* went and emerged.
There! They've become *bugyu!* "They are breathing like them," the others
say.
Another jumps in *tuphu*, and another *tuphu*, and another *tuphu!*
One burst out here *bhuuuu*, there *bhuuuu*, here *bhuuuu*, there *bhuuuu*
bhuuu bhuu!
All of the Runa became *bugyu!*

The Sound of Becoming a Boa Constrictor

The next excerpt describes a boy's transformation into a mythical boa
constrictor with a giant head (in some versions, two conjoined heads),
called the *kwung kwung* boa. The story begins when two brothers on a
distant hunting trek discover that all the meat they had been trying to
dry has been stolen from their drying rack. The older brother stays back
the following day to wait and watch for the thief, who turns out to be
a large boa. He and his younger brother then make plans to smoke the
boa out of its tree with the noxious fumes of burning dried chili peppers.
After smoking it out and killing it, they discover its nest of eggs, which
smell good enough to eat—"just like turtle eggs," according to the
younger brother. Although his older brother advises him not to, the
younger brother insists on trying the boa eggs. He then becomes
consumed by an unquenchable thirst, which he tries to satisfy by
drinking an entire pond. He then warns his older brother that he is
about to burst apart and turn into a boa. The naturalness of the younger
brother's transformation into the *kwung kwung* boa is verified by the
kwung kwung sounds he makes.[20]

> Example 14
> He exploded, sounding like a rifle.
> And with that there was *kwung kwung kwung kwung kwung kwung kwung*
> *kwung kwung kwung kwung kwung kwung kwung kwung kwung kwung.*
> Like frogs those little *kwung kwung* boas called out.

The myth fragments just presented supply a particular kind of
evidence for the sound alignment underlying Runa's views of their
relationship with nonhuman life-forms. The mythic transformations
are confirmed as accomplished through sonic performances of ideophonic utterances. In the case of the *kwung kwung* boa, the sound also
functions as the characterizing name for that nonhuman life-form.
Such sound emblems assert, in effect, that the soundings of the *kwung*
kwung boa are its most characterizing—that is, "natural"—feature. The

freshwater dolphin's name, *bugyu*, is at least a partial sound emblem of the sound *bhu*, which this animal alone makes as it bursts out of water.

Sound Alignments in Cultural and Political Contexts

Through their use of imitative sound, Runa construct, model, and align themselves with natural forces and processes. I conclude this chapter with a discussion of the wider implications of Runa sound alignments in a social and political climate of great flux. The discussion is framed as an inquiry into the diminishing use of ideophones, especially by young, politically active and economically ambitious Runa. Comparative evidence for ideophone usage in Asian and African linguistic traditions suggests that any hypothesis accounting for diminished use must include a complex configuration of factors. These factors also help explain the restricted status of ideophone use by adults in English-speaking, middle-class, mainstream society. The decisive factors, I argue, may be the constraining power of religious and philosophical constructions of humans in relation to their environment. Specifically, I believe that sonic dispositions that give rise to exuberant use of ideophones emerge in cultures that legitimate animistic forms of thought.[21]

Two Local Cultures Compared

At present, Ecuador's indigenous people are experiencing tremendous social upheaval. They are considerably more active in national-level politics than they have ever been in the past. A member of the Indigenous Peoples' Confederation was actually a participant in the military junta that attempted to overthrow the country's president in January 2000. A few indigenous people have been elected to the country's national congress. These positive kinds of changes are not without their consequences, however. When indigenous people become active in national politics, they must become comfortable with Spanish if their voices are to be heard. The habitual use of Spanish by Runa affects their ways of speaking Quechua. Ideophones become increasingly restricted as Runa become more active participants in political debates and in market-economy activities. They are restricted insofar as they are seldom used, and when they are used, they undergo much less intonational elaboration.

Two villages supply an instructive contrast that sheds light on the matter of ideophones' status in changing Runa society. The village of Puka yaku, where I did most of my fieldwork, is located on the Bobonaza

River about a thirty-minute walk from the military base Montalvo. The people of Puka yaku rely on their traditional subsistence techniques, such as swidden horticulture, hunting, fishing, and gathering. They are also opportunistic wage laborers, working for the military personnel nearby or else for geophysical companies doing exploratory seismic testing for oil. In general, Puka yakuans are reluctant to become involved in national-level dialogues and political organizations. Yet it would be wrong to consider them insular or isolated people. They travel frequently by plane to Puyo and allow relatively free access to outsiders wanting to visit or work there. In Puka yaku, ideophones are used with unrestricted abandon, and most Puka yakuans, although able to understand some Spanish, are far more comfortable speaking Quechua.

The village of Sara yaku, located farther upstream from Puka yaku on the Bobonaza River, is a hub for politically active Runa because it is the headquarters for the Organización de Pueblos Indígenas de Pastaza, or OPIP. I never attempted to visit Sara yaku because OPIP had already denied me access to another village under its control, called Canelos. I was, however, acquainted with numerous Sara yakuans and worked with a man from that place for a year in the United States. In addition to their political activism, which intersects all levels of Ecuadorean life, from the local to the national, OPIP officials are also internationally active insofar as they solicit and receive funds from a variety of nongovernmental organizations for development projects. In general, Sara yakuans are very protective of their land and allow neither oil companies nor anthropologists unauthorized visits.

When the leaders of Sara yaku organized a 240-kilometer march from the lowlands to the capital city, Quito, in April 1992, one of their goals was to acquire legal titles to two million hectares of continuous rainforest territory (Sawyer 1997). Although the march gained national and even international attention, it was not entirely successful. Suzanne Sawyer reports that the Borja administration granted only about 55 percent of the land request. Furthermore, the government carved up the territory into apparently arbitrary geometric blocks having no relevance to actual patterns of land use or to historical or mythological understandings of place (Sawyer 1997). The government's inadequate response to indigenous demands is symptomatic of a greater problem underlying Sara yakuans' debates over land use. Simmering below the surface of these debates are conceptions of natural resources that cannot possibly be reconciled. The Ecuadorean government has a rational, marketplace view of its resources as commodities for the generation of capital. As I have been attempting to show through analysis of their language, traditional Runa's culture constructs an affective relationship based on a sentiment of shared animacy with their land.

When Sara yakuans become active in political arenas of power, however, their use of Spanish and the cultural dispositions underlying Spanish linguistic culture rule out the expression of sound alignments with ideophones. The importance of the sound alignment concept and the sentiment of common animacy is that, even when they are repressed in political discourse by social and cultural factors, they are given expression in alternative form. Visual evidence for the sentiment of common animacy expressed through a sound alignment is found in a political poster created by two Sara yaku men and reproduced in Nuckolls 1996: 130, depicting an autochthonous man, his feet rooted in the earth, his mouth wide open, screaming, hands gripping weapons, all of which is echoed by the anger of the surrounding environment. The sun blazes a bright red heat, and volcanoes erupt with red lava in the distance. This poster provides a visual analogue to my claim that sound alignments are linked to a sentiment of shared animacy. The man exists as an organism that is distinguishable from his surroundings yet definitively rooted to them. The surrounding earth is also like an organism insofar as it expresses an affective state. The man's anger is expressed sonically, through a visual depiction of screaming.

Concluding Remarks

Underlying the use of ideophones by Runa is a complex of cultural constructions that link sound to sentiments of shared animacy with the nonhuman life-world. Such linkages would explain the diminution of ideophone usage under circumstances requiring cognitive reframings of human and nonhuman interrelations, as occurs when a traditional subsistence-based culture becomes increasingly dependent on market-economy activities. Interesting comparative evidence comes from G. Tucker Childs (1996), who conducted a sociolinguistic survey of attitudes toward ideophone usage among Zulu speakers in South Africa. Childs found that ideophones were disappearing among young urban Zulu speakers. His study suggests the intriguing possibility that the disappearance of ideophones might point to the loss of a language's vitality and ultimately to its demise.

Urbanism and participation in a market economy do not by themselves cause a decline in ideophone use. What is absolutely crucial is comparative data on ideophones in Asian cultures, particularly those in which ideophones exist in abundance. Japanese speakers in highly urbanized environments use ideophones quite freely. Their use has be characterized as essential to Japanese linguistic culture (Gomi 198؟). The abundance of ideophones in Japan, I propose, is related to the fact that traditional Japanese culture has not been permeated by Judeo-Christian views of nature as degraded and antagonistic to humans.[22] There is an emphasis in Japanese religions, especially Shintoism, Buddhism, and Confucianism, upon human alignments with nature. This emphasis is evident in literary traditions such as haiku poetry and extended prose such as novels, and in many genres of visual art. Robert Hass (1994: 255) has suggested that certain forms of aesthetic stylization in haiku poetry reflect "traces of an earlier animism." Hass's description of the style of the poet Issa (1763–1827) is particularly revealing for our purposes because it is said to include "lots of onomatopoeia and direct address to animals (1994: 147). The writings of the seventeenth-century poet Basho, translated by Hass, also attest to human alignments with nature. Basho urges his students to "make the universe your companion . . . and enjoy the falling blossoms and scattering leaves" (Hass 1994: 233). In another passage he states: "Every form of insentient existence— plants, stones, or utensils—has its individual feelings similar to those of men" (1994: 237).

The linguistic culture of Quechua-speaking Runa privileges the use of ideophones. Through ideophones, Runa enact a sentiment of shared animateness that aligns them with the nonhuman life-world. Sound is the perfect medium for the expression of this alignment because sound is possible only when there is movement, and movement of any kind is the prototypical criterion for animateness. Although it is certain that ideophones are becoming functionally restricted among young, politically active Runa, it is not yet clear why this should happen. Research on ideophone use among young urban Zulu speakers in South Africa finds parallel tendencies, causing Childs (1996: 83) to conclude that their diminished use signals a desire to shed one's traditional identity. The continued vigor of ideophones as a word class in Japan, however, and probably in a number of other Asian linguistic traditions as well, points to the necessity of investigating the cultural ideologies of sound that nurture or constrain them.

Acknowledgments

I thank Veit Erlmann for the invitation to participate in the symposium. I also gratefully acknowledge the following organizations under whose auspices I collected data for this chapter: the Social Science Research

Council, the Wenner-Gren Foundation for Anthropological Research, the National Science Foundation, and the American Council of Learned Societies. A summer stipend from the National Endowment for the Humanities gave me much-needed time for writing this essay. A special thanks to Luisa, Jacinta, and Faviola, whose words appear in the chapter, for helping me with Quechua, for being patient with my errors, and for managing to enjoy my company, at times.

Notes

1. Ideophones exist in many languages and language families of Africa (see Voeltz and Kilian-Hatz 2001, especially the introduction). They are also found in Asian and South Asian languages, including Dravidian, Indo-Aryan, Korean, Vietnamese, and Japanese. Reports of ideophones in indigenous languages of South America also exist, and evidence is accumulating on ideophones in Aboriginal Australian languages.

2. *Wuf wuf* is a child language ideophone, considered onomatopoeic of a dog's barking. *Ka-ching* is a whimsical ideophone for the sound of an old-fashioned cash register, in current use by adults to communicate ideas of large expense or of cashing in on something big. *Thwack* is an action-figure ideophone used in comics to describe forceful impact.

3. The term *mainstream* is intended in the spirit of Heath (1983: 391–392), who defines it as a way of life that exists all over the world and involves reliance on formal education, aspirations for upward mobility, and a perspective that seeks behavioral models outside one's family and community.

4. All translations are by the author from Quechua. Data are cited according to their tape number and page numbers from the author's transcript file. The reader is strongly encouraged to go to the Web site www.ailla.org and select from the Pastaza Quechua entry entitled "sloth's name pronounced affectively" to listen to the actual pronunciation of the Quechua word for sloth, *indillama*.

5. The pronunciation of *lomocha* is also available at www.ailla.org under the entry "affective recognition of a rodent."

6. Verb Portraits *Ab kantana*. Entry available at www.ailla.org.

7. Verb Portraits *Ab kantana*. Entry available at www.ailla.org.

8. Verb Portraits *Ba kuchuna*. Entry available at www.ailla.org.

9. In saying that ideophones are image tropes, I do not exclude the possibility that their image-tropic properties may be enlisted for other poetic effects. Noss's

analysis of Gbaya ideophones (2001: 268–269) points to their intertextuality, which links an ideophone in a familiar folktale with similar events from peoples' own experiences. Given their formulaicity, the artfulness of ideophone usage often involves manipulating listeners' expectations with unexpected hyperbole, irony, or metaphor.

10. Tape IA, Transcript File, p. 28, "Becoming a shaman."

11. Tape IIIB, Transcript File, pp. 166–167.

12. Tape IIIB, Transcript File, p. 168.

13. Ibid.

14. The ideophone *ling* describes the insertion of one thing into another. Here its meaning has been extended to describe the quick short inhalations of the dying man. I am indebted to Sergio Gualinga for explaining this particular sense of *ling* to me. See Nuckolls 1996 for a detailed discussion of the semantics of *ling*.

15. Tape IIIB, Transcript File, p. 170.

16. Ibid.

17. Ibid.

18. I do not wish to suggest that Runa have no perceptual taboos whatsoever. I noticed that people did express revulsion when experiencing certain olfactory sensations. Any hint of the smell of human excrement often triggered exaggerated retching, along with spitting of one's own saliva, as well as commentary about how nauseated it made one feel.

19. Tape IIIA, Transcript File, p. 111.

20. Tape XIVB, Transcript File, p. 178.

21. My use of the term *animism* is indebted to Viveiros de Castro (1998) and Descola (1994), who conceptualize it as a way of seeing relations between human and nonhuman life-forms in social terms.

22. There is, of course much more to be said about the factors contributing to the functional restrictedness of ideophones in mainstream Western culture. Collingwood (1976) traces the history of concepts of nature from Greek and Renaissance to modern conceptions. The Renaissance view of nature as brute substance for the fashioning of mechanisms is obviously antithetical to the development of a sentiment of shared animacy. The emphasis in modern philosophy upon the mind as a rational entity, distinct from the world of matter, may also be relevant in this regard.

Raising Spirits and Restoring Souls: Early Modern Medical Explanations for Music's Effects

Penelope Gouk

The consequences of increasing visual mastery for Western science and culture—Foucault's totalizing power of the gaze—have been subjects of scholarly fascination at least since the time of Walter Ong's writings (1958, 1970). Around the same time, Marshall McLuhan (1962) compared the early modern "communications revolution" of the printing press to the burgeoning computer revolution. It has now become commonplace to assert that a decisive shift took place in the early modern "West" from a predominantly aural to a primarily visualist culture, a transformation that in the long term made it distinctively different from non-Western societies (e.g., Classen 1993; Crosby 1998). My own work, however, suggests that simple, linear models of a once-and-for-all shift away from hearing (and the other senses) and toward vision as the principal way of knowing are inadequate, not only for understanding early modern European culture on its own terms but also for comparative and cross-cultural research (Burnett, Fend, and Gouk 1991; Gouk 1999, 2000a, 2000b, 2000c). Other scholars have made similar arguments, and it is clear that a move is now under way toward developing alternative, more integrated models of sensory perception (e.g., Bijsterveld 2001; Schmidt 2000; Smith 1999).

In this chapter I explore how changing musical practices and acoustic technologies contributed to new medical theories about music's effects in the early modern period—the sixteenth to eighteenth centuries. At the core of the larger project of which this essay forms a part lies the more general assumption that "objective" Western scientific models and causal explanations of music's power to affect human nature are mediated through and constituted by "subjective" bodily experiences of that power, which are acquired through the senses—in this case, hearing. I argue that there is an intimate and perhaps even necessary linkage between making new music and making new (scientific) knowledge. Put another way, as the nature of music and its organization changed in early modern society, so understandings of human nature and its organization were correspondingly transformed.[1]

This ambitious agenda cannot be accommodated easily within the analytical frameworks historians of medicine and historians of music have conventionally used to explore what interests them about early modern European culture (Gouk 2000). In contrast, anthropologists apparently take for granted that in order to grasp the meanings of specific institutions and practices in a given society, these have to be mapped onto a larger worldview. For example, Anthony Seeger's work on the Suyá is driven by the desire to "understand the relationship between ways that people conceive of their universe (cosmology), organise themselves into groups (social organization) and organise sounds (music and some of the sonic features of language)" (Seeger 2002: 5).

This insight has also paid off in the more specialized field of ethnomusicology, especially since John Blacking (1995) argued that "music" functions as a primary modeling system in preliterate and non-Western cultures. A growing body of texts cogently demonstrates how "music" (as embodied sound, movement, etc.) is variously used by cultures to restore balance between people and their environment (Stobart 2000) or more explicitly as a therapeutic tool in the healing process (Friedson 1996; Janzen 2000; Roseman 1993). These studies suggest that one of the most important functions of "music" is as a vehicle for altering spiritual states, not only those of humans (and animals) but also those of beings who lie beyond the visible realm.

In my experience, at least, it is hardly normal for scholars studying aspects of (modern) Western culture to assume that cosmology and music are related to each other through social systems, so the idea that they should be trying to explain how such connections might work is practically unthinkable. Indeed, one of the main narrative threads in Western intellectual history is the story of the separation of cosmology and music during a process of "disenchantment" that took place from the late seventeenth century onward (e.g., James 1993). According to this narrative, the scientific revolution marked the period when an experimentally based method of generating scientific truths began to emerge in Western society, together with a mechanized conception of the universe in which all bodies and their relationships to each other were governed by the same laws of Newtonian physics (Henry 1997). Within this new scientific paradigm, we are told, there was apparently no place for a Pythagorean-Platonic conception of an animated, ensouled cosmos held together by a network of invisible spirits and correspondences. The harmony of the spheres apparently fell silent in the wake of this new, materialist cosmology.

Of course there is some basis to this account of long-term Western "disenchantment." During the eighteenth century, European intellectuals explicitly distanced their rational, experimentally based knowledge from the credulity and superstition they perceived as still rampant among the lower orders, women, and non-Western cultures. Belief in horary astrology, witchcraft, and demonic magic certainly declined in educated urban society. For example, it became much less common for madness to be ascribed to demonic possession, a diagnosis that was acceptable in the seventeenth century but that now gave way almost entirely to explanations of physical and mental imbalance (Heyd 1984). Given this shift in attitudes, it is easy to imagine that there really was a complete disjuncture between cosmology and music, which, in the Enlightenment system of knowledge, lay on opposite sides of a newly constructed arts-science divide. Within this framework, music was definitively located among the fine arts rather than the mathematical sciences. Composers no longer sought to legitimate their art through a knowledge of mathematical principles but instead demonstrated their power to move the passions (Palisca 1985a). Indeed, because of its evident capacity to rouse strong feelings, music was clearly remote from the realm of experimental science—a practice presented by its supporters as a dispassionate, reliable method of generating knowledge, in contrast to the fanciful speculations that might be produced by an overheated imagination.

The Enlightenment myth that scientific rationalism gradually displaced (and was necessarily incompatible with) magical and religious beliefs has proved remarkably enduring (e.g., Hinde 2001). Historians have long since demonstrated the theological underpinnings of early modern science, but only comparatively recently has a more nuanced understanding of the influential role that magic played in its development begun to emerge. Nevertheless, a growing body of research indicates that although the manipulation of natural forces and the application of mathematics to the physical world are now hallmarks of the scientific method, before the seventeenth century they were a recognized part of natural, or spiritual, magic.

Broadly speaking, the occult powers that could be harnessed by magicians were thought to fall into two categories. On the one hand, demonic magic relied on the intervention of intelligent, immaterial beings that could be summoned by a variety of (forbidden) techniques to enact the magician's commands. On the other, natural magic supposedly avoided this intervention by concentrating on the manipulation of impersonal forces operating throughout God's creation.[2] The natural magician understood the universe to be constructed on mathematical principles, with nature being full of hidden spiritual properties whose virtues could be harnessed through the application of proper techniques (e.g., those used in chemistry and mechanics). In brief, the new experimental science—characterized by its emphasis on technical control and experimental trials bringing about predictable effects, coupled with the goal of improving the state of mankind—simply took over the most powerful aspects of natural magic, even while magic itself was discredited as false and valueless (Henry 1997; Webster 1982).

This revised account of the transformation in early modern scientific thinking still lacks an essential dimension, namely, an exploration of what changes occurred in the *aural* environment during the period and how these changes might have altered people's inner sense of themselves as well as their relationship to the outer world. Music historians have studied the transformations that took place in musical practice between the fifteenth and eighteenth centuries (conventionally demarcated as the Renaissance, Baroque, and Classical periods), but the effects these changes might have had on society more generally have not yet attracted systematic investigation. There are many reasons why sound has been left out of mainstream European cultural history—not least the assumption that a shift to a predominantly visualist culture took place between the Renaissance and the Enlightenment. This preoccupation with new "ways of seeing" has led to a disproportionate amount of attention being paid to the power of visual technologies to transform the world and its modes of representation. Whether aural technologies—including new instrumental sounds and musical genres—have had an equivalent power to alter physical and mental states, including the capacity to create entirely new "ways of hearing," is not yet recognized as an equally pressing question. Nevertheless, musicologists have begun to ask how we might reconstruct the experience of listening in various historical periods (Wegman 1998b) and to trace the concept of a "musical ear," which seems first to have emerged in the late seventeenth century (Kassler 1995).

I first began to address the relationship between cosmic, musical, and social harmony in my earlier work *Music, Science and Natural Magic in Seventeenth-Century England* (1999), which focused chiefly on the use of musical models in the new physics of Newton, Hooke, and the early Royal Society. I was able to demonstrate that musical technologies (instruments, notation, techniques) provided resources for those who would understand and explain, not only music, but the entire structure of the universe. In particular, the model of a vibrating string governed by mathematical laws served as a means of understanding planetary motion. What I did not try to do in that work was to track the parallel process of reconceptualizing *inner* space, the hidden and mysterious world beneath the skin that was only just beginning to be opened up to the anatomist's gaze. My current project, the working title of which is "Doctors, music, and human nature from Renaissance to Enlightenment," examines medical understandings of music and its effects on the human body and psyche over this crucial period when the Western "soundscape" of composed art music was dramatically transformed.

Soundscapes and Passions

As Bruce Smith has observed, "people dwelling in a particular soundscape know the world in fundamentally different ways from people dwelling in another soundscape" (Smith 1999: 47). Evidence suggests that the soundscape that eighteenth-century musicians and their audiences inhabited was very different from any of the fifteenth century (Christensen 1993; Fenlon 1989). Certainly, far more composed art music was being produced in the eighteenth century than even two hundred years earlier. But there seems also to have been a qualitative transformation in the nature of musical experience itself. Since the eighteenth century, it has seemed normal to consider music as an expressive language of the passions, and a substantial body of Enlightenment literature reflects on making and appreciating music (Cowart 1989; Fubini 1994). Looking back, however, it becomes apparent that no equivalent body of medieval or Renaissance literature on music's emotional power exists apart from a few brief commonplaces. Nor is there much evidence that musicians of the time were thinking about the emotions—or at least they wrote nothing on the subject.

During the sixteenth century, a fundamental redefinition of the goals of music took place. Composers began to reflect on music's emotional capacity, especially with a view to re-creating the powerful effects of ancient (especially Greek) music. Now, for the first time, they expressly sought to move and imitate what were then called the "passions" or "affections" (rather than the "emotions," which is a more recent concept). The best-known results of these experiments in following the ancient ideal of expressing the "affect" or emotional character of the words are the development of monody (flexible solo song with chordal accompaniment) and the birth of opera around 1600. During the seventeenth century, composers, librettists, singers, and instrumentalists developed ever more sophisticated techniques for expressing human passions as well as moving their audiences (Palisca 1985a).

At the same time, a literature on the passions, especially melancholy, also began to appear (e.g., Burton 1621; Wright 1604). The first systematic codification of the "doctrine of affections" appeared in Athanasius Kircher's *Musurgia Universalis* (1650). This doctrine, which underpinned early opera and oratorio, continued to inform the musical practice of later baroque composers such as Bach and Handel (Palisca 2000). Moreover, it provided a taxonomy for medical theorists and natural philosophers, who now began to theorize in detail about music's effects on people. In short, Enlightenment doctors had access to a wealth of written data and experimental evidence drawn from a soundscape that simply had not existed two hundred years previously. Framed around musical and artistic conventions that still underpin Western popular and classical music, this soundscape was also constitutive of physiological models that—as recognizably modern, objective, and apparently culturally neutral representations of both music and human nature—are both the starting point for and the conclusion to my project.

Richard Browne's *Medicina Musica, or a Mechanical Essay on the Effects of Singing, Musick and Dancing* (1729) and Richard Brocklesby's *Reflections on Antient and Modern Musick, with the Application to the Cure of Diseases* (1749) are routinely held up as the first scientific texts on music therapy (Darrow, Gibbons, and Heller 1985). They were certainly the earliest medical works in English to deal explicitly and extensively with music's effects and their potential therapeutic applications.[3] In their own time, both would have fallen into the category we now call self-help literature, practical texts that give advice about how to keep healthy and avoid disease. The reason they are now identified as scientific is because the authors assume not only that music's power to alter emotional states is experimentally verifiable (there being a correspondence between a person's mood and the character of a piece) but also that the body's inner mechanisms work according to the laws of Newtonian physics. Another recognizably "modern" feature of these texts is that they identify nerve action (understood in terms of the flow of spirits) as responsible for effecting these inner changes. This reflects the enormous impact that Thomas Willis's *Cerebri anatome nervorumque descriptio* (1664)—a seminal work in what was then the newly emerging discipline of neurophysiology—had on early modern medical thought.

After situating these texts and their contents within the intellectual milieu of eighteenth-century London in the following section, my strategy will be to move backward, rather than forward, to look at the first Western text to suggest how to manipulate the emotions through musical sound. Published in 1489, this work also proves to be a health manual, its advice directed chiefly toward scholars whose intellectual labors predispose them to melancholy. But this was not the kind of advice most fifteenth-century physicians would have been offering their patients, and indeed its author was no ordinary physician. The author of the *De vita libri tres*, or *Three Books on Life*, was none other than the Florentine philosopher and priest Marsilio Ficino (1433–1499), the foremost Renaissance expert on natural magic and the effective architect of the magical worldview that early modern experimental science is supposed to have overthrown. I show why the "music therapy" that Ficino recommends in the third book, "On fitting one's life to the heavens," is actually a magical operation, a daring experiment to realign the operator's spirit with those of the planets, in order to receive their beneficial influences through the power of song and instrument (Ficino 1989; Tomlinson 1993; Walker 1958).[4]

With the benefit of hindsight, historians now know that the *De vita* not only was the source for all later discussions of the melancholic temperament and its association with genius but also laid the foundation for the way educated Europeans were to address the question of music's effects on the body, mind, and soul into the next millennium (Schiesari 1992). These long-term implications were scarcely manifest by 1500, however, and although increasingly popular, the *De vita* had no immediate influence on either musical or medical theory. Its significance began to emerge only in the later sixteenth century, when, as we have already seen, composers sought to experimentally re-create the powerful ethical and magical effects of ancient music. The reasons they began to do this cannot be adequately explored in this chapter, but we can at least look briefly to events of the Reformation as an essential context for understanding this extraordinary quest.

Lasting for more than a century after Luther's original protest in 1517, the Reformation conflict fragmented Western Christendom as established hierarchies of church and state were overturned and the political map of Europe redrawn. As confessional lines blurred and bifurcated,

Protestants and Catholics alike struggled to reestablish mankind's proper relationship to God, as well as establish a harmonious social order. There were many competing visions of how Christians should reach the divine, which meant that music's place in worship as well as in society more generally was a hotly contested issue. In the search to establish a new social and moral order, reformers typically looked back to antiquity for appropriate models of conduct. One of the striking differences between ancient and modern civilization seemed to be that ancient music had far greater powers than it did in modern times, especially on morals and behavior. What were the reasons for these powers, and how might one go about restoring them? For anyone seriously interested in this question, an obvious place to start (apart from the scriptures) was with Ficino, whose editions of Plato and other ancient philosophers seemed to offer direct access to the sonic practices of lost civilizations. Taking Ficino's position in a moment, we will see why he particularly identified with Pythagoras as a musical healer, but first let us compare how differently such ancient authorities were treated by the thinkers of the Enlightenment.

Enlightened Mechanical Bodies

Compared with Ficino, Browne and Brocklesby are obscure figures. Browne (fl. 1720s) apparently practiced as an apothecary in Oakham, Rutland, whereas Brocklesby (1722–1797) achieved minor fame as Samuel Johnson's physician and friend (Breathnach 1998). Although we do not know what immediately prompted either of them to write on music and disease, both doctors had a similar kind of audience in mind, namely, educated, middle-class urban dwellers, including women. Browne, for example, hoped that his volume would appeal to the "fair sex," whose "tender and delicate constitutions" rendered them most liable to the diseases he identified with music. A potentially huge market existed for such literature: by the early eighteenth century, London had become the largest city in Europe, with a population of around six hundred thousand, or about one-ninth of the total English population. The metropolis acted as a magnet for the professions and all forms of conspicuous consumption, including music (Beier and Finlay 1986; Earle 1989). Indeed, for a combination of religious and political reasons that bear on this chapter, London had by this time become the largest commercial musical marketplace in Europe (Gouk 1999: 54–61). In such an environment, a specialist book about music's benefits to health might well have been considered commercially viable.

Members of the leisured urban classes could well afford to purchase remedies and advice from a wide range of practitioners in what has also been called the "medical marketplace" of Georgian London. The central message these particular doctors wanted to get across to their readers was that music could be good for health and that they could justify this in learned medical terms. In particular, they claimed that music could help cure certain ailments, especially nervous diseases and mental disorders.[5] Browne, for example, recommended music as a cure for the spleen, vapors, melancholy, and madness, and Brocklesby thought it sensible to try music in disorders arising from excessive passions such as anger, enthusiasm in religion or love, and the panic of fear. He also discussed tarantism (a disease reputedly inflicted by the bite of the tarantula and alleviated by music and dancing) and the benefits of music in pregnancy and old age. Both authors were careful to note that music was not a universal remedy, that the same music could have differing effects on individuals, that the wrong kind of music could sometimes actually worsen symptoms, and that music should be positively avoided in the case of some diseases (e.g., phthisis). It might also be used as a supplement to drugs—for example, soothing mad people by turning their mind's attention away from their bodily organs so that medicines would work better.

Although not entirely explicit, some distinction is made in the two books between effects that accrue from actually singing or playing instruments (and, in Browne's book, dancing) and those that can be achieved merely through listening. Unlike benefits derived from making music, those to be gained from listening to music are not automatic but rather depend on the refinement of the ear and the cultivation of what Brocklesby calls "internal sense," or "taste." Thus, Browne affirms that "by singing, we may cheer and elevate the soul, though the voice be harsh and inharmonious, whereas if our ears are not rightly modulated for the perception of harmony . . . no pleasure can possibly arise" (1729: 4). To modern readers, it might come as a surprise to find these Enlightenment doctors referring to music's effects on the soul as well as the body. Contrary to popular belief that the soul ceased to be important to science after Descartes, medical theorists continued to invoke this entity as a necessary part of understanding the body's workings into the eighteenth century and beyond.

Yet while these doctors were willing to incorporate God and the soul into their explanations of music's powers, they clearly had no time for evil spirits or magical operations, and it is this that identifies them with the Enlightenment. Following a well-established humanist tradition, both authors refer to the marvelous effects attributed to music in anti-quity (Orpheus, Pythagoras, and King David being the key examples), citing works such as Plutarch's *De musica* and Plato's *Republic* as starting points for their own observations about music's powers. Yet their attitudes toward antiquity are strikingly different from that of Ficino, who was one of the first Western scholars to have access to a body of texts that described the sometimes astonishing effects that incantations, hymns, and other musical sounds were capable of evoking in ancient pagan and Jewish civilizations. Fifteenth- and sixteenth-century scholars treated this literature with enormous respect, seeing it as a repository of ancient wisdom and power that was superior to modern experience and that might be recovered as a means of creating a new golden age (Gouk 1999: 251–254; Walker 1972).

By the eighteenth century, Enlightenment scholars were in a position to treat ancient music altogether more critically. Although they did not dismiss the value of some ancient learning, a consensus grew that modern society was more technologically and scientifically advanced than antiquity, its music was more complex, and its people were more sophisticated. (Not everyone considered such changes wholly positive, however.) Browne and Brocklesby were typical in their confidence that the wonders attributed to ancient music did not need demons or magic to work but could be explained by one or more of the following: some effects were exaggerated or even invented by the authors of these myths; the people who heard the effects were gullible or unsophisticated—that is, they had little or no previous experience of the phenomena and therefore responded to them more directly than "modern," or civilized, listeners would do; and this gullibility (variously described as "supersti-tion" and "enthusiasm") was exploited by politicians, priests, or both, whose "aptitude for deception" could dispose people to a belief in poet-ical fictions. In other words, there was no aural mystery that could not be explained in rationalistic terms (compare Schmidt 2000: 16–28). Hav-ing made these observations, Browne, for example, could simply reduce David's cure of Saul to the treatment of spleen—there was no need to invoke evil spirits, either as part of the diagnosis or as part of the cure.

With demons firmly ruled out of the picture, what did these authors regard as an appropriately scientific explanation of music's mysterious ability to affect mood and behavior? According to Browne, the condi-tion of "spleen" (a disease closely related to melancholy) was caused by the defective secretion of the animal spirits, which were responsible for nourishing the bodily solids and maintaining the springiness and elasticity of the animal fibers. This loss of "spirit" could lead to a variety of mental and physical symptoms, ranging from despair to poor digestion. In simple terms, the reason music could effect a cure was because it could invigorate and increase the spirits, which, thus stimulated, flowed through the nerves to every part of the body.

First, however, the vibrations of musical sound had to be mediated via the ear, a process that doctors were beginning to explain in terms of the properties of musical instruments. For example, the anatomist Joseph Du Verney, in his *Traité de l'organe de l'ouïe* (Paris, 1683), argued that the eardrum was involuntarily adjusted to resonate with different vibrations of the air in the same way that the body of a lute conformed to the various sounds produced by its strings. These vibrations were then transmitted to the cochlea and labyrinth by means of the auditory ossicles in the same way that the vibrations of a string on one lute were transmitted to a string on a neighboring lute via their bodies and the table. Thomas Willis's *Two Discourses on the Soul of Brutes* (London, 1683) likewise identified the cochlea as the organ of hearing, where the audible species were in turn impressed on the nerve fibers, and hypothesized that these impulses were carried along the nerves to the brain via the flow of animal spirits.[6]

Browne's account of the process by which sounds could stimulate the secretion of animal spirits was somewhat less sophisticated, but it nevertheless reflected these developments in neurophysiological thinking. In Browne's model, sound arose from small vibrations propagated through the external air, communicated to the internal air of the ear by the motion of the eardrum and auditory ossicles. In turn, this inner air made equivalent impressions on the auditory nerve, "the immediate organ of hearing," which transmitted these vibrations to the mind, "which by sympathy will invigorate the motion of the spirits, and communicate a correspondent sensation through the whole machine" (1729: 36). Finally, as the blood itself was set in motion, this led to the secretion of more animal spirits. Armed with this explanation, Browne's readers were in a position to conceptualize exactly why various types of music would automatically produce corresponding feelings in their bodies. Swift, short, and bold vibrations would briskly agitate the nerves, whereas the "slow languishing strokes of the fiddle" would cause the spirits to "flow back in gentle undulations." There was a direct correspondence, or sympathy, between the vibrations produced by musical instruments and the body, which was itself responding like a musical instrument.

Although both Browne and Brockelsby took the increased flow of spirits through the nerves to be self-explanatory, there was controversy about the process. First, debate existed about the precise nature of the animal spirits, which were the chief instrument of the rational soul. It was generally accepted that they were a particulate, chemical substance distilled from hot arterial blood. Physicians were undecided whether these spirits actually constituted the sensitive soul itself or were simply its agent, but they agreed that they were transmitted through the nerves and acted as the medium of all sensory and motor functions. Second, the structure of the nerves, too, was in doubt. Some physicians conceptualized them as small pipes through which the animal spirits flowed like a fine liquor. Others claimed the nerves to be more like strings that communicated their effects through elastic, vibrative motion.

Whatever their differences, all physiological models at this time were essentially based on, or were responses to, the teachings of the Leiden medical professor Herman Boerhaave (1668–1738). This was because from the early 1700s Boerhaave's physiology was institutionalized in medical schools across Europe. The Boerhaavian system taught that human beings comprised an immaterial soul sympathetically linked to a material body made out of fluids and solids, whose workings could be understood in wholly physical terms. Thus debates about the spirits essentially revolved about whether their flow should be conceptualized in hydraulic or mechanical terms (electrical phenomena not yet being understood).

Boerhaave's physiology derived its scientific legitimacy from the principles of Newtonian physics—that all bodies and forces in nature were governed by the same mathematical laws (e.g., his law of universal gravitation) and that all phenomena, including light, sound, gravity, and magnetism, could be explained in terms of particulate matter in motion. In the *Principia mathematica* (1687), Newton was the first to offer a coherent mathematical explanation connecting the properties of musical strings and other elastic vibrating bodies (Gouk 1999: 224–257). In the early eighteenth century it was confidently assumed that Newton's success at revealing the laws of planetary motion could be emulated in the quest to reveal the hidden mechanisms of human bodies and their interaction with each other. Within this overall "mechanistic" framework, music's effects were to be explained in terms of the laws of vibrating fluids and solids, both within and beyond the body.

Not all doctors, however, accepted that the body's workings could be accounted for in purely physical terms. From around the mid-century, some medical theorists began to advance vitalist models in which a nonmaterial, sentient principle was the basis of life. They postulated an active substance that mediated between the physical and non-physical realms, and they used the concept of sympathy to explain how particular affections of the mind could bring about particular disorders of the body, and vice versa. For example, George Cheyne's *English Malady, or a Treatise of Nervous Diseases* (1733)—another treatise on melancholy—described the brain as the seat of the soul, the place "where all the Nervous fibres terminate inwardly, like a Musician by a well-tuned instrument."

Cheyne, however, was not a mechanist but rather suggested that the elasticity of the stringlike nerves might be due to an extremely fine and active spirit, which might well be the same as the "subtle" elastic spirit described by Isaac Newton in the 1713 edition of the *Principia* as a medium "which pervades and lies hidden in crass bodies, and by whose power and actions the particles of bodies mutually attract each other at minute distances." A similar spirit is described in the 1717 edition of the *Opticks*, where Newton speaks of infinite space as God's sensorium, that is, the deity manifesting his existence as an all-pervasive spirit whose power could be recognized through its effects (Gouk 1999: 254–545; Walker 1984). In other words, Cheyne was using Newtonian physics to support his own medical hypothesis that the "spirit" stuff that linked the human soul and body was analogous to, or even identical with, the "spirit" that mediated between God and his creation (Guerrini 2000: 119–127). Whether Cheyne realized it or not, the first time this analogy was put forward seriously, it was used to precisely the opposite effect. When Ficino suggested that an identity existed between human spirits and natural, cosmic spirits, he was using a well-established medical theory to buttress his new and somewhat daring cosmological theory, one that also found legitimation through harmonic principles.

Scholars, Spirits, and Souls

In one sense, Ficino's *De vita* compares directly to Browne's *Medicina Musica*, in that it is aimed at readers who are prone to melancholy, provides advice on diet and regimen, suggests the kinds of music that will help alleviate this condition, and explains why it works. Yet the social and intellectual context in which this text appeared, as well as the soundscape its author and readers inhabited in fifteenth-century Florence, was wholly different from the eighteenth-century London scene I have described. Ficino dedicated the work to his patron, Lorenzo de' Medici (1449–92) "the magnificent," the foremost citizen of Florence and leader of its influential Platonic Academy. Its readership, like that of any other book published in Latin at the time—fewer than forty years after the invention of the printing press—was by definition tiny. However, its intended audience was even smaller, for its esoteric and possibly dangerous contents were notionally aimed at a group of intellectuals known personally to Ficino, whose shared love of philosophy and making music made his prescriptions especially apt for their condition. One of these was Lorenzo himself, an accomplished poet, musician, and lover of the arts and sciences.

Ficino's social and professional identity was also rather different from that of Browne or Brocklesby. He was not a physician by profession but a scholar and priest who had learned medicine from his father, a physician to Cosimo the Elder (1389–1464), Lorenzo's grandfather. Indeed, it was as a result of Cosimo's patronage that Ficino became a scholar, spending much of his life translating, editing, and eventually publishing a huge corpus of ancient texts, especially those thought to be by Plato and Hermes Trismegistus. This was an essential part of Cosimo's demand for Ficino to re-create the Platonic Academy in Medici Florence, which was to be the "new Athens." The justification for Ficino's studying these pagan and magical sources was that they contained an ancient theology that providentially harmonized with Christianity. This secret wisdom, or perennial philosophy, had initially been revealed by God to Adam and was subsequently transmitted through a select group of *magi* that included Hermes, Orpheus, Pythagoras, and Plato (Walker 1972).

Ficino was especially keen to emulate the healing effects these *magi* reputedly achieved through song and incantation, notably the ability to cure diseases of the soul and body, to expel evil passions, and to bring the soul into a state of virtuous harmony. Unfortunately, the *magi* were also able to accomplish other effects through musical art that were difficult to reconcile with Ficino's role as a Catholic priest: through the same sonic power, they could summon demons and angels, attract their power into statues and amulets, raise the dead, and force other people to act against their will by means of enchantment.[7] Because the Church condemned all forms of idolatry and magic, it is perhaps not surprising that Ficino was accused of practicing magic himself. In the event, formal charges were dropped, but although Ficino firmly denied consorting with demons, he nevertheless believed himself to be practicing a form of natural, or spiritual, magic.

This desire to emulate the powers of ancient *magi*, to transgress existing boundaries by appealing to natural spiritual laws—but without straying from orthodox Catholic values—provides the essential context for the *De vita*. The book is nothing less than a guide to conditioning one's spirit so that it may become receptive to benign celestial influences, as part of a long-term process of purification of the soul and union with the divine. The first book of the *De vita* deals with preserving health, the second with prolonging life, and the third with astral influences. It is in the third book, "On fitting one's life to the heavens," that Ficino offers a set of practical techniques for creating songs that will draw down beneficial planetary emanations, especially those of the sun (Apollo), to restore the spirits and offset the melancholic influence of Saturn. Musical sound, which consists of aerial movements that imitate the motions of the spirit and soul, serves as the link between heavenly and earthly domains.

Paradoxically, these aural experiments were based entirely on a written tradition, and although they sought to re-create ancient effects, they were a wholly modern product of the printing age. The principal texts that Ficino used as the basis for his astrological songs were the *Chaldean Oracles* and the *Orphic Hymns*. Rare manuscripts of these works had only recently arrived in Venice from Constantinople, and Ficino was among the first Western scholars to read them (producing an edition of the *Orphic Hymns* in 1462). Although current scholarship dates these poems from the second century A.D., Renaissance philosophers believed them to be authentic examples of the hymns that Zoroaster, the Persian *magus*, and Orpheus, the Greek master of Pythagoras, sang to their sun gods. Ficino had no idea what these ancient priests might have sounded like, but because he admired the way they combined theology with "medicine and the lyre," he attempted to reconstruct their solarian songs (Voss 2000; Walker 1958).

What did Ficino's spiritual music sound like? It is generally agreed that his songs were probably chanted, midway between song and speech, to the accompaniment of the *lira da braccio*, the harp, or possibly even the lute.[8] Ironically, modern scholars and musicians who attempt to reconstruct these Renaissance magical songs face much the same problem that Ficino himself encountered in trying to imitate the ancients: no examples of original instruments, musical notation, or traces of the sounds themselves remain to guide the would-be performer. Nevertheless, Ficino provided a set of rules for fitting songs to the heavenly bodies that involved learning the powers of particular stars, observing the character of their modes and songs (e.g., the sun's music was venerable, simple, and earnest, united with grace and smoothness), and then singing the songs frequently, so that the singer's spirit would take on this character. Ficino stressed that the musical sounds were drawing down natural spirits, which could in turn nourish human spirits. In other words, the nexus between natural and human spirits is "automatic" in the sense that it bypasses the will and is confined to the sensory level and imagination.

From Ficino's perspective, the procedures he recommended in the *De vita* for nourishing the human spirit, or *spiritus*, were based on sound medical and scientific principles. He began by defining *spiritus* in a way that would have satisfied any academic physician of his time, and although lacking in anatomical specificity, his description distinctly recalls the eighteenth-century mechanisms I have already outlined. For Ficino, spirit is "defined by the physicians as a certain vapour of the blood, pure, subtle, hot and lucid. And, formed from the subtler blood by the heat of the heart, it flies to the brain, and there the soul assiduously employs it for the exercise of both the exterior and interior senses" (Walker 1958: 1).

The *spiritus*, in other words, is a corporeal vapor that acts as the link between the body and the incorporeal soul and serves as the instrument for sense perception, imagination, and motor activity. There is a profound ambiguity, however, in Ficino's understanding of this human *spiritus*, which is "contaminated" by another category of spirit that Christians found deeply problematic: that is the world soul, or *spiritus mundi*, of the Neoplatonists. Indeed, the philosophical underpinning for Ficino's magical songs was provided by Plotinus's *Enneads* (third century A.D.), a classical Neoplatonic text that was unknown to the Middle Ages and that Ficino himself edited in 1492.

According to the Neoplatonists, the heavenly bodies exert their influence on the earth (and vice versa) according to two principles, both of which are connected to the physical and mathematical properties of music. The first principle is the *spiritus mundi* (*pneuma*, world soul, or astral body of the Stoics), an extremely fine medium that permeates the cosmos, intermingles with earthly matter, and can bring about changes in its form. The affinity of different parts of the cosmos is maintained by *tonos*, or tension, a dynamic property of the *spiritus*. The Neoplatonists explained this sympathy by analogy with a properly tuned lyre: when one string on the instrument has been struck, another tuned to the same pitch will also vibrate, and this vibration can even travel from one lyre to another, setting equivalently tuned strings in motion. This emphasis on vibration leads to the second, mathematically based principle: as explained in Ptolemy's *Harmonics* (second century A.D.), the same harmonic proportions govern planetary relationships (*musica mundana*), the relationship between body, spirit, and soul (*musica humana*), and musical sound (*musica instrumentalis*).

Ficino himself did not elaborate in any detail on these harmonic principles. Nevertheless, they informed his belief that the peculiar power of music was due to a similarity between the air, the medium in which music was transmitted, and the human spirit (Walker 1958: 3–11). He thought that sounds, being moving, animated air, combined directly with the aerial spirit in the ear (most anatomical details of the inner ear were lacking) and were conveyed both to the soul and to the spirit dispersed throughout the body. Sound affected the spirits more strongly than sight because it transmitted movement and was itself moving, whereas vision was concerned with static images. Because man's whole moral and emotional life consisted of actions of the body and motions of the spirit and soul, these could be imitated in music and transmitted by it. Indeed, the matter of song itself is "warm air, even breathing, and in a measure living, made up of articulated limbs, like an animal, not only bearing movement and emotion, but even signification, like a mind, so that it can be said to be, as it were, a kind of aerial and rational animal" (Walker 1958: 10).

Sonic Transformations

This striking description of musical sound as a living, rational being conjured up by the singer's voice and instrument finally leads us to reflect on the huge differences between the soundscapes in which Ficino's songs and Browne's musical remedies were located. In each case, it is clear that we have to consider the larger frame of reference (cosmological, social, intellectual) within which the "music" being discussed takes on its particular form and meaning. However, I also want to claim a more active agency for music itself in this overall transformation: namely, that changes in the organization of musical sound— brought about through a process of intense experimentation by individuals deliberately seeking to alter spiritual conditions—irrevocably altered Western understandings of human and cosmic bodies and their relationship to each other. Following Anthony Seeger's (2002) example, I have attempted to track down some of these connections between Western musical and cosmic organization that have been lost to view since the eighteenth century, the point when the laws of harmony were shown to be grounded in natural principles, even as musical language itself was recognized as a human artifact.

The connections between these realms are not always where we might have expected or hoped them to be. We cannot say that Ficino's Pythagorean experiments to realign his soul with the heavens were successful; to us his methods seem false and unscientific because he tried to control what we would now call *supernatural* influences, rather than concentrating on what we now see as music's *natural* powers. Nevertheless, his is the first recorded attempt to try to manipulate the emotions by playing music fitted to a particular character, a result that was to be achieved by harnessing natural forces to bring about predicted effects. At the time Ficino published the *De vita*, it was entirely unpredictable that "the fullest exposition of a theory of magic and its most influential such statement in post-classical times" (Copenhaver 1988: 274) would provide a basis for the powerful new forms of scientific as well as musical practice that were successfully institutionalized in seventeenth-century Europe. Again, we cannot say that sixteenth-century composers were actually successful in their experiments to restore the ethical effects of ancient Greek music, but we can recognize that entirely new ways of affecting people through sound were unexpectedly created as a result of deliberate attempts to realign cosmic, human, and social states and to bring individuals and communities closer to the divine through the power of harmony.

By reversing the flow of my historical narrative, I have sought to emphasize just how *un*natural and *extra*ordinary these affective powers once were, which was why they were first identified with magic. In the eighteenth century the ability of composers to alter inner states was still marvelous, but by this time the experience of having one's feelings manipulated through sound had become normalized, rather than being something outside of everyday experience. When Ficino conceptualized his experiment in terms of the action of "spirits" and the vibration of musical strings, there were neither universal mathematical laws nor an experimental method that he could take for granted, and so he drew on the resources of natural magic, which took for its starting point that "nature is musical." It was only after Newton succeeded in unifying the mathematical principles that underlay manifest mechanical actions and occult attractive forces in his new physics that the paradigm became "music is natural" and its effects on human nature became amenable to medical and scientific experiment.

Notes

1. Considerable problems are entailed in using terms such as "music" to address non-Western sonic practices; for a detailed discussion in relation to medicine and healing, see Gouk 2000.

2. In reality, the boundaries between these types of magic were blurred, because demons were themselves part of this creation and could accomplish effects only through the harnessing of natural forces. Further discussions of natural magic are found in Walker 1958: 75–84 and Gouk 1999: 11–12 and passim.

3. Browne's *Medicina Musica* of 1729 is apparently a "revised and corrected" version of an earlier work, published anonymously as *A Mechanical Essay. . .* in 1727. Although virtually nothing is known about Browne apart from his self-description as an apothecary, he claimed to have written the work during his apprenticeship, a stage that traditionally took place between the ages of fourteen and twenty-one, which would mean he was probably born around 1700.

4. On Ficino's likely Arabic sources, especially the writings of the ninth-century philosopher al-Kindi, see Burnett 2000.

5. None of the following examples is original to either author; there was a well-established literary tradition on this subject. See Kümmel 1977 and the essays in Horden 2000.

6. For further discussion, see Gouk 1991: 95–113, especially pp. 108–109; and Gouk 1999: 271–272.

7. For early modern thinking about the nature of *female* enchantment, and responses to powerful figures such as the sibyls and the Witch of Endor, see Austern 1989.

8. The *lira* was a seven-stringed bowed instrument of the Italian High Renaissance, "one of the most characteristic implements of the intended revival of the rhapsodic art of the ancients" (Winternitz 1979: 87).

Ether Ore: Mining Vibrations in American Modernist Music

Douglas Kahn

At least since the time of Pythagoras, and his echo in Plato's *Timaeus*, music has been used to find one's place in the cosmos, just as the stars themselves have been used for navigational purposes. Unlike the sextant, however, music has never been considered merely a tool. Its ability to place one in the cosmos has been understood as deriving from its ability to emulate—perhaps more directly, recapitulate—the deployment of celestial bodies in its innermost operations, the relationship of pitches, delivering the order, unity, and entirety that is the cosmos in an experiential form. This ability of music not only situates a listener and audiences among elevated concerns but also imbues certain types of music and certain individuals who make it possible with a grandiloquence and sanctity far above the fray of mundane realities. It also makes audible an order wrenched from chaos, presents harmonies to make mundane realities more manageable, and brings authority of various types into tune with the cosmos.

The inverse holds true as well; the universe itself becomes imbued with the human concerns of music, even though the silence of the heavens beyond the birds, wind, and thunder was experienced in antiquity, too, long before it was discovered that sound does not travel in a vacuum, at least by acoustical means. Pythagoras, who some say invented the notion of the cosmos, inferred the musicality of the universe by correlating the ratios of the positions and movements of the sun, the moon, planets, and stars to musical intervals grounded in the actions of the vibrating string of the monochord. Aristotle, in *De Caelo* (On the Heavens; Aristotle 1984: 479), disagreed with the acoustic tenets of Pythagorean cosmology. Celestial spheres were large

107

and traveling at great speed; if they were to make a sound, it would be the loudest sound imaginable. Thunder could split rocks, he said; this sound would be much louder than thunder. Pythagoras's followers flanked Aristotle's incredulity by saying that the sound was known only through reason and heard only through the special sensitivity of the blessed.

Followers of the occult in the latter half of the nineteenth century took Pythagorean and Platonic thought to heart, as such followers do to this day. Whatever the reason they might have felt out of place, they continued to seek assistance from music to place them in the cosmos and the social order. Like earlier Pythagoreans, they were required to respond to criticism. Developments in mathematics and measurement made it obvious that Pythagorean notions were no more than hopeful arithmetic and geometry. Concerns in Western art music challenged harmonic traditions with increasing dissonance. And audiophonic technologies (telegraphy, telephony, phonography, radiophony) helped transform the nature of auditory culture itself, raised expectations that phenomena should be audible, increased the sphere of what had yet to be heard, and based all sound, music included, more firmly in a materialist rhetoric of acoustical vibration.

One of the most elaborate and creative responses to this new set of challenges was developed by the French-American composer and esoteric philosopher Dane Rudhyar. At once at the forefront of Western art music in the early twentieth century and heavily influenced by theosophical thought, he rejuvenated the oldest harmonic tropes of the West by appealing to the recently appropriated tropes of South Asia— specifically, Tantric cosmogony, with its central figure of a cosmogenic vibration, which the theosophists had appropriated.

Although it had entailed a cosmogony, Pythagoreanism had come down through the centuries as cosmology, the structure and function of the cosmos, its vibrations arrayed spatially and harmonically among certain intervals, rendering it incapable of accounting for complex phenomena. In Rudhyar's conception, the Hindu cosmogenic vibration was capable of generating any acoustical phenomenon, because it was always in the process of creating everything else. The way in which he appealed to acoustics placed him among a generation of avant-garde composers who began to employ a rhetoric of sound. Among them were Luigi Russolo, with his art of noise, Edgar Varèse, with his liberation of sound, and John Cage, letting sounds be themselves. Unlike them, Rudhyar did not develop his sound through an emphasis on percussion and timbre but instead used his system to reintroduce a primacy of harmony characteristic of the composers the avant-garde sought to supersede. In effect, Rudhyar appropriated South Asian religious thought in order to employ a contemporary rhetoric of sound for the conservative purposes of Western music.

In the rest of this chapter, I show how Rudhyar found his way through several universes of discourse and practice in order to find a place in the cosmos of vibrations. I propose that his primary technique was akin to that of the early Pythagoreans when they argued that ostensibly inaudible sounds were known only through reason and heard only through the special sensitivity of the blessed. In the cosmos of Rudhyar's system, this technique was located at the place where he fused the single vibration with harmony, Tantrism with Pythagoreanism, and East with West—and this was at a point of inaudibility created by equating the "natural" harmonic series with harmonic intervals. The cosmic role for music and, indeed, the musical role for the cosmos have depended on the maintenance of this slippage between the audible and inaudible. To entertain the possibility of the inaudible requires belief, while the promise of making the inaudible audible fulfills the purposes of revelation. Making the inaudible audible, to appeal to the "super-sensory," not only underscores preoccupations of occultism to this day but also has functioned as an important metaphysical mechanism throughout the history of Western art music itself.

Dane Rudhyar has rarely been acknowledged for the central role he played in the development of American modernist music, let alone for his contribution to a musical rhetoric of sound per se. A central figure during the 1920s among the "ultramodern" ranks of Carl Ruggles, Henry Cowell, Ruth Crawford, and Charles Seeger, his ideas, as the music historian Carol Oja has recently suggested (2000: 97–110), prefigured those of the postwar avant-garde in the United States, which itself was animated by appeals to sound. Indeed, apart from the Italian Futurist Luigi Russolo, in his "Art of Noises Futurist Manifesto" (1986 [1913]) and book *The Art of Noises* (1916), no one so vociferously and systematically employed a rhetoric of sound so early.[1] Rudhyar's ideas were developed through a formidable series of publications, most of them appearing during the 1920s, in well-known musical journals such as *Musical Quarterly* and *Modern Music*, in other journals close to the community of musicians, in the theosophical press, and in self-published books and pamphlets. He was also a diligent and impassioned student of many topics other than music and subsequently became better known for his writings on astrology and spirituality.

Rudhyar's musical ideas were informed by numerous philosophical and esoteric traditions, the musics and thought of South and East Asian cultures, popular versions of contemporary science, and pseudo-science. Although what he developed was peculiarly his own, it was also an amalgamation characteristic of the theosophy movement in the late nineteenth and early twentieth centuries. Theosophy itself was one of many concerted attempts to reconcile religion with a powerfully persuasive science. Western art music as a discursive establishment was slower to respond, but as the early twentieth century proceeded, the spiritual dimension that it had prized came under materialist pressures and modernist imperatives to respond to advances in acoustical research, musical acoustics, and audiophonic and musical technologies. The ambitiousness of all such attempts, theosophical and musical, was motivated by the possibility that fragile alliances might fly apart at any moment. Rudhyar, in effect, brought the means by which theosophy had fought its war of science and religion into the specific battle to maintain the spirit in Western art music.

Rudhyar favored the theosophy of Madame Blavatsky (who died in 1891) over that of the subsequent Theosophical Society leadership of Annie Besant and Charles W. Leadbetter. Theosophy and related spiritual systems were influential with many modernists among all the arts. Although Western art music had long fancied itself as a conductor of the divine, the international success of the Russian mystic composer Alexander Scriabin, with his interests in theosophy, went a long way toward legitimating the movement within the ranks of music. Whereas Scriabin himself was not inclined to put his ideas into print, Rudhyar was forthcoming and prolific. He extended the occult role of sound and music formulated by Blavatsky into a system that attempted to apply the terrestrial conditions of science, specifically acoustics, and the metaphysical conditions of Hinduism and the esoteric tradition to the "progressive" and modern music of the 1920s.[2]

During the late nineteenth century, theosophy and science often met on a common ground of the ethers. Rudhyar, too, appealed to the ethers, emphasizing a special one that was infused with sound. The ethers, however, had been persistently equated with light, electricity, magnetism, and nerve impulses, not with sound, and by the time Rudhyar began writing they had lost much of their credibility among scientists.[3] But ethereal thinking was too well suited to a musical cosmos for musicians to let go of it. As an unknown entity, the ethers provided a place where physics and metaphysics could meet, where the minute mechanical vibrations of musical acoustics could interact with the atomic vibrations of physics, and where a Pythagorean cosmological inheritance might find a home. The Pythagorean cosmos was, after all, a musical one, with simple numbers and ratios describing harmonic intervals, the structure of the universe, and the correlation of so many discrete entities and affects. Yet just as the ethers themselves were dying out, so, too, were the mathematics subtending the Pythagorean cosmos. It seems to have come with the territory, the legend being that the cult of Pythagoras itself had done away with one of its own, Hippasos, when he challenged the cult's faith in integers (Samuel Beckett drowns him in a mud puddle in *Murphy*), and at least since the late Middle Ages Pythagorean intervallic proportions had had to be modified in light of contemporary musical tastes and mathematical practices.[4]

Some of the problems facing the Pythagorean musical cosmos were circumvented by the theosophical recourse to Hindu concepts of ethers, among them a Tantric sonoriferous ether, the *akasha*. This ether endowed the cosmos with acoustical operations of a primordial vibration that, in the Pythagorean tradition, had been underscored by music. It was a generative ether whose movement from a state of undifferenti ation to differentiation, in the to-and-fro of a single vibration or breath, was elaborated in a descent from spirit to matter as the source of everything, from the finest perturbations of atoms to the miasmic seas of chaos, and it could easily handle any of the cruder proportional systems belonging to Pythagoreanism. Rudhyar took full advantage of the acoustical and vibrational character of this Tantric ether to refurbish, in an array of negotiations between "East" and "West," the depleted resources of Pythagoreanism and Western art music.

With respect to modernist musical discourses, Rudhyar was most notably involved in legitimating a certain type of "natural" or "spiritual" dissonance based on acoustical properties of musical sounds. His appeal to distant cultures was not in the service of appropriating musics at a stylistic level but was part of a perennial philosophical approach correlating cultures at a more theoretical level. He developed a musical discourse privileging the "Single Tone" and resorting to "sound" outside of received musical sound that predated similar developments in the avant-garde of American music. Therein lies the irony of Rudhyar's position. He was in a pivotal position with regard to a subsequent avant-garde, with its shift to nonharmonic priorities of timbre, percussion, and noise and its focus on technologies, yet his own music was "relentlessly harmonic in conception" (Joseph Strauss, quoted in Oja 2000: 110) and thus remained loyal to the harmonic tradition of Western art music. The avant-garde was also engaged in a predominantly inscriptive and materialist rhetoric of sound, not a vibrational and metaphysical rhetoric (see Kahn 1992: 14–19). Rudhyar was able to employ a rhetoric of sound per se common to the avant-garde in order to reinstate what the avant-garde sought to supersede.

Sources of Sonic Plenitude

Within modernist artistic strategies, Rudhyar's pivotal position between the tradition of Western art music and the avant-garde was made possible by his going outside the given confines of musical sound to other sources of sonic plenitude. The source of sound was so rich that it was ubiquitous, although no one could hear it. The general strategy within music entailed going outside the givens of Western art music and importing elements back as provocation, musical material, and legitimation. Such excursions were a way in which modernist plenitude itself was generated, creating the sense of vitality characteristic of the arts at the time and, by default, an acknowledgment of a prior or constant state of vitiation, to be remedied by benign raids and destructive embraces. Before discussing Rudhyar's music theory specifically, I want to situate his recourse to sounds outside of music by briefly describing five general sources of sonic plenitude pertaining to sound and music. That they are not mutually exclusive becomes obvious in any discussion of specific cases, including the present one. Also, it is good to keep in mind that the sounds under consideration can exist in symbolic or actual sonic form or both, and they can be dramatically transformed depending upon the nature of the encounter with the source, the means of appropriation, and their situation in a new context.

The first and most familiar set of sources lying outside Western art music was popular musics, the musics of racial and ethnic minorities, rural and peasant musics, the musics of distant cultures, and combinations thereof. Encounters with such sources might occur through travel, performances, recordings or texts, and anthropological or religious projects, whereas the appropriation might be anything from fleeting stylistic intimations to outright repetition and deeper alignments that might or might not have immediate auditive consequences. Although the appropriations often reiterated the imperialist and other oppressive relations of the time, even as many of its composers and artists struggled among powerless ranks of bohemianism, there were numerous factors that ran contrary to the prevailing conduct of power.

A second source lay in going outside of Western art music not to other musics but to "sound." What precisely might constitute "sound" varied from one instance to another, yet there was at the least an appeal to a rhetoric of sound, if not an incorporation of actual extramusical sounds. Likewise, what was "outside" music was under constant negotiation, but the main sources of these sounds were nature, urbanism, war, the quotidian and domestic, other languages and dialects, the outward expressions of exceptional psychological states, and technology, whether it was the technology of new instrumentation (musical or scientific), communications (especially phonography and radio), or the wider world of machines and motors. These sounds were usually subjected to considerable transformation, often until they were beyond recognition, as they ran headlong into certain musical and modernist proscriptions against representation. We can find a classic technological call for "any sound whatsoever" in Rudhyar's own discussion of a new type of electronic musical instrument: "Such an instrument will permit us to produce by combination *any sound* whatsoever. . . . We shall have the wondrous splendor of an infinitude of cosmic sounds. For with such an instrument as we imagine, every quality of sound is theoretically possible" (1922: 115).

A third source was the plenitude of nature and other extramusical realms, which were invoked as a means to break down restrictions internal to music itself, forming "new musical resources" without going too far afield of Western art music. We can find this trend expressed by Ferruccio Busoni in his *Sketch of a New Esthetic of Music* (1907: 89):

> We have divided the octave into twelve equidistant degrees, because we had to manage somehow, and have constructed our instruments in such a way that we can never get in above or below or between them. Keyboard instruments, in particular, have so thoroughly schooled our ears that we are no longer capable of hearing anything else—incapable of hearing except through this impure medium. Yet Nature created an *infinite gradation—infinite!* who still knows it nowadays?

Besides nature, there were several "worlds of sound" that could pry open the possibility already residing within the givens of music. Henry Cowell's short essay "The Joys of Noise" exemplifies this focus on "resident noise," as did the modernist infatuation with percussion and timbre (as an intermediary to noise) and with glissandi and sliding tones (as counters to the segmentation of scales) (Kahn 1999: 70–91).

A fourth source was private sounds that one person alone might hear. These included the sounds and voices of exceptional psychological states and some not-so-exceptional ones—most commonly, drug-induced states, psychopathological states, mysticism, synaesthesia, and the like. They also included the murmurings and tangents of the unconscious, which the Surrealists sought to transcribe through automatic writing, as well as stream of consciousness, taken literally, or any manner of voice in the lineage of the Socratic demon. Experienced as private auditions, these voices and sounds lacked a technology adequate to their audiophonic reproduction.

The fifth source was the world of unheard, inaudible, and "super-sensible" sounds, which pertains to the inaudible sounds permeating the cosmos. In the West these ubiquitous and persistent sounds were primarily the legacy of Pythagorean and Platonic discourses, but they also occurred as nondissipative sounds and voices within a variety of mythological and fictional contexts, and they received added support during modernism by the physics and pseudoscience of atomic and molecular vibrations. As we will see later, during the late nineteenth century this Western cosmos resonated with the sympathetic vibrations of Hinduism, reintroducing Pythagorean thought as a whole by reconstituting its historical suppression of auditory space (as opposed to mathematical, proportional, intervallic, and musical space). As in private listening, these sounds could be heard only by select individuals or by individuals with the proper technology or promise of technology.

These sources were related to the modernist and avant-garde musical predilection for the paradigmatic set of *a sound* and *all sound.* Whereas the latter correlated directly with these sources, the repercussions of *a sound* were felt most immediately in the changed character of single sounds and, indeed, the very attention brought to them. This way of thinking about sounds paradigmatically, at least across a diapason of all possible phenomenal sounds audible to most people in the world, was developed throughout the nineteenth century before being articulated in American musical modernism in the 1920s. This development was characterized by two notable features. The first was a displacement of the centrality of the human utterance, found in both the acts and figures of the voice or musical performance, by intervening notions and practices of audition that suggested the equalization of all sounds of the world, human and nonhuman alike. Second, this equalization of all sound was buttressed by the individuation of a sound, initially through the graphical techniques of acoustical research, whereby any individual sound lost its ephemerality and assumed the stable nature of a text, and eventually through the inscribed repetitions of phonography.

One Sound: The Single Tone

The composer Chou Wen-Chung, in his essay "Asian Concepts and Twentieth-Century Composers" (1971), argued that the most salient similarity between Asian music and new developments in Western art music was to be found in their mutual emphasis on single tones. Many Asian musical cultures, he said, had emphasized the autonomy and integrity of tone, as opposed to the historical legacy of Western musical culture, which favored relationships among a set of given tones:

> [A] pervasive Chinese concept: that each single tone is a musical entity in itself, that musical meaning lies intrinsically in the tones themselves, and that one must investigate tones to know music. This concept, often shrouded in poetic and mystic metaphors, is fundamental to many Asian musical cultures. It is manifest in the great emphasis placed on the production and control of tones, which often involves an elaborate vocabulary of articulations, modifications in timbre, inflections in pitch, fluctuations in intensity, vibratos and tremolos.... Such concentration on the values of a single tone is the antithesis of traditional Western polyphonic concepts, in which the primacy of multilinearity and the acceptance of equal temperament make the application of such values limited and subordinate. (Chou 1971: 214–226; see also Chou 1977 and Lubet 1999)

Chou was not saying that Asian cultures did not employ complex relational systems but only that a greater and prior emphasis was placed on musical sound than was the case in Western musics, which were concerned primarily with relationality. Although he supported this immediate claim by referencing Chinese sources, he stated that it held true for other Asian musical cultures as well, including the raga system in Indian music, in which tone had been defined as "that which shines by itself" and in which "the expression of individual tones is emphasized systematically" (Chou 1971: 217). Chou discussed a wide range of twentieth-century composers in relation to "Asian influences," whether their music derived from contacts with Asian musics or simply exhibited similar characteristics, with the works of Edgar Varèse being emblematic of the latter (1971: 214–216). The earliest instance Chou cited of a Western composer who recognized a primacy of sound in Asian musics was the composer Edward MacDowell, the founding member of Columbia University's Department of Music (1971: 220).[5]

The first important advocate of the Asian concept of the single tone in twentieth-century composition, according to Chou, was Dane

Rudhyar, an avid student of Eastern philosophies and musics who, unlike MacDowell, championed the primacy of sound (Chou 1971: 219–220). Chou appears to have been correct in his assessment; Rudhyar himself could be no more explicit: "For a musician who is a mystic a Single Tone is the foundation of music," he wrote in a 1930 essay in *Modern Music* (Rudhyar 1930: 34). What Chou does not say is that Rudhyar's Single Tone was, simultaneously, an emphasis on the autonomy of sound against the relationality of Western art music and a reassertion of this very same relationality.

Rudhyar established his Single Tone in three ways. First, he argued in terms of musical practice by contrasting it against the relationality of Western art music, a relationality that has only an abstract bearing upon actual "living" sound and that prohibits the full continuum of sound characteristic of nature and certain Asian musics. In an argument reminiscent of the one Busoni set out in *Sketch of a New Esthetic of Music*, Rudhyar wrote that the conventions and instrumental technologies of Western art music had diminished the value of the continuity of sound characteristic of nature:

> We are habituated to such a degree to this *discontinued* music of ours, to our melodies "in scale," leaping from step to step, from note to note, that the *continuous* music of the elements, the melodies of Nature herself, flowing without breaks, without leaps, with a great sustained impetus, rising by insensible crescendos and dying away in glissandos which never stop at points conventionally determined (such as notes); that this music not of the intellect seems to us to be mere incoherent *noise*. (Rudhyar 1919: 171)

For Rudhyar, discontinued music also failed to acknowledge the origins of music in nature: "The prodigious cosmic symphonies of the winds, the oceans, the forests, the sounds of many waters and the song of birds, every song of multiple life made man new-born aware that he was alive, that music was" (1919: 171). Like other modernists, he was not arguing for admitting to music actual sounds from nature or anywhere else outside of music, or for other such mimetic moves that might have opened the door to the vulgarities of program music; his was instead a rhetorical appeal to the plenitude of nature in order to access the musical resources already at hand, similar to "all those vocal glissandos, all these infinite melodic palpitations of Hindoo music, which represent what remains of 'continuous' music" (Rudhyar 1919: 172). Tone was coterminous with an immediate, *lived* experience of continuity (*pace* Rudhyar's reading of Bergson's *duration* over the regularized parceling out of *time*), rather than with the segmentation of notes within a scale. Indeed, he reveled in the fact that *tone*, an anagram of *note*, could represent such contrasting systems.

As his second way of establishing his Single Tone, Rudhyar celebrated the sounds of gongs and bells as sources of single tones. The singularity of their sound was infused with a "life-principle" from an age before abstraction, before living was lost, in the use of gongs in Buddhist ritual musics of "Burma, Java, Thibet [*sic*], etc., the original source of which seems to have been the inland portion of Indo-China, cradle of the mysterious Khmers. In these gongs we find the greatest instrumental perfection of tone yet reached by man" (Rudhyar 1930: 34). In a way he does not explain, the gongs are manufactured so "that the form element is present *within* every tone; not outside in the sequence of abstract entities called musical notes, black dots on paper, edges of intervals, having no meaning in themselves, therefore no life-principle" (1930: 34). Gongs also recalled the (lapsed) importance of bells in Christian religious life and thus established a common association for Rudhyar: an "Eastern" practice of ancient origin, with continued significance to the present day, associated with a "Western" custom that had fallen out of practice, perhaps having been repressed. Acoustically, the complexity of gongs and bells cannot be dismissed as noise, because their resonance lends itself to duration and is similar enough to the sustained aspect of periodic tones, versus the aperiodicity of noise. Instead, their complexity hints at the point where a chaos of rampant multiplicity meets the fecund void of an undifferentiated ether. However, although gonglike and bell-like sounds can be heard in Rudhyar's compositional practice and form an important rationale for his Single Tone, they play only a fleeting and very limited role in his overall musical theory. The more important role was fulfilled by the third way in which he argued for the significance of the Single Tone.

In that third way, Rudhyar correlated the Single Tone with the ether through an intrinsic metaphysical status in unity or nondifferentiation and through the capacity to generate difference from that unity. The Single Tone was granted this generative role by its becoming the fundamental in a harmonic series, generating a series of partials or overtones, just as the ether generates everything. Both the tone and the ether are first of all single; both then produce difference. The Single Tone has its ultimate claim on the Ultimate because the ether itself has sound at its foundation. Rudhyar used various terms associated with theosophical discourse, but the key idea for this ether was that of the *akasha,* the Hindu-derived undifferentiated field of energy-substance of (supersensory) Sound, the site of the cosmic root vibration, the sonoriferous ether. This etheric Absolute is both the All and the One, singular in its ubiquity. The Single Tone is its sonic simulacrum and terrestrial manifestation. Because the *akasha* generates everything, the domain of all life, all realities in multiple and ever-developing universes of spirit and matter, the Single Tone becomes the embodiment of all that as well. Here, the material element of music becomes infused with the cosmos. What was once a black note becomes a black hole. The sound of music does not get much more significant than that.

The reason Rudhyar opted for the Single Tone as fundamental in a harmonic series, rather than for the complex sound of gongs and bells, was that the two generate very different things. Whereas the harmonic series generates *ratios* that are at the (etymological) root of rationality and reason, the acoustical product of gongs and bells is too complex to count within a rational and relational system. The Western esoteric tradition to which Rudhyar appealed was in a certain respect rational to a fault, relying on simple proportions and correspondences, whereas science and mathematics at the time Rudhyar was writing had proceeded to irrational numbers, relativity, and uncertainty.

Rudhyar rationalized the Single Tone as the fundamental by, first, setting it as an elemental entity against musical systems based upon relationality, but he did this through the internalization of another set of relations, those produced by the fundamental itself. The acoustical phenomenon of the harmonic series is *mapped* onto the intervals of the harmonic system in music. This mapping may seem innocent enough, but it is the most crucial juncture in his entire theory of music. It is where metaphysical and physical sounds and vibrations shift, effectively at the last instant, from an acoustical basis to a musical one. It becomes an occasion to reintroduce the musical mathematics and proportions of Pythagoreanism and the endlessly permutating correspondences of the esoteric tradition. What was initially posed as a bulwark against musical relationality becomes a conduit through which relationality is asserted with renewed vigor, preserving the harmonic basis of Western art music and returning it to an intrinsic spirituality. What was at first rationalized through an implicit "Eastern" critique of the contemporary "West" becomes a means through which "the West" is fortified.

The harmonic series was an important topic in Western art music discourses during the 1910s and 1920s, when it was used to rationalize certain types of dissonance. *Natural* or *spiritual* dissonance was based upon partials in the series, some of which were "out of tune" in terms of prevailing harmonic conventions. These discourses were informed by nineteenth-century studies of the harmonic series and acoustical vibrations by Lord Raleigh, John Tyndall, Hermann Helmholtz, and others, the fruits of which were available in both technical and popular texts. However, the harmonic series of acoustical research must be distinguished from the use of it made by composers and writers on Western art music. The sounding of a fundamental will produce a series of overtones, and as they rise in the series they decrease in intensity and are audible only under certain conditions, aided by special acoustical instruments or by the trained ears of certain individuals. Most of the partials, especially the ones used to provide the rationale for dissonance, are simply too faint and too ensconced among other sounds to be audibly appreciated in their own right.

When Rudhyar and others mapped these increasingly differentiated and ephemeral partials of the harmonic series back upon a system of harmonic intervals—effectively mapping acoustics back onto music—certain unspoken shifts in the frame of reference were required. The partials had to undergo an isolation, shifting from being elements at play within a "compound tone" to being individual "simple tones," in Helmholtz's terms. They had to be amplified, in a manner of speaking, in order to recover them from their ephemerality, and they were textualized through notation and enumeration in the series according to their rate of vibration. This shift in the frame of reference, of course, would happen unannounced and instantaneously. Once in place, partials that might be functionally inaudible could serve nonetheless as elements in natural or spiritual dissonance. As one person wrote of the dissonance of Scriabin's music: "Scriabin derived all harmony from Nature's harmonic chord, and this by a curious method of his own. We all know that there are some upper partial sounds given off by a vibrating string or pipe, which have hitherto been considered so badly out of tune with our system as to be useless. . . . Scriabin assumes that they are quite near enough for the purpose, and takes them all into his net" (Hull 1916: 608–609).

Not all dissonance was sanctioned. The transgression that was dissonance was permitted only because it obeyed the natural "laws" of acoustics, rather than being introduced under irrational or subjective auspices. Just as certain dissonances were disallowed, so, too, were other types of acoustical phenomena known, in the musical parlance of excluded sounds, as noise. The most common way to produce overtones, both in clinical practice and in musical rhetoric, was to sustain a tone with the regularity of a periodic waveform. As Rudhyar wrote without effort: "A musical sound is a series of periodical vibrations and as such has a certain definite frequency" (1931: 51). This would fail to account for timbre, of course, but would also rule out the aperiodic waveforms types of percussion with their little bursts of noise and a vast number of complicated sound events that might otherwise seem common and simple. This battle, waged at the minute level of the waveform, could also occur on the large scale of the noisy sounds of nature, by filtering nonmusical sounds through musical principles. An article in an 1879 issue of *The Theosophist* stated that "the aggregate sound of Nature, as heard in the roar of a distant city, or the waving foliage of a large forest, is said to be a single definite tone, of appreciable pitch. This tone is held to be the middle F of the piano-forte, which may, therefore, be considered the key-note of nature" (Trimbuk 1879: 47, citing B. Silliman, *Principles of Physics*).

Rudhyar also found it necessary to limit the harmonic series at the seventh octave, since the intervals at the start of the eighth octave had become so small "that the ear (as presently constituted) can no longer differentiate any two successive intervals; in other words, it can perceive only continuous sound" (1931: 59–60). That he would set the demarcation on a standard of hearing was arbitrary, not only because of the variability in different individuals' capacity to distinguish the increasingly fine gradations of overtones but also because he did not acknowledge the use of technological aids.[6] In an esoteric sense, however, it was not arbitrary that Rudhyar's musical universe reached its limit in seven octaves, for seven also happens to correspond to "the seven stages of Life, the seven principles of Cosmic differentiation . . . the seven spheres, globes or heavens, and ruling Hierarchies of the Theosophists and mystics . . . [and] the division of a cycle of planetary manifestation in 7 great Races or cycles of human activity" (Rudhyar 1931: 60, 89). Similarly, other primes, proportions, and relationships among the harmonic series go on to produce a dizzying array of correspondences— evolutionary, planetary, zodiacal, racial, theological, sensory, and so forth—through a juggling of figures characteristic of Western esoteric traditions.

The *ascent* of pitches through the harmonic series likewise has symbolic value. Spirituality increases as the pitches rise heavenward into ever increasing ephemerality, sublimity, and rarefaction, to a point where ostensibly only continuity and no differentiation can be perceived, thereby arriving at another counterpart of the undifferentiated cosmic ether. This ascent, however, also gives rise to a problem for Rudhyar. The penultimate of spirituality is understood to be a unification with the undifferentiated Absolute (as the ultimate unity and *primal* differentiation). It is understood as a return, because the material world that humans occupy is generated from the Absolute through a process of differentiation. The state of differentiation is itself a mark of descent from spirituality into materiality. The rise up the harmonic series into increasingly differentiated octaves would therefore be no ascent at all, but a *descent* into matter, no matter how fine. To remedy this situation, Rudhyar appealed to the earlier authenticity of Greek scales, which could be represented as descending from the fundamental through a series of material lengths in the string of a Pythagorean monochord.[7] He equated this ancient practice with the spiritual—"The H.S. [harmonic series] was at first considered a descending progression and *spiritually* speaking remains always the same" (Rudhyar 1931: 63)—but he did not want to relinquish either modern acoustics or the vernacular of common experience in favor of the idea that pitches naturally rise or that rising itself connotes a movement toward the spiritual. Thus, in a seemingly contradictory manner, he chose to retain both ascent and descent of the harmonic series, reconciling them through a dual movement of the Great Breath and the primordial vibration.

Rudhyar often used the Great Breath (*prana*) in close association with the undifferentiated Absolute to describe primordial differentiation, either in its potentiality for differentiation or in its simplest to-and-fro manifestation, its "one primordial, eternal, ultimate vibration" (1931: 66). This theological physiognomy and physics is rhetorically very useful, for it can reconcile any contradiction, unify any set of opposites, and describe movement of any sort whatsoever. It has the benefit of being experiential, and thus a person inhaling and exhaling can empathize with the ebb and flow of the cosmic ocean, a favorite theosophical metaphor for the operations of the ether.[8] Although Rudhyar repeatedly referred to the breath and the oceans as a means to explain cosmic functioning, he was restricted in a more general application of this analogy to his theory of music because the breath calls up the voice and thus speech, language, and the musical problems of cultural mediation and program music. The voice would have provided an insufficiently neutral basis from which to construct a theory of music, let alone a cosmological theory, amenable to the traditions of absolute music to which Rudhyar's compositional thinking conformed, and it would have run afoul of a musicalized modernism with its distrust of language.

Breath calls up the body (not to mention animality), which was also a difficult proposition for Western art music (McClary 1995).[9] There might have been an option in the practice of mantras, which, in certain yogic versions, have sounds located at the chakras (energy centers) in the body and a discipline involving an ascent up through the chakras. Rudhyar's appropriation of Tantric sources, however, was much like John Cage's appropriation of Hinduism and Zen Buddhism, in that both borrowed spirituality in a philosophical way but failed to integrate the body practices through which spiritual states were experienced. Similarly, there was an ascent and descent of spiritual sound in Tantrism that had a social character among gurus and students in an oral and pedagogical tradition.[10] Rudhyar's emphasis on the harmonic series in this way involved proscriptions against noise, the voice, the body, and sociality. In other words, the cosmos was required to undergo a typical set of purifications before it could imbue music with spirit.

All Sound: The *Akasha*

For Rudhyar, the etheric and inaudible figure of *all sound* was derived primarily from the Hindu notion of the *akasha*. What the *akasha* might be precisely, and how the term was used in different contexts, was a matter of some controversy within the ranks and surrounds of theosophy at the time. At its most basic, *akasha* means "space," but it was also understood to be etheric and generative (of everything) and, per Rudhyar's interest in it, sonoriferous or soundful.[11] Like the fundamental, the Absolute was also involved in autogenesis and was also sonic. As a pair, the two inhabited the paradigmatic set of *a sound* and *all sound* that had developed in scientific and cultural discourses in the nineteenth century and was being increasingly adopted by the avant-garde tradition in the twentieth century.

In opting for a sonoriferous ether, Rudhyar was going against the grain of general conceptions of ethers. Most notably, he ran counter to the prevailing scientific theories of ether, which sought to account for light, magnetism, electricity, radiation, and nervous impulses, but not sound (Cantor and Hodge 1981). Even someone as useful to occultists as Sir Oliver Lodge equated the perceptual attributes of ether with the eye alone: "The eye is truly an etherial sense-organ—the only one which we possess, the only mode by which the ether is enabled to appeal to us; and that the detection of tremors in this medium—the perception of the direction in which they go, and some inference as to the quality of the object which has emitted them—cover all that we mean by 'sight' and 'seeing'" (Lodge 1909: 114). Where Lodge saw an optics, Rudhyar needed an acoustics.

Blavatsky stressed that the etheric nature of the *akasha* had to be distinguished from the scientific "ether of space," Lodge's term to distinguish it from the chemical. She noted that the physicists' full comprehension of the ether was elusive, meaning that it frayed at its material edges and entertained explanations for certain psychical, occult, and spiritual phenomena. But because of their frame of reference, their efforts were doomed to be reductive—to remain on the manifest, gross, perceptual, exoteric physical plane and not to reach the unmanifest, fine, supersensible, and esoteric metaphysical plane.[12] Nevertheless, that science had its ether provided a good position from which the occult could speak. First, both the *akasha* and the ether of space were assigned a substantiality and functionality far in excess of any evidence of their existence. Second, whereas the scientists might be held to confirmation, the occultists were both more practiced in this type of speculation and quite satisfied with a deferred confirmation. The real inducement, however, came from the fact that the *akasha* itself was a force; there was a physics to its metaphysics. This was developed in theosophy as a veritable Hindu physics cast in terms of vibration (see Chevrier 1907; Franklin 1907). In this sacred physics Rudhyar could find support for his acoustics, musical acoustics, and music.

Before he could do this, Rudhyar had to make sound more important than it usually is in Hinduism. The *akasha*, it seemed, was not generally accepted as being as soundful as he liked. Compared with the other major religions of the world, Hinduism includes an elaborate and important standing for sound, yet a distinction must be made between sound as it pertains primarily to the voice and sound as it relates to all phenomena, whether terrestrial or cosmic. Commentary on sound, in Hinduism generally and in its theosophical diffusion, concentrated on the oral/aural aspects of the mantra, which in turn became located in linguistics, the voice, logos, prayer, and the Word, even as Om or AUM become the embodiment of a cosmic sonic order. No matter how attractive this may have been (or might still be) in cementing a perennial philosophical connection between Hinduism, Christianity, and the scriptural order, it nevertheless would have predisposed Rudhyar to the aforementioned problems that accompany the voice.

Rudhyar found confirmation in Hinduism for his acoustical cosmos in various sects of Tantrism, where an elaborate and consistent role for nonvocal sound could be found alongside the more familiar practices of mantra. Nevertheless, this was a selective reading of Tantrism, one that had to be cautious about certain body practices and an eroticism that ran counter to American morality, among other things. As Guy

Beck (1995: 124) points out, "several Tantric cosmogonies describe Nada-Brahman (cosmic sound) as being the vibration resulting from the sexual act of Siva and his consort Sakti, a kind of rumble in the cosmic mattress, as it were." Indeed, Tantrism, with its sexual associations, fared as well with Victorian morality as the body did with Western art music (Majumdar 1880: 173).

A major influx of Tantrism appeared in *The Theosophist* in the prolific series of translations and writings on "nature's finer forces" by Rama Prasad, which ran from November 1887 to December 1888. It formed the basis, with important differences, for Prasad's *Nature's Finer Forces: The Science of Breath and the Philosophy of the Tattvas* (1894 [1889]) and was regularly cited as one of the primary texts of the theosophical movement. In his writings, Prasad repeatedly equated *akasha* with "sonoriferous ether" and stated that the *akasha* "must, as a matter of course, precede and follow every change of state on every plane of life. Without this there can be no manifestation or cessation of forms. *It is out of akasha that every form comes, and it is in akasha that every form lives*" (Prasad 1894 [1889]: 19).[13] This is the *akasha* that Rudhyar utilized.

Rudhyar actually proposed a sonically intensified version of Blavatsky's cosmos. Blavatsky was not as inclined as Rudhyar to equate the *akasha* so cosmically with sound: *akasha* was "Divine Space," and sound, its "primary correlation." To consider sound an "attribute" of the *akasha* was to anthropomorphize what was properly beyond the present-day faculties and terrestrial circumstances of humans. This qualification did not dampen Blavatsky's enthusiasm for the occult significance of sound, as she expounded in "The Coming Force" section of *The Secret Doctrine* (1971 [1888], 2: 279):

Sound is a tremendous Occult power; it is a stupendous force, of which the electricity generated by a million of Niagaras could never counteract the smallest potentiality when directed with *Occult Knowledge*. Sound may be produced of such a nature that the pyramid of Cheops would be raised in the air, or that a dying man, nay, one at his last breath, would be revived and filled with new energy and vigour.

For Sound generates, or rather attracts together, the elements that produce an *ozone* the fabrication of which is beyond chemistry, but is within the limits of Alchemy. It may even *resurrect* a man or an animal whose astral "vital body" has not been irreparably separated from the physical body by the severance of the magnetic or odic chord. *As one saved thrice from death* by that power, the writer ought to be credited with personally knowing something about it.

Apart from this anecdotal evidence, her resolve was not derived from a reading of Hindu texts but was instead supported by the pseudo-science, some would say simple fraud, of John Worrell Keely, whose motors and guns based on sound and etheric forces were, in effect, the cold fusion of the late nineteenth century.

A Philadelphia inventor internationally championed by occultists at the time, Keely was depicted as being always on the brink of making the most profound discovery of all time, tapping into vibratory forces given various names depending upon the speaker, including *akasha*. "It is the fact that Keely is working with some of the mysterious forces included under the name Akasa that makes his discoveries interesting to theosophists" (Bloomfield-Moore 1983: xix). Most of his renown in occult circles can be attributed to his citation in *The Secret Doctrine*. "Drawing a fiddle-bow across a tuning fork" could generate twenty-five horse-power in the Keely motor, Blavatsky stated, but it seems Keely himself was better known outside occult circles for being unable to reproduce such effects when needed. Keely's lack of success and validation were no obstacle for Blavatsky, who believed he was not being "permitted" to succeed by higher spirit entities because in his theory of "sympathetic vibrations" he had unwittingly arrived at the secret of a dark, destructive force, a vibratory force mentioned in Hindu texts that, Blavatsky allegorically states, "would reduce to ashes 100,000 men and elements" (1971 [1888], 2: 286). This would itself become an allegory for atomic weaponry. She wrote, "Had Keely been permitted to succeed, he might have reduced a whole army to atoms in the space of a few seconds, as easily as he reduced a dead ox to that condition" (1971 [1888], 2: 279).

More importantly for Rudhyar's work, the way in which Keely and Blavatsky theorized sonic and etheric force was in terms of vibrations (Blavatsky 1971 [1888], 2: 286): molecular vibrations took place at 100 million per second, intermolecular vibrations at 300 million per second, atomic vibrations at 900 million per second, interatomic vibrations at 2.7 billion per second, etheric vibrations at 8.1 billion per second, and interetheric vibrations at 24.3 billion per second. For Rudhyar, this was consistent with the sonic nature of the *akasha* and was a way to extend a soundfulness to all matter through a commonality in vibrations:

Sound is one of the many types of substantial energy. It is matter liberated as energy, in its manifested aspect at any rate—very much as perfume or heat or magnetism are [sic] radiations or emanations from some substantial entity. Among the few scientists who have come to similar conclusions may be mentioned J. W. Keely of Philadelphia, the prophetic discoverer of a new type of energy, which he tried to harness by means of a motor of his invention, a motor which however could only work when he energized it by his own human magnetism. (Rudhyar 1928: 36)

Most importantly, physics and pseudophysics provided Rudhyar with an association between atomic and molecular vibrations and the concert hall; it could render all mute matter continuously soundful and musical and thereby provide an experiential corollary to the soundful ubiquity of the *akasha*, which was also inaudible. Where God might once have occupied ubiquity, now there were vibrations, sound, and music.

Vibrations in the Service of Music

For Rudhyar, the ideas of life, energy, radiation, vibrations, sound, and musical sound flowed freely from one another, establishing a continuum that included the atomic and molecular constituents of matter, the soundful primordial vibration of the *akasha*, all terrestrial and supersensory sound and movement, and even, with Western art music, a repressed eroticism of palpitations and throbbing. However, this continuum or, rather, space of continua, of vibrations itself vibrated in a specific manner, which belied a recuperation into music. All the key features within it complied with acoustical and physical figures and operations that related to a general category of sound that was not immediately musical. The sound was socially, culturally, and ecologically deracinated, to be sure, but neither was it musical. Nevertheless, in the last instant, Rudhyar's vibrational and soundful cosmos was brought into line with the harmonic tradition of Western art music. The *akasha*, atomic and molecular vibrations, the continuous sound of nature, the complex acoustical properties of gongs and bells, the acoustics of the harmonic series, even the *tone* of the Single Tone, as contrasted with *note*, were all exterior to the musical exigencies of the fundamental as a generator of harmonic music.

Indeed, all that forms the bridge between this mass of vibrations and its delivery into music is the unspoken mapping of the harmonic series onto harmonic intervals. This one act recuperates the Hindu cosmos into the Pythagorean one and recuperates acoustical discourses, however unorthodox, into an allegiance with Western art music. And this is possible only because the Pythagorean cosmology has been so consistently equated throughout the centuries with music and intervallic proportions instead of with acoustical properties beyond music.

Rudhyar's musical shift from harmonic series to harmony was a delicate deception, a means to contrive the Single Tone into the last gasp of Pythagoreanism. Yet it was nevertheless sufficient, given the powers of the esoteric tradition and Western art music, as a hedge against a cosmos of already deracinated and denatured vibrations, to restore the spiritual to Western art music.

Although the esoteric traditions of proportions and correspondences may have faded, this does not mean that the tenets of Pythagoreanism as a whole have been exhausted. They still reside in the inherited metaphysics of music and will resurface, for a similar set of negotiations is presently under way among physics, technology, religion, and spirituality, and they will no doubt influence and validate musical thought and practice. Certain features may be found in musics that rely on mathematics, revisiting hopes of absolute music, cybernetic formulas of digital mantras, the transmutation of signals to vibrations (e.g., radio astronomy), and the tiny microphones and other instruments promised by nanotechnology. I am thinking specifically of John Cage's desire to amplify the small sounds of atomic and molecular vibrations. "Look at this ashtray. It's in a state of vibration. We're sure of that, and the physicist can prove it to us. But we can't hear those vibrations. . . . It would be extremely interesting to place it in a little anechoic chamber and listen to it through a suitable sound system. Object would become process; we would discover, thanks to a procedure borrowed from science, the meaning of nature through the music of objects" (Cage and Charles 1981: 220–221; see also Kahn 1999: 195–196). Rudhyar not only prefigured the concentration upon single sounds and rhetoric of all sound of the subsequent avant-garde in the United States but also developed a vibrational logic extant in Cage and, indeed, still audible somewhere between the avowed quantum behavior of "microsound" and echoes reverberating off the Big Bang. That this involves another spiritual physics at play is evidenced in the easy equation of vibrations and music.

Notes

1. Within the context of American modernist music, Varèse's "liberation of sound" became most developed in lectures beginning in 1936, whereas Rudhyar

proposed a "liberation through sound" in a series of lectures published under the same name in 1931. For a bibliography of Rudhyar's publications pertaining to music, see Oja 2000. John Cage's 1937 lecture "The Future of Music: Credo" championed the use of electrical and recording technologies to usher in an "all-sound music of the future" (Cage 1961: 3–6), inaugurating what would become the most influential rhetoric of musical sound in the postwar era with his famous dictum to "let sounds be themselves."

2. Correspondingly, William James thought that there was something "musical" in the language of mysticism itself and of Blavatsky's mysticism in particular. "In mystical literature such self-contradictory phrases as 'dazzling obscurity,' 'whispering silence,' 'teeming desert,' are continually met with. They prove that not conceptual speech, but music rather, is the element through which we are best spoken to by mystical truth. Many mystical scriptures are indeed little more than musical compositions." He then quotes Blavatsky's translation from "The Book of the Golden Precepts," in which Nada is equated with "the Soundless Sound" and "the inner ear will speak THE VOICE OF THE SILENCE," and then he continues: "These words, if they do not awaken laughter as you receive them, probably stir chords within you which music and language touch in common. Music gives us ontological messages which non-musical criticism is unable to contradict, though it may laugh at our foolishness in minding them" (James 1974: 405–406).

3. An important exception can be found in the attempt by Dayton Clarence Miller, an acoustician well known among modernist American composers at the time, to disprove Einstein's withering argument against ether (see Thompson 2002: 105, 355 n. 138).

4. See Porush 1993 and Berger 1990. Claude Palisca (1985b: 60) has also written: "The tradition that stemmed from Pythagoras discouraged further investigation of sound, and those most influenced by him as late as the sixteenth century refused to recognize new scientific facts that were at odds with the doctrine."

5. MacDowell, however, mentioned the primacy of sound disapprovingly and with respect to Chinese music; indeed, serious questions arose for him about whether this practice belonged properly to the realm of music at all. The Chinese appreciation of the texture of a sound, "the long, trembling tone-tint of a bronze gong, or the high, thin streams of sound from the pipes . . . enjoyed for their ear-filling qualities," belonged instead to "mere beauty of sound [which] is, in itself, purely sensuous. . . . For it to become music, it must possess some quality which will remove it from the purely sensuous," a sensuousness he places at the lower end of the musical evolutionary scale with "the savage's delight in noise" and "the most primitive form of suggestion in music . . . in the direct imitation of sounds of nature" (MacDowell 1912: 263, 265, 267).

6. Henry Cowell (1969: 5, 18) wrote that "Professor Dayton Miller, well-known acoustician and author of *The Science of Musical Sound*, speaks of having heard the forty-fourth overtone with his unaided ear . . . [and] Professor Leon Theremin, in a demonstration of his electrical instruments, showed that the interval of one-hundredth part of a whole step can be plainly discerned by an audience."

7. As Kathi Meyer-Baer (1984: 71–72) explains, "Plato knew that the place of a tone in the system depended on the length of the string of the kithara. But he did not call one tone 'longer' and another 'shorter,' because these terms were used for the rhythmic qualities of sound. He related the pitch of a sound to a faster or slower motion of the sound. The faster the motion the shriller the tone. . . . Plato held the sounds with the fastest motion to be 'low' and the sounds with the slowest motion to be 'high,' the reverse of modern usage, and he did so because for him the celestial bodies with the shortest orbits, e.g., the moon, corresponded to the fast motion. Today the sound wave is decisive, but it was not for Plato."

8. As Blavatsky wrote (1971 [1888], 5: 382): "In Space there is not Matter, Force, nor Spirit, but all that and much more. It is the One Element, and that one the Anima Mundi—Space, akasha, Astral Light——the Root of Life which, in its eternal, ceaseless motion, like the out- and in-breathing of one boundless ocean, evolves but to reabsorb all that lives and feels and thinks and has its being in it."

9. On the voice and animality, see Bulwant Trimbuk's (1879) proposal for a "science of music" based on ancient precepts, including the correlation of musical sounds with the "notes" produced by the peacock, ox, goat, crane, blackbird, frog, and elephant.

10. According to Sir John Woodroffe (1969: 79–80), the guru communicates what his "Supreme Ear" hears and communicates this with his "Supreme Tongue" to the student, who hears imperfectly, because it is being communicated through manifest sound and heard with *relative* ears. "In this way the primordial sounds descend down to our relative planes, where the natural sounds, that is, causal sounds of many objects, are not represented at all, and those that are represented are represented suitably to conditions of relative ears and relative tongues." Being equipped with a taste for the higher sounds then aids the student in an ascent to the spiritual. That Pythagoreanism is attractive to the secret societies of the esoteric tradition is itself due in part to the broken descent of his word within oral transmission, a breach that requires an internalization and recuperation of uncertainty and speculation.

11. The term *akasha* should not be confused with the Akashic Library or Akashic Record, a term associated in the late nineteenth century with Éliphas Levi and which was a kind of clairvoyant Olympian view of the past and

future as inscribed upon the ether, an early and unusual form of documentary film.

12. "Official science *knows nothing to this day of the constitution of ether.* Let science call it Matter, if it likes; only neither as akasha, nor as the once sacred Æther of the Greeks, is it to be found in any of the states of Matter known to modern physics. It is Matter on quite another plane of perception and being, and it can neither be analyzed by scientific apparatus, nor appreciated or even conceived by the 'scientific imagination,' unless the possessors thereof study the Occult Sciences" (Blavatsky 1971 [1888], 2: 210).

13. The other major source of information on Tantrism came in the writings of Sir John Woodroffe (Arthur Avalon), including those written in collaboration with Bengali scholars (Woodroffe 1969, 1995). Both Rudhyar and Woodroffe placed the same obvious stress on "stress," so to speak, as an intermediary and conflation of force and action in a process of disruption of unmanifest ethers toward their manifestation in the terrestrial world, whereas Prasad stated similar processes differently.

Hearing Modernity: Egypt, Islam, and the Pious Ear

Charles Hirschkind

The first thing we know from God and which became connected to us from Him was His speech and our listening. . . . Therefore all the messengers came with speech, such as the Koran, the Torah, the Gospels, the Psalms, and the Scriptures. There is nothing but speech and listening. There can be nothing else. Were it not for speech we would not know what the Desirer desires from us. . . . We move about in listening.

> Ibn al-Arabi, quoted in *The Sufi Path of Knowledge: Ibn al-Arabi's Metaphysics of Imagination*, William C. Chittick, ed.

In this essay I explore a practice of ethical listening in Egypt and some of the transformations this practice underwent in the context of social and political modernization in the twentieth century. The inquiry is informed by a growing recognition in anthropology that central to the historical configuration of what we call modernity is a vast reorganization of sensory experience. In order to contribute to our understanding of this process, I look at some of the ways in which the concepts and practices of the nationalist project impacted on the organization and ethical function of auditory experience in Egypt. A key aspect of this impact involved the gradual introduction of new notions of agency, authority, and responsibility into practices of pious audition as these came to be oriented toward new purposes in the emergent domain of modern politics.

From early in the development of Islam, sermon audition has been identified as essential to cultivating the sensitive heart that allows one to hear and embody in practice the ethical instincts undergirding moral

131

action. Beyond the cognitive task of learning rules and procedures, careful listeners hone those affective-volitional dispositions that both attune the heart to God's word and incline the body toward moral conduct. Although sermons retain this ethical function in contemporary Muslim societies, their audition now takes place in a social and political context increasingly shaped by modern structures of secular governance, on one hand, and by the styles of consumption and culture linked to global mass media, on the other. Practices such as national political oratory and popular media entertainment now shape the discursive space in which sermons are practiced and, as a result, the aural responsiveness that is both invoked and refined through the activity of listening.

In Egypt, where I conducted fieldwork for a year and a half, cassette-recorded sermons of preaching "stars" have become immensely popular among middle- and lower-middle-class Egyptians. The voices of these well-known orators spill into the streets from loudspeakers in cafes, the shops of tailors and butchers, and the workshops of mechanics and TV repairmen; they accompany passengers in taxis, mini-buses, and most forms of public transportation; they resonate from behind the walls of apartment complexes, where men and women listen alone in the privacy of their homes after returning home from the factory, while doing housework, or together with acquaintances from school or office who are invited to hear the latest sermon from a favorite *khatib* (preacher; pl. *khutaba'*).

For religious and secular reformers from the late nineteenth century until the present, the sermon has provided a favored problem space for reassessing the virtues and dangers of the ear and for attempting to establish the conditions enabling its re-education.[1] The innovations these reformers brought about did not result in the replacement of a premodern listener by a modern one, a pious ear by a political one. Rather, in Egypt's institutions of Islamic authority and the forms of public discussion these institutions articulate, we find the practices, languages, and techniques of ethical listening overlapping with a set of often competing forms linked to the nationalist effort to construct a modern public sphere. One of my central aims in the latter part of this chapter is to suggest how these contrasting regimes of aural sensibility structure public debate and political life in Egypt. Such an inquiry into the politics of listening raises important challenges to normative models of public discourse and deliberation. Notions of the public sphere presuppose not only particular perceptual habits, as I will argue, but also a particular conceptual articulation of the act of listening in relation to individual agency and authority. What forms of dialogue can be imagined that may navigate the conceptual and sensory divide that separates different listening subjects? My attempt here is to frame this question and suggest its importance.

The Rhetoric of the Listener

I begin by discussing a certain tradition of thinking about listening in relation to language and human agency, one that has exerted considerable influence on the way Muslim scholars and nonscholars alike have understood the act of sermon listening. Until the early twentieth century, Muslim scholars—*at least in print*—were relatively unconcerned with elaborating an art of sermon rhetoric or devising techniques to ensure the persuasiveness of a preacher's discourse, as found, for example, in Christianity. The scholarly tradition of *'ilm al-balagha* (the Islamic discipline frequently glossed as "rhetoric") did not take the Friday sermon as either its object of analysis or its point of practical application. Rather, as formulated by the grammarian Abd al-Qahir al-Jurjani (d. 1018), *'ilm al-balagha* explored Arabic semantics, taking the particular eloquence of the Qur'an as its central topic of investigation.

One of the doctrines through which earlier scholars had sought to identify and substantiate the uniqueness of the Qur'anic revelation was that of *i'jaz al-Qur'an*, an expression often translated as "the miraculousness of the Qur'an" but whose literal meaning refers to the idea that the Qur'an's sublime beauty rendered humans "incapable" (*'ajiz*) of producing anything of equal value.[2] This doctrine took on a fundamental importance in the development of *al-balagha* by al-Jurjani and his successors. Although they frequently drew examples from poetry in their investigations, the basic framework of the field revolved around an analysis of the linguistic devices through which the Qur'an achieved its aesthetic excellence. In other words, Muslim scholars of language never rigorously pursued a concern for the civic function of speech— for the techniques by which an orator might move an audience to action as had been elaborated by Roman and medieval Christian rhetors. Instead of elaborating formal rules of speaking, they gave priority to the task of listening, a fact reflecting the particular status ascribed to the revealed text over the course of the development of Islam. In this sense, *'ilm al-balagha* can be considered one branch of Islamic hermeneutics: whereas the discipline of *fiqh* (jurisprudence) sought to derive the principles of divinely sanctioned human action from the text, *'ilm al-balagha* indicated how the text should be listened to, read, and appreciated in what we might call its poetic aspects.[3]

That Muslim scholars have been relatively uninterested in elaborating an art of persuasive speaking owes in part to the way revelation affected their conceptions of the efficacy of speech. As the miraculous word of God, the divine message convinces, not via an artifice of persuasion— the rhetorical labor of skillful human speakers—but by its own perfect unification of beauty and truth. When humans fail to be convinced by this word, the fault lies not in the words but in the organ of reception, the human heart. The message itself has been articulated in the most perfect of possible forms, the Qur'an. This is made evident in many parts of the Qur'an where the failure to heed the words of God is attributed to a person or community's inability or refusal to hear (sam'). When humans in the Qur'an do respond in an ethically positive manner, either to the speech of other humans or to that of God, the agency is largely attributed to the hearer. Indeed, an incapacity to hear the words of God is one of the distinguishing traits of those humans and demons (jinn) who are destined for hell: "They have hearts wherewith they understand not, eyes wherewith they see not, and ears wherewith they hear not [la yasma'na bihi]" (Surat al-A'raf, 179).[4] Hearing, in other words, is not something one passively submits to but a particular kind of action itself. For this reason, what the divine message requires in this tradition is not so much a rhetor as a listener, one who can correctly hear what is already stated in its most perfect, inimitable, and untranslatable form.[5] It requires not a speaker's persuasiveness but the instrumentality of God acting through his words on the heart of a listener. One might say, in other words, that within this interpretive tradition, the rhetorical act is accomplished by the hearer and not the speaker.

One finds a similar privileging of the listener in the extensive theological and mystical writings on music that Islamic scholars produced from the ninth century onward. Fueled by a concern with the ability of music to bypass the faculty of rational judgment and directly affect the senses of the listener, debates over the admissibility of music listening engaged many leading Muslim scholars up through the nineteenth century (During 1997; Shiloah 1963). In general, those who opposed the audition of music pointed to its dangerous ability to arouse unruly passions, stimulate sensual pleasures, and distract one from thoughts of God, whereas those who advocated the practice— frequently those writers who were well-disposed to mystical currents in Islam—saw in it a means to move the heart to greater piety and closeness to God.[6] For scholars adopting the latter argument (including al-Ghazzali, al-Darani, and Ibn al-Rajub), it was wrong to view music as intrinsically dangerous. In the words of the ninth-century mystic al-Darani, "Music does not provoke in the heart that which is not there." The agency of music to either corrupt or edify, to distract from moral duty or incline the soul toward its performance, lay not in the sound in and of itself but in the moral disposition of the heart of the listener. If the listener brought to the act the proper intentions, goals, and ethical attitude, then he or she would benefit from the audition. In short, as with the proper audition of the Qur'an, the responsibility fell again to the listener.

The effect of this concern for the moral and emotional state of the listener is evident, moreover, in the fact that many key musical concepts in the Arabo-Islamic tradition simultaneously indicate both the responsiveness of the listener and the qualities of the performance. Within this tradition, listener and performer form an interdependent dyad such that the former is often seen to precede and make possible the performance of the latter, as we see in the following remarks by the contemporary Syrian musician Sabah Fakhri: "In order to deliver something you must have it in yourself first and then reflect it, as the moon shines by reflecting the light it receives from the sun. In a large measure, this state emanates from the audience, particularly the *sammi'ah* (talented and sensitive listeners), although the singer must also be endowed with *ruh* (soul) and *ihsas* (feeling)" (quoted in Racy 1998: 96). Here we might also note that, within the mystical currents that contributed much to the tradition of reflection on the powers of music to which Fakhri is heir, *sam'* (the conventional term for "hearing") refers to the act of audition, the ritual dance that may accompany it, and the music or cantillation that provides its occasion (During 1997: 129–133).

This tradition of reflection on agency and audition remains one of the key points of reference for the contemporary practice of preaching in Egypt. Although the human heart, known only to God and oneself, can never be made the object of a science of persuasion, its capacity to hear can be impaired, particularly through the repeated performance of sinful acts.[7] Sermons are a means to its recovery. As one of the most prolific contemporary Egyptian writers on the sermon notes:

> From acts [of sins and disobedience] come the sicknesses of the heart and their causes. God said: "By no means! But on their hearts is the stain of the ill which they do." It covers them like rust, until they are overcome. And they continue sinning and postpone repentance until [their acts] become imprinted on the heart such that it will neither accept good nor incline toward it. There is no medicine for this except the ointment of

the *shari'a*, in the form of a precise scientific, chemical compound composed of sermons [*khutub*], exhortations [*mau'iza*], and religious counseling [*nasiha*], all drawn from the Qur'an and *sunna* [prophetic traditions]. Without this treatment, hearts cannot be corrected. (Mahfouz 1952: 63)

Sin corrodes the heart, the organ of both audition and moral comportment. Listening to the godly speech of sermons and exhortations, if done repeatedly and with proper intention, can remove this corrosion.[8] Today, cassette sermons provide an attractive medium for accomplishing this task.

Another author, writing in *Al-Tauhid*, a popular religious digest often read and cited by the sermon listeners with whom I worked in Cairo, likens an impaired hearing to a short-circuit in the wiring that prevents an electrical current from reaching the lamp it is supposed to illuminate. Drawing out the metaphor, he suggests:

The Qur'an is effective in itself, just like the electrical current. If the Qur'an is present [to your ears], and it has lost its effect, then it is you yourself that you must blame. Maybe the conductive element is defective: your heart is damaged or flawed. Maybe a mist covers your heart, preventing it from benefiting from the Qur'an and being affected by it. Or maybe you are not listening well, or your heart is occupied with problems of money and thinking about how to acquire and increase it. (Badawi 1996: 13)

For the possessor of such a defective heart, the only solution, according to the author, lies in cleansing (*tahara*) the heart, both by giving up the sinful acts that led to such a state and by repeatedly listening, with intention and concentration, to sermons, exhortations, and Qur'anic verses.

Within the Islamic homiletic tradition I describe here, listening is privileged as the sensory activity most essential to moral conduct. Once revelation had brought the most powerful and sublime form of speech into the world, the problem of persuasion shifted onto the listener and the clarity of human hearts. An orator in this tradition requires, not the knowledge of audience psychology so central to Greek rhetorical study, but rather a complete performative grasp of the true word, revealed in the Qur'an and exemplified in the *sunna*, the record of the Prophet's exemplary acts and sayings. This is not to suggest that a skillful *khatib* is not appreciated for the excellence of his sermon. Rather, I am simply pointing out how a specific view of the means by which words convince has undergirded a certain depersonalization of the utterance, so that its agency is located less in the speaker and more in God and the disciplined ears and hearts of listeners.

Augustinian rhetoric, it should be acknowledged, does share certain features with the tradition I have described here. Augustine transformed Greek rhetorical theory into a kind of hermeneutic discipline, one not entirely unlike the 'ilm al-balagha fashioned by Muslim scholars. Rhetoric taught the Christian scholar how to uncover deeper layers of biblical meaning. "[Christ] did not hide [truths] in order to prevent them from being communicated," Augustine claims, "but in order to provoke desire for them by this very concealment" (quoted in Todorov 1982: 76). Yet Augustine also envisioned rhetoric as the primary weapon of the orator. In his De Doctrina Christiana (1973: 494), he opens the section that most explicitly deals with preaching with a defense of the arts of rhetoric for Christian educators:

> Now, the art of rhetoric being available for the enforcing of either truth or falsehood, who will dare say that truth in the person of its defenders is to take its stand unarmed against falsehood? . . . Since, then, the faculty of eloquence is available for both sides, and is of very great service in the enforcing either of wrong or right, why do not good men study to engage it on the side of truth, when bad men use it to obtain the triumph of wicked and worthless causes, and to further injustice and error?

For Augustine, rhetoric is a tool of persuasion bearing a purely instrumental relation to moral truth: no intrinsic connection exists between the eloquence of statements and their veracity. For classical Muslim scholars, however, the Qur'an represented the highest form of truthful discourse as well as the model from which the criteria of aesthetic excellence were derived. Placing divine speech at the core of their inquiries, Muslim linguists and philosophers have tended to base their analyses of beautiful elocution on the fundamental unity of the aesthetic and the true. One consequence, as I have suggested, is that the figure of the listener took on a paradigmatic status in the field of moral inquiry and practice, including the tradition of Islamic homiletics with which I am concerned here.

A Sense of Nation

Although this tradition of ethical audition continues to inform sermon practice in Egypt today, it now bears the imprint of social and political projects presupposing very different kinds of listeners. One key aspect of the reform policies undertaken by Egyptian nationalists from the late nineteenth century to the present has been the state's legal and administrative intervention in the domain of religion, in order to render it consonant with the secular-liberal and technocratic discourses central to the state's own legitimacy, functioning, and reformist goals. This project has entailed incorporating the institutions of religious authority under the wing of the state and creating various educational and bureaucratic institutions to train, certify, and supervise *khutaba'* (preachers) and other religious specialists. Redefined as an instrument of state propaganda, the sermon and its affiliated institutions were placed within the purview of the bureaucracies concerned with media, information, and culture.

Indeed, in state planning documents from the 1950s and 1960s, as well as in some of the preaching manuals published at the time, sermons were often assimilated to the category of "mass media" and understood according to the behaviorist models that dominated the field at the time. Preachers were seen to offer the state a preestablished channel of direct communication between itself and the population under its management. Sermons would now provide both useful information and an oratorical form geared to the moral improvement of an Egyptian population still seen to be bound by the ideological constraints of a deep-rooted traditionalism. Informed by an Orientalist critique linking the backwardness of Muslim societies to an Islamic, and particularly Sufi, fatalism, said to be evident in a general denigration of practical, this-worldly concerns in favor of otherworldly ones, sermons could be used to encourage modern virtues of hard work, individual initiative, self-improvement, cooperation, and obedience to state authority.

Not surprisingly, the model for the new sermon was to be found in the press, the primary political instrument for articulating and disseminating the new cultural standards upon which a reformed Egyptian nation was to be founded. Like the press, a revitalized sermon was to serve as an engine of moral progress, inculcating nationalist sentiments while providing useful (i.e., modern) information. One of the leading religious reformers of the time, Jamal al-Din al-Afghani, outlined the complementary functions of these institutions: "We cannot arrive at the goal of happiness without both oratory and the press; and the only difference between them is that oratory moves the blood through the movement of the speaker and the power of voice, while newspapers serve to fix the issues in peoples' minds" (quoted in al-Kumi 1992: 137).

Although *khutaba'* had always been recruited by Muslim rulers to provide support for their policies and legitimacy to their rule, the kind of political project into which religious orators were now to be incorporated was without precedent. Instead of an acclamatory function—the public recognition of the legitimacy of the regime—the sermon was now to be rendered an instrument of state-guided social and individual discipline, a pedagogical technique for the dissemination of the attitudes and orientations appropriate to a modern national citizenry. Needless to say, this attempt to harness the sermon to the task of nation building has run into numerous obstacles. Though I discuss some of these later, let me mention here that one such obstacle has resided in the fact that popular preaching has always been grounded less in institutions of formal study (i.e., those more easily placed under direct state control) than in social knowledges reproduced more informally in the local community.

The professionalization of the activity of preaching in Egypt that began around the turn of the twentieth century has been accompanied by the development of a pedagogical literature on the art of oratory (*al-khataba*), one distinct from the investigations into poetics and semantics found in the classical field of *'ilm al-balagha* discussed earlier.[9] Prior to the emergence of this literature, most *khutaba'* relied on classical exhortatory works and collections of prophetic traditions (*hadith*) for their material. The preaching manuals that did exist focused primarily on the virtues required by the *khatib* in order to perform his role and often concluded with a sample of exemplary sermons on common topics. As for the composition of the sermon itself, little was offered beyond a list of doctrinally specified requirements, usually limited to the following: the sermon (*khutba*) is divided into two sections, and the *khatib* sits down briefly between the two; the opening should include the customary locutions of praise to God (the *hamdala*), prayers to the Prophet (*salat 'ala al-nabi*), and the *shahada*, the testimony to the unity of God and the status of Muhammed as his messenger; the *khatib* should recite verses from the Qur'an during the first section; during both sections he should exhort listeners to greater piety and end with an invocation to God (*du'a*). Few manuals went beyond this.

Much of the new literature for preachers that emerged from the end of the nineteenth century departed radically from the earlier, ethics-based tradition in its general omission of any discussion of the virtues required to preach. Indeed, the whole question of the virtues that had been central to preaching as an ethical practice got largely dropped as sermons, increasingly modeled on the press, became reoriented around the task of providing and inculcating "useful information." For example, eschatological issues, which had always been central in shaping the ethical sensibilities or virtues that underlay correct conduct—such as humility (*khushu'*) and fear of God (*taqwa*)—now became subject to the charge of irrelevance and obscurantism. Thus, Abdullah Nadim, a well-known orator and student of al-Afghani, complained:

> Sermon oratory [*al-khataba*] was not limited to recalling death, asceticism, to warnings against worldly pleasures and luxuries; rather, oratory during the time of the Prophet and the early caliphs included current events and news of the community [umma]; it did not focus on the promise of heaven [*wa'd*] or the threat of hell [*wa'id*] except when the week had produced no new events or important affairs. (1881: 237)

In other words, the afterlife, for Nadim, though not entirely to be forgotten, no longer had implications for shaping how the self might understand and respond to "new events or important affairs," topics worthy of the modern citizen's attention. Rather, the structure of knowledge and sentiment invoked by Nadim is that cultivated in the public sphere of the emerging nationalist bourgeoisie, one articulated through forms of discourse such as newsprint, political meetings and speeches, and talk in private clubs.

By the time of the Nasserist revolution, the emphasis on individual ethics in preaching manuals had been replaced (at least in the writings of state-affiliated scholars) by an amalgam of Aristotelian rhetoric and work in the field of American communication studies. Thus, a manual entitled "The Art of Rhetoric and the Preparation of the Preacher," used to train *khutaba'* at the government-administered School of Guidance and Preaching at Al-Azhar University, defined its subject matter as "that set of laws by which one is able to convince others in regard to whatever topic one desires, by causing the listener to surrender to the correctness of an argument or action" (Mahfouz 1979 [1952]: 13). Rather than serving as a catalyst for the ritual act and ethical exercise of drawing near to God, the *khatib* now deploys a morally neutral art of rhetorical manipulation, instilling in his audience the opinions and attitudes that will constitute modern Egyptians.

Importantly, what is signaled by this innovation is not simply the adoption of new rhetorical methods or styles of argumentation but also a new conceptual framework for the relation of the *khatib* to his audience: the latter is stripped of its agency, which now lies entirely in the techniques of opinion manipulation exercised by the *khatib* as representative of the state. This is evident in the following comment from another popular sermon manual written during the Nasser period:

> [A *khatib*,] with the eloquence and persuasiveness of his speech, can incline his listeners toward whatever good he wishes, impart to them moral qualities and lead them away from wrongdoing, rectify their characters; and plant in their souls [the importance of] practical work [*i'mal al-dunya*] as well as good work [*al-i'mal al-saliha*]. He can also be a support for the government in issues of state order and security. (Muhammed 1972: 6)

The new set of assumptions is clear in Muhammed's comment: by adopting the proper rhetorical style, a *khatib* can mold his audience like clay, transforming it into the sort of people that he and the government he represents seek to create. As an instrument of the state—the agent responsible for the progressive development of the nation's people and resources—the sermon is to become a device for working on and improving the raw human material that is to be the national citizenry. This shift can be highlighted by comparing the foregoing passage with one from a preaching textbook from the same period, though one clearly indebted to the earlier tradition I have already discussed:

> Thus, the khatib's voice must embody [*yujassim*] the ideas of his sermon and give form to their meanings; he must perfect his ability to enunciate each letter in its natural way, such that the inflection of his voice gives each expression its due [*haqqihi*]. . . . A good voice and a correct pronunciation [*sidq al-lahja*] accompanied by sincerity [*al-ikhlas*] produces the words that come from the heart of the speaker. [These words] go beyond the ears of the listeners, to arrive at their hearts without even obtaining permission. (Abu-Samak 1995: 95)

Notably, the *khatib* in this conception does not make his discourse persuasive by embellishing it, nor is his relation to his speech purely instrumental. Instead, he submits to its discipline, fashioning his voice in accord with the demands of the words he recites, giving them their "due" (*haqqihi*), their "natural" pronunciation. This achieved, his task ends, while that of the listener begins.

Although this shift is most evident in manuals written by state-affiliated authors, its impact is also clear in writings by figures associated with the Islamic opposition movement. Thus, a recent book titled *Al-da'wa al-mu'athira* (Effective preaching), written by an author associated with Hizb al-'Amal, the most prominent Islamic political party in Egypt today, defines the three primary effects of successful preaching as leading the listener to a firm conviction, enabling him or her to develop personal perspective, and helping him or her to choose the right solution to a problem without compulsion (Madi 1995: 16). In this regard, we might also note that Egypt's most popular preacher during the 1990s, Muhammed Hassan, is a graduate of the Department of Communications at Cairo University.

By the 1980s, with the rise of a militant Islamic oppositional movement, the pedagogical role of the sermon was increasingly backgrounded in favor of an emphasis on security concerns. During the Sadat era (1970–1981), it was assumed that all mosques could be staffed by preachers appointed directly by the Ministry of Religious Affairs, in order to solve the problem of militant preaching. As it became obvious that this plan was well beyond the state's actual financial and administrative capacity, the goal shifted to the stationing of government censors in all mosques to monitor activities in the mosque as well as sermon content. This shift in strategy has been accompanied by a growing pessimism among many in the state regarding the potential of sermon oratory to serve as a vehicle of enlightenment. A sociologist I spoke to who had been enlisted by the Religious Affairs ministry to give a course in "modern perspectives" to graduating *khutaba'* suggested:

> From what I've seen, by the time they arrive here it is too late, as they are far too steeped in traditional Islamic perspectives and thus immune to all our attempts. They've spent years reading and talking about hell, the danger of women's skin, how much beneficence from God they earn by repeating meaningless phrases. And as *khutaba'*, they will go out and spread more ignorance and superstition, even as employees of the Ministry of Religious Affairs.

With oratory's power to reform increasingly in doubt, the utility of mosques has been redefined, to some extent, in panoptic terms, as structures for the localization, control, and supervision of bodies. In a dramatic shift, mosques have become sites where the state now listens to the audience for the incipient rumblings of contestation and militancy.

To summarize, to the extent that Islamic discourses are put to the fundamentally different task of producing a modern citizenry in a national framework, sermon listening loses some of its ethical function. Listeners no longer bear responsibility for the effects of their audition, because the efficacy of the act no longer depends upon the dialogic, agentive activity that characterized the earlier tradition. Like other mass media forms to which it is now compared, the sermon—as an instrument of the state—is to be deployed as a technology of the modern subject, a device for the production of modern attitudes, desires, and modes of self-identification.

The notions of persuasion, agency, and government implied here contrast sharply with the model of ethical listening I laid out earlier. As I suggested, a *khatib*, in accord with this earlier tradition, does not shape his audience at will but serves as a mediator, providing the linguistic and gestural resources through which the listener can undertake the ethical labor involved in properly attuning his or her faculties to the word of God. Religious institutions, in other words, have a mediatory function and are not responsible for the creation of moral subjects. This task lies with God and the individuals themselves. Within the context of this tradition, the institutions and practices wherein moral action occurs and is assessed presuppose such an aural subject, one whose particular sensory capacities, honed through auditory disciplines, gave rise to ethical performances. While it is the responsibility of the community to prevent corruption and the spread of erroneous behavior, the community is not, properly speaking, assigned the task of enforcing a normative morality, for each individual is ultimately answerable to God on the Day of Judgment. Indeed, it is this event, one in which moral responsibility is radically individualized, that provides the basis for this moral model. In this light, it is not surprising that the narration of the Day of Judgment has always been a staple of ethical preaching in Islam.

Loss of Voice

The shift in the model and status of the listener that I have been discussing is tied to the incorporation of the institutions of preaching into the state. But other important transformations in sermon listening have taken place in modern Egypt that have not involved the state's direct administrative control. As in other modernizing states, in Egypt the process of recruiting citizens into the structures of national political life produced expectations, aspirations, and participatory demands before the administrative, ideological, and security apparatuses that could accommodate those demands were fully developed. In this context, sermons became one of the critical sites for the expression of demands engendered by political modernization, especially among those ill-versed in the literacy of newsprint. Given the state's complete monopoly over television and radio broadcasting in the country, and strict censorship policies that severely limit unofficial viewpoints in the press, sermons—both in mosques and circulated on tape—have come to play a key role as media of national contestation. As such, they have helped define the attitudes, interests, and modes of appraisal of an Egyptian Muslim citizen.

Two media events were particularly key, both in introducing a nationalist sensibility to the pious ear and in linking its cultivation to media technology: the radio broadcasts of Gamel Abd al-Nasser's speeches and the weekly concerts of the singer Umm Kulthum. Enabled by the vast proliferation of radios during the 1950s and 1960s, as well as by a populist political movement centered on the personality of the president himself, Nasser's rousing speeches provided Egyptians with their first experience of a collective national audition. Many contempo-rary *khutaba'* cite Nasser as among the speakers whose oratorical prowess had the greatest influence in shaping sermon oratory during the twentieth century. Notably, as Nasser's successors were unable to match his unique rhetorical skills or rely upon the revolutionary enthusiasm that accompanied Egypt's socialist experiment, they gradually forfeited the ability to enlist the ear as the sense organ of a national imaginary. Instead, hearing and the human voice were rapidly recuperated by an opposition movement grounded in Islamic institutions and the tradi-tions of oratory and ethical audition these institutions embedded. Taking advantage of the mass dissemination afforded by the cassette medium, popular preachers, beginning in the early 1970s, emerged as rallying points and exemplary figures in a national (and international) political arena (Hirschkind 2001b). A modern political discourse was, in this way, increasingly incorporated into practices of ethical listening linked to the sermon.

Egypt's definitive moment of collective audition, however, came with the weekly radio concerts of the singer Umm Kulthum, again during the 1950s and 1960s (Danielson 1997). Trained in the art of Qur'anic recitation and the genres of Islamic folk performance popular through-out the Egyptian countryside, Umm Kulthum performed music that embodied the sensibilities of Egyptians in a way other contemporary performers, lacking experience in the Islamic traditions of vocal performance, could not. In many ways, her vocal style, particularly in the early part of her career, foregrounded the same affective dynamics that underlay the tradition of ethical sermon audition. As sermons moved outside the mosques to become a popular media practice,

competing with other forms of media entertainment, listeners came to
expect some of the same pleasure and cathartic experience that Umm
Kulthum's music had made available. Importantly, just as Nasser's death
in 1970 marked the end of a national audition in the political arena,
so Umm Kulthum's death in 1972 coincided with the dissolution of
the music industry in Egypt that had made such national superstars
possible. The entire structure that had raised Umm Kulthum and a few
other musicians to such prominence, one grounded in the highly
centralized control and coordination of film, record, and radio production, was crumbling, a condition indebted in no small way to the weak-
ness of copyright protections in the face of the possibility of infinite
duplication afforded by the cassette.

In short, Nasser and Umm Kulthum, in different ways, helped define
a modern national auditory practice that connected traditions of ethical
listening with emerging media practices of political discourse and
musical entertainment. Importantly, because neither of the two had a
successor in his or her field, the sole inheritors of their legacies were
the media-based popular preachers associated with the rising Islamist
trend. Able to circulate outside the regulatory purview of the state,
cassettes became the privileged media form for a contestatory Islamic
discourse on state and society. Many of the young men I worked with
explicitly identified cassette sermons as alternatives to the televisual and
press media promoted by the state. Attempts to produce and distribute
recorded sermons by state-approved *khutaba'*—including Shaykh
Sha'arawi, a *khatib* whose television and print-based popularity rivals
that of all other contemporary religious figures in Egypt—never
succeeded. Not surprisingly, Sha'arawi's immense attraction has always
centered on his avuncular grimaces and gestures—that is, on his
televisual image—and not his vocal performance.

Once hearing lost its privileged relation to the version of Egyptian
national culture promoted by the state, the ear and the institutions that
previously organized its cultivation now become suspect. Associated
with religious customs and knowledges that were now seen as obstacles
to modernization, the aural traditions came to be viewed as morally
and epistemologically untrustworthy, if not directly responsible for the
rise of a violent militant movement carried out in the name of Islam.
Today, articles in the government-controlled national press frequently
bemoan the ongoing practice of traditions that cultivate a "reverence
for the sacred word" and an attention to the sonic qualities of language
over and above the symbolic. Hearing bypasses the rational faculties,
it is claimed, penetrating directly to the vulnerable emotional core of

the untutored Egyptian peasant. Reading, in contrast, encourages reasoned reflection and reasoned assent. The nineteenth-century European critique of the superficiality and artificiality of Muslim practices has found a new purchase in this context: tradition-bound Muslims, it is said, are too involved with surfaces and externalities— the sound of reciting voices, the prescribed movements of the body at prayers, rules of fasting and ablutions—all of which define a kind of life incompatible with more refined and developed modes of reason, understanding, and piety.

The Contemporary Politics of Hearing

The shifts in the orientation and function of hearing that have accompanied the modernizing project in Egypt have not led to the wholesale abandonment or replacement of the earlier tradition. In the remainder of this chapter, I indicate briefly how tensions between diverse styles of listening get articulated onto social and political conflicts in Egypt today. Disagreements about the role of listening do not simply reflect different ideologies of eye and ear, speech and writing, but also concern the range of institutions that embed these practices, the goals they promote, and the forms of sociability they sustain or are indifferent toward.

To cite an example, one of the axes around which contemporary divisions in Egyptian society position themselves concerns precisely the question of whether the Qur'an's divine aspect lies in the material word itself or only in its symbolic meaning as discovered through the operation of human understanding. The two models of language authorize very different interpretive regimes, structures of power linked to contrasting social and political projects. Arguments over this topic are part of public debate and appear frequently in both sermons and the popular press, both state-controlled and independent.

In a recent article in the Labor Party (*Hizb al-'Amal*) newspaper, *Al-Sha'b*, for example, the writer, Muhammed Wagdi, draws on the Qur'anic account that the divine text entered the Prophet's heart before it was uttered by his tongue in order to assert the validity of a more literalist interpretive approach. Having cited a verse from the chapter of the Qur'an entitled "Al-Qiyama" that refers to this matter, he explains, "And this means that the Qur'an was inserted into the heart of Muhammed, and thus that he heard it [*sam'*] through revelation before he pronounced it. That is, that he memorized it in his heart before he understood it, or, in other words, that the verbal expression preceded the explanation of its meaning" (*Al-Sha'b* 1995). The author

then speculates on the reason God imparted such a miraculous nature
to the verbal expression itself, suggesting that in this way, "the beauty
of the composition [*jamal al-siyagha*] became inseparable from the
greatness of its message, and this unity creates [in the listener] remem-
brance [*al-dhikr*] and humility [*al-khushu'*]." The argument, in other
words, has an ethical dimension that belongs to the same tradition I
discussed earlier. The ethical dispositions that the author deems essential to a Muslim society (such as humility and a mindfulness of God's
commands) depend upon an appreciation of the "sheer words" of the
Qur'an, or, rather, on the practices of aural discipline that incorporate
such an appreciation (e.g., sermon audition, Qur'anic recitation [*tajwid*],
memorization [*hifz*]). That is, entwined in the debate about the status
of the Qur'anic word is an argument about the virtues that underlie a
Muslim society and the role of those virtues in public life (e.g., in public
education).

Sa'id al-Ashmawi, one of the Islamic thinkers whose opinion on this
matter is cited in the article and who writes prolifically on matters of
Qur'anic interpretation and history, asserts an opposing view. Writing
in a popular leftist magazine, al-Ashmawi argues that it is the meaning
of the Qur'an that is preeminent, a meaning that, moreover, has no
necessary relation to a precise verbal form. In his view, an overprivileg-
ing of the literal word has been an impediment to freethinking and
reason in Islamic history and has kept Muslim societies from progress-
ing. While it is unnecessary to repeat here the details of al-Ashmawi's
argument, what I want to point to is the context in which the argument
occurs. Specifically, al-Ashmawi is a legal scholar allied with liberal
currents in the judicial and political system in Egypt. For those who
support these currents, the virtues cited by the author of the *Al-Sha'b*
article and the institutions that uphold those virtues have no dominant
role to play in contemporary society. For thinkers like al-Ashmawi, often
called "neo-Mu'tazila" by contemporary Egyptians, in reference to the
eighth-century rationalist movement in Islamic history,[10] God's wisdom, as embodied in the Qur'an, must be consonant with or at least
not impede the modes of reasoning and pragmatic demands that
underlie the progressive movement of modern national life. The
contemporary reading of the Qur'an (and it is a *reading*, not a recitation)
must take as its goal the uncovering of symbolic meanings through an
interpretive approach founded upon the same notions of language,
history, and context as those applied to contemporary literary texts.

This disagreement, I suggest, can be usefully illuminated by taking
into consideration the contrasting ways of understanding agency and

authority in relation to auditory experience. More is involved here than simply a contrast between a literalist and a symbolic interpretive emphasis. For Muhammed Wagdi, writing in *Al-Sha'b*, word sound lies at the heart of those traditional practices by which the self acquires the virtues that enable moral action. Al-Ashmawi's argument, on the other hand, draws on an expressivist understanding of language whereby speech is conceived of as a material apparatus for the externalization of a nonmaterial meaning. An overconcern with the sonic qualities of the Qur'an—mere externalities in this view—threatens to corrupt the purity of the interpretive exercise, to infect one's reasoned engagement with the text with nonrational modes of discrimination. Vocal expression, especially religious expression, can be an instrument of power when applied to a passive listener. These traditions of language theory and practice presuppose distinct conceptual and disciplinary conditions on the part of their respective readers or listeners. Without an understanding of the prior cultivation of certain sensibilities—habits of the ear—it will be difficult for one to appreciate the force of the respective arguments.

Let me clarify these points further by reference to an event in Cairo that generated considerable discussion in both Egyptian and international media: the case of the Cairo University professor Nasr Hamid Abu Zayd, who was initially denied tenure on the grounds that his writings showed him to be an apostate.[11] Although most of the people I worked with were unfamiliar with the details of the case, except for the fact that Abu Zayd had been accused of having denied the divinity of the Qur'an, a few had followed the debate as it unfolded in the national press. One man, a preacher and part-time university professor named Mustafa Ahmed, expressed his opinion on the matter in the following terms:

> Many of those who dismiss Abu Zayd out of hand must never have looked at his work. For clearly he demonstrates considerable knowledge of the Qur'an and is doing important work in terms of bringing new theories to bear on its study. We need this. Unfortunately, his irreverent and dismissive attitude toward classical Islamic scholars is incompatible with serious work in this field by a Muslim. He writes of the Qur'an without humility, respect, or fear of God: while this may be fine for other books, it is not acceptable for a Muslim to do so with the Qur'an. I don't think he should be treated the way he has been, but he should be made to understand that such an attitude is injurious both to Islam and his work.

Ahmed is suggesting that the Islamic virtues of humility, fear, and respect endow the scholar with the commitments and orientations that ensure right reasoning and action. Without these qualities, the performance of either preaching or scholarly inquiry may achieve a kind of technical proficiency but never the standards of excellence internal to these activities as Islamic practices. The assertion is that Abu Zayd's writing betrays an attitude or an emotional disposition incompatible with and subversive of the intellectual and social good realizable through an engagement with the Qur'an. We would be tempted to read these criticisms in terms of a concern with tone over substance. In framing the matter this way, however, we fail to acknowledge the extent to which the affective register alluded to here is recognized to be of considerable consequence for the scholarly excellence of the work and its potential contribution to the Islamic society in which it has been produced. Insomuch as the reading and recitation of the Qur'an play a role for Muslims in the shaping of virtues, the text cannot be approached as an abstract statement to be assessed dispassionately. A properly disposed heart—a figure for something like "the right attitude"—is necessary in order to learn from it, to achieve sound judgment in one's engagements with it *as a Muslim.*

Of course the argument here concerns a written text, not an oral performance or a moment of actual audition. Nonetheless, the particular sensitivity that the commentator finds lacking in the writings of Abu Zayd is precisely one historically grounded in and acquired by means of practices of ethical audition. The cultivated ear, in other words, is intrinsic to the normative form of literacy one brings to the scholarly treatment of the Qur'an in this view; it is a sensory condition of its understanding.

The preceding observations represent a preliminary attempt to trace what might be called a history of the pious ear in modern Egypt. In approaching this history, I have drawn attention to the place of ethical discipline in creating the nondiscursive background of sentiments and habits upon which public deliberation depends. My aim has been to demonstrate how an analysis of public discourse can benefit from a more complicated understanding of the embodied listener, a figure that democratic theory, despite the efforts of many, cannot quite get rid of. Practices of listening inhabit distinct forms of public life and are assigned specific functions and goals in accord with those forms. This is not an issue captured in the familiar story of the decline of the religious ear in a secular age. Rather, what is at stake, I suggest, is a politics of the ear—one that, as I hope I have made clear in this discussion, we should be interested in.

Acknowledgments

This chapter is based on fieldwork carried out in Egypt between 1994 and 1996 with the support of dissertation grants from the Wenner-Gren Foundation for Anthropological Research and the Social Science Research Council. Additional funding was provided by a Charlotte Newcombe Dissertation Write-up Fellowship and a Rockefeller Post-doctoral Fellowship at the Centre for the Study of Religion, University of Toronto. Earlier versions of the essay were presented to audiences at Columbia University and the University of Amsterdam. The chapter has benefited from the comments of Hussein Agrama, Penelope Gouk, Saba Mahmood, and Hillel Schwartz.

Notes

1. For a discussion of the emotional and gestural repertoires that enable the practice of ethical listening in contemporary Cairo, see Hirschkind 2001a.

2. *Mu'jiz*, an Arabic word from the same root as *i'jaz*, is usually translated into English as "miracle (especially one performed by a prophet)" (Wehr 1980: 592). The etymologies of the English and Arabic terms provide a revealing comparison. Lane (1984 [1863–1893]: 1,961) elaborated the theological meaning of the Arabic term *mu'jiz* as "an event at variance with the usual course [of nature], produced by means of one who lays claim to the office of a prophet, in contending with those who disacknowledge [his claim], in such a manner as renders them unable to produce the like thereof." *Mu'jiz*, in other words, denotes an action performed in the context of an argument. As such, it presupposes a rhetorical situation of debate and contestation. Paradigmatically, this act is one of speech, with the Qur'an as its primary reference. The English word *miracle*, on the other hand, derives ultimately from the Latin *mirari*, meaning "to wonder at," an act involving the eyes and the face (the English word "smile" comes from the same root). As a manifestation of divine intervention, its primary mode of perception is visual. This distinction between a visual and verbal experience of the divine attests to the different emphases given to these modes of perception in the two overlapping traditions.

3. As many scholars have pointed out, Islamic piety combines more rational-istic approaches to the divine text with an attitude of reverential celebration for its miraculous beauty and the grandeur of its eloquence (Denny 1980;

Graham 1987; Madigan 1995). However, when we speak of Muslim practices as *combining* rational and aesthetic strands, we must avoid the supposition—embedded in our grammar—that those strands may be conceptually and analytically disarticulated in accord with our own categories. Qur'anic recitation, for instance, combines what we would identify as both rational and aesthetic elements: its study, according to the fifteenth-century scholar Ibn Khaldun, is as essential to the development of capacities of moral reasoning as are the disciplines of exegesis and theology (Ibn Khaldun 1958: 436–447).

4. All translations of the Qur'an are from Asad 1980. Numbers refer to verses cited.

5. Although translations of the Qur'an into other languages exist, the vast majority of Islamic scholars generally accept that no translation can capture the full richness, beauty, and meaning of the Arabic text.

6. For a discussion of a similar debate in contemporary Cairo, see Hirschkind 2001b.

7. See Calverly 1943 for a useful overview of Islamic understandings of the soul.

8. Plato, moreover, expressed a similar view. As Iris Murdoch, commenting on Plato's psychology, succinctly put it: "We cannot escape the causality of sin. We are told in the *Theaetetus* (176–7) that the inescapable penalty of wickedness is simply to be the sort of person that one is, and in the *Laws*, that evil-doers are in Hades in this world" (1977: 39).

9. Gaffney (1991) provides an excellent overview of the professionalization of preaching in Egypt from the beginning of the twentieth century up to the 1980s.

10. The Mu'tazila placed reason on a par with revelation by arguing that God, in His essential constitution, is rational. In accord with this rationalist tendency, they asserted that those parts of revelation containing anthropomorphic images of God as sitting on a throne or raising His right hand had to be interpreted metaphorically. For the orthodox, the demand that God be reasonable constituted an unacceptable restraint on divine will and power. For a concise account of this movement, see Rahman 1979: 86–90.

11. For an extensive discussion of this case, see Hirschkind 1995.

Edison's Teeth: Touching Hearing

Steven Connor

The senses are multiply related; we rarely if ever apprehend the world through one sense alone. Indeed, under conditions in which any one sense predominates, closer inspection may disclose that the predominating sense is in fact being shadowed and interpreted by other, apparently dormant senses. Indeed, we might enunciate a paradoxical principle: that the more we concentrate or are concentrated upon one sense, the more likely it is that synaesthesic spillings and minglings may occur. To look intently may be to long to grasp and consume; to be surrounded by sound is to be touched or moved by it. The more dominant a particular sense or the apparatuses used to support and supply it may seem to be, the more it will implicate other senses, and therefore the more complex and the less "pure" its dominion will become. The development of the microscope in the seventeenth century allowed the extension of the powers of the eye into regions and dimensions that had previously been unavailable to it, but in provoking a new sensitivity to the swarming surfaces of things, it also extended or rarefied the sense of touch. The microscope not only looked intently at the skin, at the populous surfaces of living things, it also looked with the skin: it gave the skin eyes.

Similar synaesthesias are precipitated by more modern visual machineries. If it is true, as is often said, that our contemporary lives seem dominated by the technologies of vision, then the effect may be to give visuality the same complex hegemony as the English language: because it is everywhere dominant, it is everywhere subject to corruption and contamination. Douglas Kahn and others have pointed to the interest in synaesthesia that characterized modernism (Kahn and Whitehead 1992: 14–19). If it is true that the impulse to compound the senses belongs to an avant-garde desire to go beyond the ordinary sense economies of the everyday world, then we would be wrong to see synaesthesia as always exceptional, revolutionary, or transcendent. To understand the workings of any of the senses, it is necessary to remain aware of the fertility of the relations between them.

Intersensoriality

The relations between the senses are not all of the same kind. We can mark out a distinction, for example, between the sound-sight relation and the sound-touch relation, as they currently subsist. In our culture, and perhaps others besides, the relations between sound and sight may be said to be largely indexical, by which I mean that the evidence of sight often acts to interpret, fix, limit, and complete the evidence of sound. Seeing may then appear as the destination or terminus of sound—"Oh, now I see what you mean." Perhaps because of the imperfect nature of hearing in humans, hearing tends to ask questions that get answered by the evidence of the eyes. As the two senses on which human beings seem most to rely, hearing and sight are closely interwoven but not necessarily synchronized. Though light moves faster than sound, these relations are reversed in the logic of human perception; it is sound that seems to be immediate, and sight, as the sense with which we achieve balance and understanding, that follows after it. Hearing proposes; sight disposes.

The relations between sound and touch, by contrast, tend to be mimetic: touch accompanies, mimics, performs sound rather than translating or defining it. Touch doubles sound rather than dubbing it. This may imply a hierarchy of senses with regard to the information they give and the finality of that information, with touch participating on a level with sound, as opposed to sight, which processes, transforms, counters, and commands it.

There is a long tradition of the denigration of touch in Europe. Touch signifies the proximity, the undifferentiation of the body. The Renaissance philosopher Ficino wrote, "Nature has placed no sense further from the intelligence than touch" (1989: 124). Kant argued, "By touch, hearing and sight we perceive objects (on the surface); by taste and smell we partake of them (take them into ourselves)" (Kant 1974: 35). Kant's distinction seems to leave touch as a hinge sense, able to be lifted into perception by the differentiating senses of hearing and sight but also able to sink into the grosser participations of taste and smell. Touching yourself is the worst kind of touch, because it disallows even the minimal differentiation involved in being touched by another body.

There is good reason to posit the disproportionate role of touch in the coordinating of the senses one with another. Because all of the primary senses are lodged in the skin, on the outside of the body, one might say that in literal terms they are connected to each other by a membrane of tactility and that this is reproduced in the way in which we experience them—as may perhaps be testified to by a term such as "sense impressions." More than this, though, touch seems to be the primary or favored mode of our sensory self-attention, which is perhaps why our models of the workings of the senses tend to be topological. This is not to say that we have knowledge of our senses only through touch: knowledge and understanding of the senses will also be encoded in visual terms. But our investments and identifications and above all our feelings of love for the senses, along with their reversals and negative correlatives, such as the wish to mortify or deny the senses, tend toward the tactual. As Michel Serres (1999: 35) suggests, the act of beautifying the face involves the touching, the touching up, as we may say, of the senses as they are manifested in the head and face—the lips, the ears. It is with the hand that we stop the nose, block the ears, or cover the eyes.

Touch appears to be the most versatile and various of the senses, partly because it threads through all the other modes of sensory apprehension and also because it seems itself to be formed differently depending upon the particular kind of apprehension it delivers, whether of shape, texture, volume, space, tightness, heat, or weight. It may help in understanding and appreciating the comminglings of hearing and touch to suggest some distinctions among some broad modalities of touch. There is the apprehension through touch of what we might call qualities of measure, by which I mean qualities of shape, distance, space, volume, and texture. There is the apprehension of what might be called pitch; included under this heading would be all the sensations of weight, force, tension, and balance. Then there are relations of temper; these include the whole range of sensations of greater or lesser degrees of excitation, whether in heat, cold, itch, inflammation, or sexual arousal. (I have of course skewed the matter by giving these categories names that suggest the elements of music.)

Another reason the relations between the senses are so complex and variable is that we do not have merely a client relationship to them. We not only use our eyes, ears, skin, nose, and tongue to convey information to us about the world; we also establish strong bonds of pleasure, identity, and even love with those senses and their associated organs. Amid all the vast literature about the powers and protocols and pleasures of looking, there is actually surprisingly little about the particular pleasures taken in one's own activity of sight. It is perhaps only when we confront the possibility of our senses being dimmed, damaged, or taken away from us that the intense love that binds us to them becomes apprehensible. This love for the senses expresses itself in and may derive from the need to protect organs that are at once extremely important to us and also, by definition, sensitive and easily damaged (damage will recur later in what I have in mind to say). The love for the senses takes cultural as well as individual forms: in the formalizing of particular kinds of sensory pleasure—in the experience of perfume, music, food—the senses themselves are set apart and invested with a kind of collective narcissism.

It was thought by medieval philosophers that there must be some sixth, overarching sense, a *sensus communis*, that allowed the individual senses to be coordinated with one another. Often we seem to assume a radial model, in which each of the senses conveys a different form of information to a central command-and-control module that receives and processes the sensory input from these five channels. But we do not merely "use" different senses to give ourselves a more three-dimensional fix on the objects of our apprehension. The sense we make of any one sense is always mixed with and mediated by that of others. The senses form an indefinite series of integrations and transformations: they form a complexion. So there may be no such central module, no statue on which the senses may be thought of as being hung or draped. The senses communicate with each other in cooperations and conjugations that are complex, irregular, and multilateral. This complexion of the senses knits itself together anew with each new configuration. We cannot merely reflect on the operations of sense without performing active sensory operations or enacting sensory apprehensions. Writers seeking to account for the demotion of the sense of hearing and to redeem it from that demotion may nowadays often evoke the idea of a cultural sensorium, or a mansion of the senses. But what a culture offers is not just a static consortium of the senses, disposed like a molecular structure in a particular configuration, but rather a field of possibility, a repertoire of forms, images, and dreams whereby reflection on the senses can take place. Intersensoriality is the means by which this is enacted. Cultures are sense traps that bottle and make sense of sensory responses, but they are also sense multipliers.

In Touch

One of the most important features of hearing, for example, or of the human relation to hearing, is that it seems incomplete and interrogative; hearing provides intensity without specificity, which is why it has often been thought to be aligned more closely with feeling than with understanding. We need not necessarily think of this in terms of the definition or rounding-off that sight gives to hearing. We might, for instance, think of it as an orientation toward the future in sound, rather than toward the past: hearing, we might say, is usually more provocative than evocative. But precisely for this reason, sound may be supplied with compensatory substance, its indeterminate force given an imaginary but determinate form—for example, in the form of the "voice-body" about which I speculated in my book *Dumbstruck* (2000).

One apparent paradox of hearing is that it strikes us as at once intensely corporeal—sound literally moves, shakes, and touches us—and mysteriously immaterial. Mythology provides examples of the power of sound to form and manipulate substance, as in the story of Amphion, who used the magic sounds of his lyre to cause the fortification of the walls of Thebes, the stones moving into place apparently of their own free will. Perhaps the tactility of sound depends in part on this immaterial corporeality, because of the fact that all sound is disembodied, a residue or production rather than a property of objects. When we see something, we do not think of what we see as a separable aspect of it, a ghostly skin shed for our vision. We feel that we see the thing itself, rather than any occasion or extrusion of the thing. But when we hear something, we do not have the same sensation of hearing the thing itself. This is because objects do not have a single, invariant sound, or voice. How something sounds is literally contingent, depending upon what touches or comes into contact with it to generate the sound. We hear, as it were, the event of the thing, not the thing itself.

But if sound necessarily parts from, comes apart from, its source, it rarely does so completely. To think of a sound as the "voice" of what sounds is not only to humanize or animate the sounding world, ascribing an Aristotelian quality of soul to it; it is also to think of the sound as owned by and emanating essentially from its source, rather than being an accidental discharge from it. Precisely because of its default condition of disembodiment, sound may be apt to be thought of in terms of how it clings or stays in contact with what begets it. During the medieval period and afterward, a distinction was commonly marked between unvoiced, or whispered, sound, which lingered in the mouth, and voiced sound, which went forth bodily from it. Bacon, for example, described whispering as an "interior" sound, which "is rather an Impulsion or Contusion of the Aire, than an Elision or Section of the same" (Bacon 1626, no. 288). Even some "voiced" sounds seem to have this continuing tactile relationship with their source, as though they emanated, seeped, wept, leaked, or spread from that source rather than having been emitted or launched by it. There is a lingering continuity in the mode of the separation of source and target that resembles the effect of aroma. The most important determinant on thinking about the executive power of breath and voice is the Christian idea of the Word. The African theologian Lactantius distinguished between the Son of God as speech and the angels as the silent breath of God:

> The Son of God is the speech, or even the reason of God, and ... the other angels are spirits of God. For speech is breath sent forth with a voice signifying something. But, however, since breath and speech are sent forth from different parts, inasmuch as breath proceeds from the nostrils, speech from the mouth, the difference between the Son of God and the other angels is great. For they proceeded from God as silent spirits, because they were not created to teach the knowledge of God, but for His service. But though He is Himself a spirit, yet he proceeded from the mouth of God, with voice and sound. (Lactantius 1871: 224–225)

But most early theologians also insisted that the Son of God was a particular kind of voice that must be thought of as coming into being "by partition, not by section," as Tatian put it, comparing the giving of voice to the lighting of a torch, which in no way diminishes the fire that is its source (Tatian 1982: 11). The voice as fire suggests air made substantial and active. We can see this as an idealization of the umbilicus, the physical link between beings that is cut shortly after the issuing of the first cry (Vasse 1974).

There is no more telling enactment of this idea of the umbilical continuity of the voice than the telephone, the most important feature of which was not that it separated the voice from the person emitting it but that it conducted that voice along a wire that the receiver of the call knew had to be in real-time contact with the speaker. It was the magically condensed tactility of the new medium that thrilled and intrigued users as much as the capacity to hear at long distances. The telephone revived or confirmed mesmeric ideas about the migration or transposition of the senses (mesmerists claimed that deaf subjects

could hear sounds transmitted to their abdomens through the mes-
merist's fingertips). Sound had previously been counterposed to sight
in terms of the quality of its movement: where sight traveled in straight
lines, sound was understood to radiate and diffuse evenly in all
directions, like a gas. But the wire seemed to provide a new tactual image
of the voice as capable of immense extrapolation or extrusion, its powers
concentrated and accelerated into a vector rather than a radiation.

The telephone uses the principle of electromagnetic induction to
translate sound vibrations into fluctuations of electrical charge, which
are then translated back into movement at the other end. It is the
capacity of electrical impulses to be transmitted long distances without
significant degradation by and into noise that accounts for the illusion
of bodily presence, the sense that the voice that arrived at the other
end of the line had not been transported so much as stretched out. It
was, and is, this that makes for the surprisingly undisturbing disturbance it effects in our sense of the relations between proximity and
distance. And it is this that accounts for the sense that, despite its reliance upon the new, clean, dry power of electricity, the telephone remained a moist and dirty medium (hence its still-operative associations
with sexuality and disease). We may nowadays have dispensed with the
wire and may even, in the era of disposable phones, be on our way to
disposing of the very apparatus of speech; but this may be part of a
volatilization rather than a complete abolition of the idea of touch in
technologies of hearing.

Perhaps the most important feature of the wire was that it embodied
the possibility of two allotropic states: the coiled, or compacted, and
the extended. The extended wire gave an image of the voice thinned
almost to nothing; the coiled wire is an image of the voice stored,
concentrated, and magnified by compression. The coil of wire recalls
the whorls of the inner ear. From the earliest times, the idea that such
coiled structures might detain sound, preserving it from decay, has been
in evidence. Early representations of speech in pictures took the form,
not of bubbles, but of scrolls, unrolled into the empty air. The religious
and legal powers traditionally embodied in the scroll pass across into
stories of the magical power of rolled-up words, such as those the Golem
brought to life with a slip of paper put under its tongue. The orality of
the scroll is suggested also in a magical threshold object like the Jewish
mezuzzah, the little cylinder affixed to the door post of the house,
containing on a scroll of parchment the profession of faith that begins
with the words "Shema Israel"—"Hear, Israel." The scroll coiled in an
enclosed space suggests an ear, though the awareness of the injunction

to hearing inscribed on the scroll also suggests a recording apparatus—
a way for an ear to be a speaking mouth, as it is in the horn gramophone. Is the scroll imagined as being secreted in the mezuzzah as it is
laid under the tongue of the Golem (in Hebrew, matter without shape),
to make the door post speak (the devout Jew will touch the mezuzzah
and then his lips, on entry and exit)?

The technologies of recorded sound revert with an odd insistence to
such helical images: in Edison's phonographic cylinders, the spirals of
the gramophone disk, the spoolings of audio- and videotape, and the
spiral sequences of optical data inscribed on the compact disc. Helical
sound not only allows the endlessly uncoiling and irreversible line of
natural sound to be suspended or wrapped around a single point; it also
confers the magical power of running sound backward. Like saying the
Mass backward or speaking on the in-breath rather than the out-breath
(believed by many for centuries to be the explanation of ventriloquism),
the reversal of sound is profoundly unnatural. That it is still regarded
so is suggested by the periodic panics induced by revelations of secret
satanic messages secreted backward in gramophone records, the most
famous being the mysterious phrase, "Never could be any other" to be
heard right at the end of the Beatles' "Sergeant Pepper's Lonely Hearts
Club Band."

The practice of ventriloquism, which, in the West and in modern
times, has become associated with a precise relationship between sound
and touch, provides a commentary on the tactualizing of sound in the
telephone. Edith Lecourt helps explain some of the allure of ventriloquism when she evokes the phenomenon she calls the "untouched
voice" (Lecourt 1990: 215). Ventriloquism plays variations on this
fantasy of a voiceless or mouthless voice. But the voice of which the
ventriloquist's countenance gives no sign, which appears to be separated
absolutely from him and to be issuing from the dummy or doll, is
nevertheless tethered to him. The wireless transmission of sound
between the performer and the ventriloquial figure is in some way
guaranteed by the "wiring" represented by the hand that connects the
two. There is no practical reason why the dummy needs to be manually
operated by the ventriloquial performer himself or herself, and indeed,
performers have experimented at intervals with remote control of their
figures. But ventriloquism seems to need the confirming circuit of
touch, which acts both to intensify and to protect against the disembodiment of the voice.

The lingering of touch in sound is particularly in evidence in music.
Bruce Smith (1999: 96–129) and Penelope Gouk (1999: 115–153) have

pointed to the importance in the early modern world of schemes of entablature for preserving and spreading the sense of touch in musical notation. We can define an instrument as a sounding posture of the body. We learn to hear the postures imprinted in sounds: the fat, farting buttock-cheeks of the tuba, the undulant caressings of the cello, the hooked, crooked intensity of the violin (the violin is an instrument of acute angles—chin, elbow, armpit). I am grateful to Roland Barthes for his evocation, following Jacques Attali, of the "muscular music" that one plays, rather than merely listening to it passively, in which it is "as if the body was listening, not the 'soul'"; but I think he is wrong to imply that the hand is superseded by the ear in modern habits of listening (Barthes 1991: 261). The more the artificial production and reproduction of sound—in amplification, for example—threatens to lead away from this sense of embodied source, the more we learn to replace or refuse this loss, as with the extravagant, martyred postures of the electric guitar, enacted both in the ecstatic writhings it evokes and in the ever more baroque contortions of its own shapes. What a marvelous invention is the despised "air guitar"!

When we hear an instrument that we have never heard before, we cannot fully or properly hear it until we have guessed or supposed in it the manner of its production, the mutual disposition of body and instrument that results in the sound and of which the sound bears the impress. Sometimes, perhaps a little at a loss for an adequate sound-posture to project, we will treat the instruments of reproduction or transmission as instruments, as in the manipulations of tape and vinyl practiced since the time of the *musique concrète* of the 1950s. We are not simply touched by this kind of sound. We take it into us, hear it in the mode of producing it, in an instrumental coenesthesia. This mode of touch gives us not so much touch as pressure, or the impending of things upon us, the touch of shape, or touch as the guarantee of shape.

Pathos

The imaginary power of maintaining continuity of contact in sound is in conflict with another feature of the physics and phenomenology of sound, namely, its stubborn association with violence and suffering. Unlike the other senses, which have been conceived in terms of the neutral or contingent commingling of traces, sound can come about only as a result of some more or less violent disturbance: the collision of objects with each other (we never hear the sound of one thing alone, any more than we can hear the sound of one hand clapping) and the transmission of this agitation through the air to the ears or skin of another. Sound beats, stretches, compresses, contorts. Sound always brings a difference into the world and is associated with sometimes painful change or disruption. Sound has a "gestalt of force," to borrow a term that Bruce Smith borrows from Mark Johnson (Smith 1999: 23; Johnson 1987: 41–64). It is for this reason, perhaps, that Aristotle used the word *pathos* in describing sound in Book 3 of his *De Anima*. It may be this very power of unbalancing settled states of affairs that suggests the possibility that sound itself might be subjected to, or itself have, powers to balance and steady. Thus, the psychoanalyst Otto Isakower (1939) made much of the vestibular function of the inner ear, suggesting that the coincidence of location of hearing and balance might account for an association between the ideas of power and truth projected onto the figure of the superego and the voice.

Sound is both process and object of pathos. Sound is produced by pathos—suffering, agitation—and reproduces it in others. The psyche seems more at risk from excessive sound, sound that threatens what William Niederland calls "auditory extinction" (1958: 474), than from any other sensory input except perhaps the excessiveness of touch we register as pain. Sound itself may also appear to be subjected to these processes, as though sound were both the assaulted body of the world and the cry of pain it emits. Sound is closely and recurrently associated with the deliberate application of pain to the body. In the contest of Apollo and Marsyas, a sonorous victory leads to a literal flaying away of the organ of touch. The association of sound and violent touch is prominent in the practices of penal and sexual flagellation. An inquirer to *Notes and Queries* in 1866, mindful possibly of Aristotle's remarks about the pathos of sound, asked readers to help him locate the passage in which Aristotle recommends the use of a lighter cane in the punishment of young slaves, because "the reverberation of the lighter rod made its strokes more stinging and severe than had a heavier instrument of punishment been used" ("Quaere" 1866). (None of the readers of *Notes and Queries* seems to have been able to supply the reference.)

Hearing has the reputation of being more passive than seeing. The association of hearing with feeling rather than cognition probably comes from our modern sense that feelings happen to us rather than being willed or subject to conscious direction. This has sometimes impelled claims that a culture based more around sound and hearing than around sight might be a gentler, more participative, less dominative culture (Fiumara 1990). The strong association between cultural acoustics and ecology would seem to offer further evidence of this irenic dimension of the ear. However, the pathos involved in sound can itself have two contrasting sides or dimensions. Hearing is not always listening, which is to say, silent, reserved, withdrawn, passive or alert responsiveness to sound. Most of the time, hearing is accompanied by different kinds of action, most typically, perhaps, in the production of sound in speech, which is perhaps best thought of as a kind of continuous, indistinguishable composite of hearing and speaking rather than a simple, so to speak, deaf production of sound. Just as we cannot speak without listening to or overhearing ourselves, so we cannot listen without taking into ourselves the sounds we hear. Hearing always operates to some degree on both sides of the active-passive, productive-receptive dichotomy. This means that hearing can participate in both forms of the sadism of sound, which is to say domination exercised both through and over sound. The one who barks a demand or screams an insult is using sound as a weapon to effect his will, but the means whereby this is effected is through an assault on sound itself. Sound is imagined in the same two-sided way as skin: both as that which touches and that which is touched, both as a medium through which we feel and as something that is itself subject to touching and assault.

Certainly there is as much evidence of violence in an oral-aural culture as there is in a visual-alphabetic culture. Walter Ong (1981) made it clear that the very difficulty of holding on to time that is a feature of oral-aural cultures can result in formulaic rigidity and occasional outbreaks of ungovernable rage. The distance and objectifying power that may strike us as inseparable from the regime of the eye are also what provide the space of reserve and withdrawal against the sadism or violence of hearing, a space that shrinks, for example, in the experience of some paranoid schizophrenics subject to the appalling tortures of sounds and voices from which it is impossible to retreat.

Hand to Mouth

The modes of touch that I distinguished earlier in this essay—measure, pitch, and temper—may be thought of in terms of how we are affected by what touches us. But touch doubles the duplicity of hearing, in that it has an active or executive side as well as a passive one. Just as we have the capacity to touch as well as the susceptibility to being touched, we also have the capacity to produce sound as well as to receive it. There seems to be a striking homology between the power to send out voice and other sounds of the body into the world and the executive power possessed by the hand. The hand and the voice cooperate with and in part become each other. The history of attempts to prove universal patterns of oral enactment in language, ultimately deriving from the idea that spoken language replaced gesture language when the hands were full—the association of "i" sounds with littleness in English, for example, or, even more improbably, the smoothing action of the mouth to convey the idea of "flatness" by having the tongue "outstretched in the bottom of the mouth . . . [while] drawing the top or front of the tongue backwards from the teeth to a velar position" (Jóhanneson 1958: 9)—testifies to the recurrent will-to-belief in the power of this "primal cavity" (Spitz 1955) to dance out space and shape.

Although we are accustomed to thinking of touch as focused on the hand, the most active and exploratory portion of the skin, a primary association of hearing and touch is formed, not on the exterior skin, but in the interior skin of the mouth. For it is in the mouth that we form our first sounds and may at first apprehend sound as a sort of plastic tangibility: the burring of the lips, the sibilant puffs of air between teeth and tongue, the uvular gulps and gurgles. Sound and touch meet, mingle, and part in the mouth.

Once again ventriloquism provides us with an enactment of this relation. In archaic ventriloquism, the performer would attempt to create the illusion of being nowhere near his voice, of throwing his voice out of his reach. In modern ventriloquism, the performer keeps a grip on the voice that he pretends to put away from his mouth. His hand operates the dummy, dancing along to the play of his vocalizations. For those watching the act of ventriloquial dummy performance, what is being suggested (without in fact ever being shown) is the idea that one might be literally manipulating a voice, squeezing, extruding, and palpating the sound into being, just as the nineteenth-century performer Professor Faber seemed to do as he pressed the keys that operated the wheezing vocal apparatus he named Euphonia (Hollingshead 1895, 1: 67–69). The hand of the ventriloquist becomes a vocal apparatus.

No more intimate and delightful a mirroring and interchange between the postures of the mouth and of the hand occurs than in the glove puppet. William Hogarth, in his 1755 painting *An Election Entertainment*, illustrated an early version of this kind of puppet in which the mouth is formed simply by the seam between thumb and index finger, and a number of ventriloquial performers have specialized in this kind of "soft dummy." What is a muppet, after all, than the mumbling together of the two words "mouth" and "puppet"? The shape that most people mime in the air when evoking ventriloquial performance involves a crooking of the wrist and elbow and the performance of a pecking motion with the fingers and thumb, indicating clearly enough the fantasy of a hand that reaches through the body of the dummy. Ventriloquism with a dummy gives us the mouth rendered as an oral hand; the dummy is an oral allegory.

There is, perhaps, no more ubiquitous example of the persistence of tactility in the age of apparent technical disembodiment than the microphone. The sound of the microphone is a touched sound. It not only selectively amplifies the noises of the mouth's own slidings, impacts, poppings, and palpations but also joins to these noises the sound of the tactile contact between the mouth and itself: the bangs, bumps, and scratches. The distinction between classical and popular performance has come to be a distinction between self-projective singing at a distance from the microphone and close, wet, and "dirty" proximity to it. It is appropriate that so many performers should seem to wish to incorporate the microphone into their singing, because the microphone has already been made into so obvious an extension of the oral apparatus. Few have missed the phallic significance of the microphone, especially when it is mounted on its own prosthetic support, the microphone stand. But the phallic aspect of the masturbatory relation may be less important, or at least less interesting, than its manual aspect. The grippings, bendings, brandishings, and more violent repertoire of "tactations" effected upon the microphone seem to enact the determination that the production of sound should be not so much highly and spectacularly visible as visibly tangible, a plastic work of hands and mouth combined, an exteriorization of the minor agon of sound production in the mouth.

Hard and Soft

The mouth presents a particularly complex and fascinating tactual landscape in terms of the different shapes and textures that cooperate to produce sound. The role of the teeth in the mouth is particularly striking. Teeth seem alien elements within the mouth, their hardness and impersonality making them seem older, stranger, and less truly of oneself than the fleshier, more elastic, and more sensitive portions of the mouth, especially the mouth's most mobile element, the tongue, which is so continuously at risk from the teeth's harsh inattention. The teeth are the hard in the soft. They are the fundamental means of transforming the not-self into the self. Language is born, not with the accession to the symbolic order, but with the growth of the teeth. Adult words, as opposed to the toddler's shrieking, lisping, and gurgling, can be perfectly formed in one's mouth only when there are teeth to capture them and chop them up.

Ventriloquism dramatizes the contrast between the hard and the soft mouth. Most ventriloquial figures have not been soft but hard. The woodenness of dummies has often been associated with their unfeelingness, their violence. The contemporary ventriloquial performer David Strassman is like many in having both a hard and a soft, a nice and a nasty character—his Chuck Wood is violent, demonic, grotesque, and unnaturally precocious, while his Huggy Bear is cozy and furry (and subject, we are led to believe, to violent mistreatment by his wooden sibling). Strassman manufactures a familiar sassy voice full of strident attack for Chuck Wood and a dopey, dozy, rural voice for Huggy Bear. Edgar Bergen similarly played the hard and the soft voice out into a distinction between the streetwise city kid Charlie MacCarthy and the sluggishly rustic Mortimer Snerd. We may think of the distinction between these two characters in terms of Bacon's distinction, quoted earlier, between the cut, or articulated, voice and that insufficiently voiced voice that is a mere contusion of air in the mouth. There is a sexual dimension, too: the hardened voice spits itself out, whereas the soft voice chews its own cud in autoerotic fashion. We commonly refer to "articulate speech," but it is never quite clear whether our emphasis is on the idea of breaking up or on the idea of joining together what has been broken up.

Recurring through all of these contrasts between the hard, hyper-articulated voice and the soft mumblings of the imperfectly delivered voice is the antagonism of teeth and soft tissue in the mouth. The teeth are not involved in the production of all consonants, but the stopping or blocking of the breath always seems to involve the hardness that is the quality of the teeth. Hence the links, on which I attempted to enlarge in the final chapter of my *Dumbstruck*, between ventriloquism and anatomy, mutilation and surgery. (The dentist's chair was a popular ventriloquial setting in the nineteenth century.) Ventriloquism is always more than a touching: it is a tearing, a cutting, a severing.

Ventriloquism acts out in advance some of the violent imaginary assaults upon the idea of continuous bodily shape that are characteristic of cinema. Douglas Kahn (1999: 150) has suggested that sound accompanies and redoubles the stretching of the body that is characteristic of Disney cartoons, the quality of "plasmation" that struck Eisenstein. The function of sound in cinema, he says, is not to highlight or punctuate or distinguish but to blend, associate, and transform, seeming to heal the violence involved in editorial cutting. "Sound stretching across the cut drew from the same elastic force that worked on bodies. In terms of cinematic montage, sound did not resemble a suture, which as a figure is too inscriptive; it resembled a gum or a glue, an adhesion that could stretch" (Kahn 1999: 150).

Cartoons reveal by exaggeration the sonoro-tactile pathos of cinema. Cinema is driven, not by lip-synched dialogue, but by certain violent sound tactations, six grades of which may be distinguished: the kiss, the punch, the cut, the shot, the crash, and the explosion. Contemporary cinema, especially action cinema, is conspicuously full of Deleuze's sound images, images that have been, so to speak, molded or penetrated by sound; imagings of violent sound agitating, blasting holes in, bursting out of the ideal, embattled "dream-screen" (Lewin 1946). I have elsewhere (Connor 2000a) described the "mutative commixture of substance" of which so much cinema sound seems to consist. But the very tactility that cinema promises, the ecstatic collapse of projective seeing into loud, blinded touch preserves that reference to the skin (the sounding tympanum) even as it dissolves the film—the *pellicule*, as it is in French—that is the support of sight.

Perhaps the many mediations and magnifications of sound in contemporary culture are an assault on shape, on the possibility that stimuli might be held or articulable in some coherent bodily volume or body image. But sound always seems to carry touch with it, perhaps more than ever in our era of "disembodying"—the preservative touching within the evaporations of shape and substance. As such, touch will also always preserve the something-to-be-touched: the skin of the world, the skin that joins us to the world.

If our culture of sound technology is one of cut and paste, then indeed it may be sound that provides the paste, the emulsification, that can join together what those same technologies of sound capture have parted. I have pointed to the close analogy in human experience between manuality and orality—the purpose of our hands being after all in our beginnings to grasp and convey to our mouths objects of our hunger and curiosity. But there is a closer analogy still. Acting as this imaginary paste or rubbery adhesive, sound not only exudes a universal imaginary skin but also seems to refer the actions of manipulation— the drawing out and distortion of bodily forms by the hands and fingers of the artist and the editor—to actions of mastication: the ideal joining of substances in the baby's mouth, which corresponds to the joining of skins at the breast. The play of teeth and soft tissue in the mouth reenacts the primal divisions and amalgamations of sound in the animated cinema or in the practice of montage, the teeth tearing and morselizing, the tongue rolling and folding and blending. (All of this implicates the remaining two senses, taste and smell. Speech is an idealized form of self-consumption, self-tasting. Speech is a way of consuming your own mouth without annihilating it, tasting your own mouth without swallowing it. Speaking eats itself, is a way for you to eat yourself.)

Like fingernails and toenails and hair, teeth seem to have no sensation. And yet, unlike those other forms of tissue, we can and do feel through our teeth. We feel our teeth and feel through them because we can hear with them. Hearing is the mode of tactility of our teeth, the way in which teeth feel. For most of us, the pain of the dentist's chair is inseparable from its characteristically concentrated and amplified sounds. The unpleasant sensation caused in many people by the sound of fingernails drawn across a blackboard—even just the thought of this sound—is described as "setting one's teeth on edge." In this sensation, one hears the sound of the fingernails through one's teeth, establishing a close, enactive analogy between teeth and fingernails. This sensation is not wholly localized in the mouth but also involves the prickling or raising of the skin. Perhaps it also involves the subtle cooperation of hair with teeth. For just as teeth convert sound into sensation by transmitting and amplifying it, so hair also transmits and amplifies sensation, especially delicate sensations such as the movement of air or breath. I do not know whether the hair has ever been shown to play any role in the transmission of sound to the skin, but the cat's-whisker radio-receiver is one enactment of this imaginary sense of the hair as the receiver and magnifier of sound sensation.

As the mediators between the skull and the mouth, the teeth play a large part in effecting that "hearing oneself speak" or short-circuiting of speaking and hearing that Jacques Derrida (1997) said was essential to notions of identity in the West. This short-circuiting, which seems to allow for a contact between the mouth and the ear that is faster and more direct than that delivered by the airborne sound of the voice, also makes for the dream of the mouth itself as a kind of ear. Teeth have long been implicated in the idea of the mouth as a receiver as well as an emitter of sound—for example, in the many stories of radio signals picked up by the fillings in people's teeth, stories that we may read as the reclaiming or rehabituating of what Douglas Kahn has called the "deboned" voices of modern sound technology (Kahn 1999: 7).

Teeth seem to be involved in the transition from the touched sound of a prerecording era to the untouched sound of a postrecording era. This is because teeth represent an alternative route into the ear or even a way of short-circuiting the ear. It is said that the deaf Beethoven gripped a stick between his teeth to convey the sounds of the piano to him. Similarly, Thomas Edison would chomp on the wood of a gramophone in order to hear faint overtones that, as he claimed in a 1913 interview, were normally lost before they reached the inner ear: "The sound-waves thus came almost directly to my brain. They pass through only my inner ear. I have a wonderfully sensitive inner ear . . . [that] has been protected from the millions of noises that dim the hearing of ears that hear everything. . . . No one who has a normal ear can hear as well as I can" ("Edison's Dream" 1913: 798). Edison's other method of monitoring sound was to inspect the grooves incised by the actively listening tooth of the stylus: he was particularly alert to the visual distortions of line produced by the tremolo effects he so disliked (Israel 1998: 437). The use of teeth represents a markedly active way of taking in sound: a listening that is also a kind of aggressive consuming. One of the most remarkable of the sensory conversion machines produced in the wake of the telephone and the phonograph was Edison's "phonomotor," which turned sound impulses into rotary motion; Edison hoped to be able to make his machine powerful enough to bore through wood (Israel 1998: 152).

These applications of teeth may be seen both as a primal resort to the medium of touch—the earliest, because the most proximate, medium of sensory contact, in which hearing is possible only at the cost of speech—and as a rewiring of the body's hearing-speaking circuitry that anticipates or mimics some of the mechanisms of modern sound production. Beethoven's stick is a stylus; Edison's teeth are in part an aerial. Beethoven's stick, along with hearing trumpets and other devices for channeling and amplifying sound, are reversible speaking ears: they gather and concentrate sound in order to broadcast it inward into the body. Nowadays, hearing aids—Edison called his versions "autophones"—work with electronic versions of this acoustic structure. The very minerality of the teeth, that which makes them seem inorganic and archaic, strangers in the most intimate parts of ourselves, also renders them sensitive to the most rarefied auditory signals, receiving and amplifying vibrations. By bypassing the outer ear, the teeth highlight the role of the ear as a transmitting station in something of the way that Michel Serres evokes when describing the involuted structure of the ear, which transforms the "hardness" of exterior sounds into the "softness" of information or meaning:

In this new trap, the hard is made soft: the box defends itself against unfamiliar assaults, deaf to all that exceeds its powers; the membrane of the tympanum presents a skin surface to the outside and a membrane of mucous to the inside, the skin harder and the mucous softer, separated in the milieu of the membrane by a more resistant armature; the acoustic wave emanating from a shock changes into a chemical signal carrying the information electrically towards the centre. . . . What centre? Does this box receive or transmit? To hear means to vibrate, but vibrating means emitting. Unfold the cochlea, for example, and an inverted piano appears, on which high and low are inscribed from left to right. But a piano sounds, it does not hear. The reasoning continues: The ear needs a more central ear in order to hear what is transmitted by the three ears, the external, the median and the internal, which are heard in succession. The centre hears. What centre? (Serres 1999: 182–183)

Serres imagines the senses as part of a cluster or network of black boxes, each synthesizing a noisy, "hard" input and yielding it up as a "soft," or informational, output. But the senses do not merely move in this direction. The softening of sensation into information—what Serres calls the progressive *ad-diction* of the body to language—may be accompanied by knottings or clusterings of the hard in the soft as information is returned to sensation in the mode of pathos, the mode of collision, the mode of the "mixed body." It is hearing, its organ a magical transformer of hard skin into the soft touch of sensation, that preserves the complex, unintegrated language of the senses, the way in which we are spoken to by the world in which we participate.

Serres's use of sound and hearing to provide an image of a labyrinthine delay in the entropic conversion of hard into soft is anticipated by Roland Barthes's (1991) arguments about the immanence of the body in music, song, and certain modes of speech. Barthes connects the apprehension of the "grain of the voice" in music with a new kind of listening that he believes is coming into being. Primary listening involves "listening out"—for signs of danger. In a second stage, listening is becoming a forensic or hermeneutic sense, a way of detecting unseen secrets. Like Serres, Barthes centers on the image of the ear, the "folds and detours" of which appear to prolong the contact between the individual and the world while in fact acting to reduce and synthesize. The ear "receives the greatest possible number of impressions and channels them toward a supervising center of selection and decision. . . . [I]t is essential . . . that what was confused and undifferentiated becomes distinct and pertinent" (Barthes 1991: 248).

The third stage of listening, into which Barthes hopes we are now entering, is instanced both in the everyday use of the telephone and in the alert openness of psychoanalytic listening. Barthes says the telephone is an instrument that "has abolished all senses except that of hearing," but straightaway he contradicts himself in his characterization of its effects and capacities: "the order of listening which any telephonic communication inaugurates invites the other to collect his whole body in his voice and announces that I am collecting all of myself in my ear" (1991: 252). In telephonic listening, the body is not abolished into meaning but collected and preserved in the soft touch within the act of communication. The telephone leads, via an approving appropriation of Freud's own appropriation of it as a model of psychoanalytic listening, to Barthes's evocation of a new mode of open and intersubjective listening that is at once a foretaste of a new sensory dispensation and a return "at another loop of the historical spiral, to the conception of a panic listening, as the Greeks, or at least as the Dionysians, had conceived it" (1991: 258). Although Barthes is often attentive to the pathos of sound—its buffeting or lacerating force—it is the soft, plasmatic body that dominates in this new, dialogic listening, in which hearing and speaking peacefully, erotically alternate.

This phantasmatic soft body, held in suspension in the synaesthesic coilings of the ear, between the inside and the outside, the self and the other, the dominative distance of the eye and the immersive melding of substance in taste and smell, governs much of the return to hearing of which we are currently hearing. One way of interpreting the pressure of touch in contemporary hearing is as a restoration of this equilibrium in the face of the extreme disembodiment of hearing, a reclaiming of the proximal tactility of the here-and-now body. But it would be better for us not to think in terms of such relations of simple equilibrium (while noting that equilibrium is a tactual metaphor in itself—for in what scale might one weigh hearing and sight?). The more apparently distanced, disembodied, or deboned a sound might seem to be, the more substantial, the more bodily our relations find a way of becoming.

We will err if we try to use the history of the senses as a way of softening the rigor mortis of a social body that we imagine has gone deaf and dumb, blind and numb. If there seems to be plentiful evidence of a demand to "feel the noise," for sonoro-tactile pathos, this need not be taken as evidence of a deficit to be made good in the social body. Sound and hearing are not the coil of parchment that will bring the social Golem back to breathing, responsive life. We should give up thinking of a culture or collectivity as a kind of super-body, a scaled-up sensorium, and give up thinking of a history of the senses as a way to restore to us the soft, lived body of a culture. There is no such sensorial church, no summary social body that could feel these quantities of plenitude or need. The body of a culture is, in Serres's phrase, a mixed body. It is neither hard nor soft, though it is made up of intricate passages between them. It is not an orchestra but the shimmering body of a multitude; it has the kind of mobile, diffuse intactness possessed by a swarm, or shoal, or horde, or cloud. We cannot bring it any more, or less, to life than it already is.

Thinking about Sound, and Distance in Western Ex The Case of Odysseus's Wa

Michael Bull

The individual is constantly here and elsewhere; alone and linked to others. . . . the twentieth century stroller with a Walkman or cellular phone remains alone, communicating not with passers-by but to those to whom he or she is connected.

Patrice Flichy, *Dynamics of Modern Communication*

Bishop Berkeley, in commenting that "sounds are as close to us as our thoughts" (quoted in Rée 1999: 36), recognized the spatial nature of sound and experience, an observation that has subsequently been buried within a largely visually inspired epistemology of experience that informs much of contemporary social scientific investigation. In this chapter I discuss the absence of sound in contemporary accounts of media consumption and the social science disciplines' consequent failure to understand the complexity of proximity, distance, and mobility in forms of media consumption. I then offer an alternative, "historically" informed analysis of sound experience by looking at three iconic moments of sound consumption in Western culture: the meeting between Odysseus and the Sirens as described by Max Horkheimer and Theodor W. Adorno in *The Dialectic of Enlightenment* (1973) and early-twentieth-century accounts of the use of the radio and phonograph, drawn from the work of Sigfried Kracauer and Michael Taussig, respectively. One example is situated in the mythic prehistory of Western culture, the other two in its "heroic" period of mechanical reproduction.

...amples to point to what an analytical framework for ...anding contemporary states of aural proximity and distance ...ight look like. In doing so, I argue that the use of sound technologies can be understood as part of the Western project of the appropriation and control of space, place, and the "other." In particular, I focus on the specific relational qualities attached to sound through which subjects relate to their surroundings, others, and themselves, especially the central role that aestheticization plays as a strategy of control over place and space. The context for this argument is an analysis of that most mobile and privatized of media artifacts: the portable radio or cassette player popularly known by the name Walkman.

Reevaluating Proximity and Distance in Media Consumption from a Sound Perspective

The structuring role of the media in daily experience has long been recognized (Livingstone 2002; Lull 1990; Silverstone 1999). Yet social scientists have largely ignored the contribution of sound, as distinct from the role of vision, in the daily consumption of media, just as they have largely ignored the increasingly mobile and predominantly sound-oriented nature of much media consumption (DeNora 2000; McCarthy 2001; Urry 2000). The analysis of sound experience presented here permits me to cast fresh light on the historical antecedents underpinning the experience and desire for proximity and distance in much of contemporary urban life.

The exclusion of the aural in media accounts of the experience of proximity and distance has led many media sociologists to neglect or misinterpret the historically situated meanings attached to these terms. A well-known and significant example of this failure is Raymond Williams's understanding and use of the term "mobile privatization" to describe the act of television viewing more than twenty-five years ago (Williams 2003 [1977]). In effect, Williams observed that, increasingly, "experience" was no longer located primarily in public spaces such as the street but rather in domestic spaces; the living room was to become the modern emporium of visual and auditory delight for the contemporary Western urban citizen. Williams thought mobile privatization was a largely unproblematic phenomenon: "It is not living in a cut off way, not in a shell that is just stuck. It is a shell you can take with you, which you can fly to places that previous generations could never imagine visiting" (Williams 2003 [1977]: 171). By watching television, urban citizens were to experience on screen, through acts

of privatized consumption, events that took place beyond the screen.
Dwelling places were to be filled with the mediated public world of
sounds and images of the television and radio.

Underlying Williams's observation was the normative expectation
that experience and aesthetics were indissolubly linked. This expectation has been perpetuated in the work of a wide range of cultural
theorists who invariably view the aestheticization of everyday life as
normatively neutral (Baudrillard 1993; Bauman 1993; Debord 1994;
Denzin 1995; Friedberg 1993). Unrecognized in Williams's formulation
is not only its "romantic" depiction of the experiencing subject but also
the unreflective appropriation of all that stands before the subject.
Williams's concept of mobile privatization is firmly rooted in the
Enlightenment project of the domination of space, place, and the other.

Mobile privatization has subsequently become a significant concept
in the analysis of media consumption:

> It is necessary for us to ask about the ways in which technology serves
> to "mediate" between private and public worlds—connecting domestic
> spaces with spheres of information and entertainment that stretch well
> beyond the confines of family and locality. Communication technologies
> have, I will argue, played an important part in the symbolic construction
> of "home"—whilst simultaneously providing household members with
> an opportunity to "travel" elsewhere, and to imagine themselves as
> members of wider cultural communities at a national and transnational
> level. . . . The multiple ownership of television sets allows household
> members to make independent journeys to distant locations and locate
> themselves within different collectivities. (Moores 1993: 22–23)

While this perspective might well be perceived as symptomatic of the
emptying out of urban public experience into fantasies of privatized
empowerment, it also poses a question about the relationship between
communication technologies, experience, and space. In doing so,
however, it fails to adequately address the nature and meaning of
mediated interaction. What, indeed, is meant by "distant locations,"
"independent journeys," and "different collectivities"? The subject who
"looks out" through the television screen remains as opaque as the
ambiguity of experiencing "the world" aesthetically through the
mediated messages of the culture industry.

Whereas notions of media-generated "distance" remain to be adequately explained, the meanings attached to "proximity" have recently
been recognized, if not the specifically "sound" nature of that proximity.

Robert Putnam has commented upon the "false sense" of companionship and intimacy created through the use of television (Putnam 2000: 242). This observation mirrors the much earlier work of Adorno, who was one of the few sociologists to recognize the significance of mediated sound in the ecology of urban life. It is no accident that much of Adorno's work concentrated on the auditory nature of urban experience, and it is there that we find an initial analysis of proximity in a mediated and increasingly media-saturated world.

Adorno argued that the consumption of mechanically reproduced music was increasingly used as an effective substitute for community, which was often lacking in capitalist cultures. It achieved this effect by producing states of "we-ness" or "accompanied solitude" among twentieth-century consumers. "We-ness" refers to the substitution of direct experience by technologically mediated forms of experience. The consumption of music integrates and permits the subject to transcend the social precisely by integrating him or her more fully into the everyday:

> The feebler the subjects' own sense of living, the stronger the happy illusion of attending what they tell themselves is other people's life. The din and to-do of entertainment music feigns exceptional gala states; the "we" that is set in all polyphonous music as the a priori of its meaning, the collective objectivity of the thing itself, turns into customer bait. . . . Thus the jukebox in an empty pub will blare in order to lure "suckers" with the false pretence of revelry in progress. . . . Music as a social function is akin to the rip off, a fraudulent promise of happiness which instead of happiness, installs itself. (Adorno 1974: 45)

The experience of the social is thus transformed through the subjects' colonizing of "representational space," enacted through the consumption of forms of aural communication technologies. Adorno, writing well before mobile sound technologies came into use, was nevertheless sensitive to the transformative role of reproduced sound in the potentially mobile spaces of consumer culture: "Loudspeakers installed in the smallest night clubs to amplify the sound until it becomes literally unbearable: everything is to sound like the radio" (Adorno 1991 [1928]: 58). Adorno never succumbed to the temptation to split off spheres of experience in his analysis of Western consumer culture; for him the experiences of the street and the spaces of the home were always intimately linked. His work on media technologies reflected upon the role these communication technologies played in the experience of increasingly mediated spaces of urban everyday life. For Adorno, the Western consumer desired "connection" in an increasingly privatized world. Sound provided this connection more readily than any other medium.

Recent work on media consumption demonstrates how solitary domestic consumption often appears to fuel feelings of omnipotence within realms of dependency (Bull 2000; Livingstone 2002). Equally, domestic use of the media teaches consumers how to "fill in" the spaces and times between activities as they become increasingly accustomed to the mediated presence of the media in their own private settings. Forms of "accompanied solitude" thus become increasingly habitual.

Ironically, as Williams was developing his "stay-at-home" epistemology, more consumers were spending increasing amounts of time "on the move" (Putnam 2000). Over the past forty years, Western consumers have been provided with a wide range of communication technologies that enable them to transform both the experience of movement and the spaces they move through. These technologies of "movement" are largely aural—the cassette player in the automobile, the personal stereo, and now the mobile phone (Bull 2001; Katz and Aakhus 2002). Much movement through the city is solitary, between destinations and meetings. This is a more literal form of mobile privatization in which sole occupancy is often the preferred mode of travel in automobiles (Brodsky 2002), while personal stereo use is by its very nature privatizing.

These technologies of accompanied solitude appear successfully to deliver a desirable and intoxicating mixture of noise, proximity, and privacy for users on the move. They inform us about how users attempt to "inhabit" the spaces of the city they move through. Mobile privatization is about the desire for proximity, for a mediated presence that shrinks space into something manageable and habitable. Sound, more than any other sense, appears to perform a largely utopian function in this desire for proximity and connectedness. Mediated sound reproduction enables consumers to create intimate, manageable, and aestheticized spaces in which they are increasingly able to, and desire to, live. As consumers increasingly inhabit media-saturated spaces of intimacy, so they increasingly desire to make the public spaces passed through mimic their desires. The meaning and nature of these desires have cultural prehistories that are, as yet, inadequately charted.

Sound, Distance, and Proximity, Historically Speaking

In a well-known passage in *The Dialectic of Enlightenment*, Horkheimer and Adorno analyze a section of Homer's *Odyssey* in which Odysseus pits his wits against the Sirens, whose song evokes "the recent past, with the irresistible promise of pleasure as which their song is heard. . . . Even though the Sirens know all that has happened, they demand the future as the price of that knowledge" (Horkheimer and Adorno 1973: 33). All who hear the song inevitably perish. Odysseus's aim is to outwit the Sirens by having himself tied to the mast of his ship, thereby enabling him to listen to the enticements of the Sirens' song without being destroyed on the rocks like all others before him. In order for his strategy to succeed, he orders his oarsmen to block their ears with wax, rendering themselves deaf. The oarsmen become unable to hear either the Sirens' song or Odysseus's increasingly desperate orders to steer the ship onto the rocks. Horkheimer and Adorno correctly identify Odysseus's desire for pleasure as being sublimated into aesthetic experience; he can hear the Sirens' song but can do nothing about it. However, they gloss over the specific auditory nature of the experience. It is precisely the aural configuration of the experience, especially Odysseus's confrontation with the Sirens, that I wish to investigate here in terms of the seduction of sound and its relation to the space that Odysseus and the Sirens inhabited.

The auditory nature of their meeting means that for Odysseus to experience the Siren's song and thereby gain knowledge of "all that can be known," he merely needs to hear their song. It is not the seeing or touching of the Sirens that motivates Odysseus but the hearing of their song; it literally enters him. As he listens, tied safely to the mast, the song transforms the distance between his ship and the rocks from which the Sirens sing. Their song colonizes him, and yet he uses the experience to fulfill his desire for knowledge. In doing so, Odysseus becomes a rational and successful shopper of experience. Aesthetic reflection is a price worth paying for gaining the seductive experience of song.

Although Horkheimer and Adorno point out that Odysseus's ability to experience the Sirens' song is purchased at the expense of the sailors' lack of this experience, and that Odysseus's aestheticization of the world is predicated upon the absence of the auditory for the oarsmen, they concentrate on the "social class" element of the experience to the exclusion of the sound and spatial elements. Yet what Odysseus desires, the sound of the Sirens' song, originates beyond him. It is the Sirens who construct Odysseus's soundscape.[1] Yet Odysseus intervenes in the nature of this soundscape by having the oarsmen's ears blocked with wax. The soundscape now encompasses only Odysseus and the Sirens; it exists only between him and them. Socially speaking, Odysseus is in his very own soundworld. This passage from Homer is significant, in part, because it is the first description of the privatization of experience through sound.

Odysseus is also a traveler who makes himself through his journey. He outwits the Sirens and in doing so furthers his self-development. He becomes an early "tourist" of experience (Todorov 1993), in search of aestheticized experience. Unlike the contemporary consumer seduced by sound, Odysseus has to experience the Sirens' song only once; he does not need to replay it. The Sirens form an aesthetic presence in his biography, representing in part the draw of the exotic and the forbidden as encountered in his travels and mastered through his intellect.

Horkheimer and Adorno describe sound before the dawn of mechanical reproduction, before its commodification and routinization. With the rise of mechanical reproduction, the exotic appears to come home in the space where it, the magical, and technology meet. After Thomas Edison sang "Mary had a little lamb" into the first phonogram in 1877, he exclaimed in delight and fascination upon hearing his own voice played back to him, as if by magic. The magical and the scientific became blurred in the transformation of experience that was often pursued by both inventors and users of the new communication technologies of the voice at the beginning of the twentieth century. Leigh Schmidt has described the "psychophone" created and used by Spiritualists in the early 1920s to hear "supernatural voices," and he notes that the telephone became a technology "of the disembodied voice . . . turned from exposing the illusions of supernatural voices to providing acoustic proof of them" (Schmidt 2000: 241). Many early accounts of aural reception remark on the "magical" quality of the experience of hearing the recorded voice, before this experience became routinized through the steady incorporation of reproduced sound into domestic and public spaces.[2]

It appears that technologies of sound and their use disclose something about both the user and the culture from which they come. For example, Michael Taussig (1993) described the early use of the phonograph among explorers, who often took gramophones with them into the colonial spaces they were to study and exploit. Their aim, he argued, was to display the scientific magic of the West to the rest, to record the exotic and to play records to themselves. In his analysis, the gramophone already has an element of routinization attached to its consumption.[3] The sometimes obsessive nature of this activity is captured in

Werner Herzog's delirious effort in his film *Fitzcarraldo*, set in the early twentieth-century Upper Amazonian rubber boom and constructed around the fetish of the phonograph, so tenaciously, so awkwardly, clutched by Fitzcarraldo, the visionary, its great earhorn emerging from under the armpit of his dirty white shirt, Caruso flooding the forests and rivers, the Indians amazed as Old Europe rains its ecstatic art form upon them. Bellowing opera from the ship's prow, it is the great ear-trumpet of the phonograph. (Taussig 1993: 203)

Taussig's description differs considerably from that of the use and reception of sound found in Horkheimer and Adorno's account of Odysseus and the Sirens. On display in Taussig's account is the magic of Western technology and sound. Fitzcarraldo takes his own Western soundworld with him, and it is this soundworld that re-creates the Amazon jungle for him, making it what it is. The jungle becomes aestheticized as a function of Fitzcarraldo's imagination, mediated through the sounds of Caruso voice. The presence of "Caruso" in the jungle is maintained only through continuous sound, through the repeat. For Fitzcarraldo, the aesthetic impulse is both literal and dependent upon the sound of Caruso's voice, unlike the case for Odysseus, whose experience of the Sirens travels with him, internalized and sublimated. In contrast, Fitzcarraldo needs the voice of Caruso to maintain his image of the jungle and his place in it. Compare Fitzcarraldo's use of sound with the soundworld of an indigenous population of a rainforest to discover the seductive similarity and dissimilarity of non-Western appropriations of sound:

> [Turnbull] elaborates on how Mbuti imagination and practice construct the forest as both benevolent and powerful, capable of giving strength and affection to its "children." For this to happen Mbuti must attract the attention of the forest, must soothe it with the strength of sound that is fully articulated in the achievement of song. The sound "awakens" the forest . . . thus attracting the forest's attention to the immediate needs of its children. It is also of the essential nature of all songs that they should be "pleasing to the forest." (Feld 2000: 255)

Colin Turnbull, like Steven Feld in his analysis of the Kaluli of Papua New Guinea (Feld 1990), points to the symmetrical nature of the soundworld of the inhabitants of the rainforest, whereas Odysseus and Fitzcarraldo are both "colonizers" of space and experience. Just as sound colonizes them, so they use sound to re-create in their image the spaces they inhabit. Their experiences take place in the grand and heroic vistas of a world "tamed" through their aestheticization of it. This stands in contrast to Kracauer's description of early radio use in the domestic spaces of Berlin in the 1920s:

> Who could resist the invitation of those dainty headphones? They gleam in living rooms and entwine themselves around heads all by themselves; and instead of fostering cultivated conversation (which certainly can become a bore), one becomes a playground for Eiffel noises that, regardless of their potentially active boredom, do not even grant one's modest right to personal boredom. Silent and lifeless, people sit side by side as if their souls were wandering about far away. But these souls are not wandering according to their own preferences; the news hounds badger them, and soon no one can tell who is the hunter and who is the hunted. (Kracauer 1995: 333)

Kracauer's radio users transcend geographical space; listening takes them away from the mundanity of their domestic place. Radio sounds transform the immobile space of domestic habitation as users no longer commune with those next to them but with the "distant" voices transmitted though the ether. The radio enables them to prioritize their desires. Just as Odysseus prioritizes his desires over those of the oarsmen, so the privatization of aesthetic desire of Kracauer's radio user has social consequences. The radio listeners privatize their already "private" space of experience. Who, indeed, can compete with the "Eiffel" noises of the radio as the inhabitants of this privatized space sit "silent and lifeless" next to one another? The technology of the radio is used to prioritize the experience of the listener, who is taken far away into the aestheticized space of the "Eiffel" noises. Kracauer accurately identifies the reconfiguring of space in which the power relationship between the consumer of sound and the producer remains ambiguous. Yet what remains clear is the enticement of the radio sounds for the user, who is transported out of his domestic boredom into the magical realm of communion with the "faraway" and enticing sounds of the radio.

These brief examples suggest a framework within which to situate the role that sound may play in the contemporary geography of Western urban culture. They indicate a powerful motivation to use sound to reorganize users' relation to space and place.[4] In each case, sound colonizes the listener but is used to actively re-create and reconfigure the spaces of experience. Odysseus, Fitzcarraldo, and Kracauer's radio listeners all repossess their spaces of habitation in order to make them conform to their desires. Through the power of sound, the world becomes intimate, known, and possessed. These examples highlight the powerfully seductive role of sound, which appears to root the user in the world with a force that differs from those of the other senses (Simmel 1997; Welsch 1997). In demonstrating the role sound can play in reconfiguring the relational qualities of experience, the examples also point to a specific Western mode of appropriation and transformation of experience through the manipulation of sound. The manner in which Odysseus, Fitzcarraldo, and our radio users inhabit social spaces calls attention to a specifically Western narrative about the cognitive, aesthetic, and moral makeup of social space as experienced through sound.

The Aesthetic Nature of Mobile Aural Solipsism: Odysseus's Walkman

Odysseus and Fitzcarraldo aestheticize their world and in the process make themselves through their travels. Odysseus's success is dependent upon both the Sirens and his own guile, whereas Fitzcarraldo relies on the technology of the phonograph and the voice of Caruso. In contrast to Odysseus and Fitzcarraldo, Kracauer's radio listeners are immobile—the world comes to them through the radio and transforms their domestic and mundane world from within. In all three examples, time and space become aestheticized.

In contemporary consumer culture, we no longer have to travel to the far away in order to aestheticize it. The communication technology that enables the drawing together of the threads of the previous examples is the Walkman, which enables contemporary urban users to create a seamless web of mediated and privatized experience in their everyday movement through the city and to enhance virtually any chosen experience in any geographical location.[5] Walkman sound is direct, with the earpieces placed directly in the ears of the user, overlying the random sounds of the environment. Walkman users can aestheticize both the mundane everyday of the city streets and the faraway spaces they visit with their Walkman sounds. Indeed, the everyday and the far away appear to become increasingly similar in the experience of many Walkman users.

Walkman users represent the amalgam of Odysseus, Fitzcarraldo, and Kracauer's radio listeners. They are often mobile, the Walkman becomes the wax in the ears, and the privatizing of space is enacted through continual use of mediated sound. Walkman users habitually take sound with them during those "in-between" times while traveling, often replaying the same track over and over in order to maintain their mood, rather like Fitzcarraldo, communing with the disembodied yet intimate sounds of the culture industry. This "colonization" of urban space is deeply social, yet the relational nature of any such aestheticization is often downplayed in urban and cultural studies:

> The beauty of "aesthetic control"—the unclouded beauty, beauty un-spoiled by the fear of danger, guilty conscience or apprehension of shame—is its inconsequentiality. This control will not intrude into the realities of the controlled. It will not limit their options. It puts the spectator into the director's chair—with the actors unaware of who is sitting there, of the chair itself, even of being potential objects of the director's attention. Aesthetic control, unlike any other, gruesome or sinister social control which it playfully emulates, allows to thrive the contingency of life which social spacing strove to confine or stifle. Inconsequentiality of aesthetic control is what makes its pleasures unclouded. . . . I make them [people] into whatever I wish. I am in charge; I invest their encounter with meaning. (Bauman 1993: 6)

Although Bauman captures the asymmetrical nature of aesthetic experience, the ramifications of this form of social asymmetry, when broadened into a mode of "being in the world," tend to be rendered harmless through a conceptual slippage concerning the aestheticization of daily experience as distinct from the viewing of a painting or the listening to a piece of music. Bauman, despite his interest in the nature of "moral" spaces of experience, fails to note this distinction. Axel Honneth (1995: 23) more accurately perceives the aesthetic as inversely proportional to the realization of a habitable social: "I think all concepts of the 'post-modern' have at least one affirmative feature in common, viz., to see in the process of the 'dissolution of the social' the chance for an expansion of aesthetic freedom for individuals."

Aesthetic colonization plays a significant role in people's daily use of Walkmans. Walkmans are used both as mundane accompaniments to the everyday and as a way of aestheticizing and controlling that very experience. Their use greatly expands the possibilities for users to aesthetically re-create their daily experience. Walkman users construct their own privatized and intimate spaces of reception. They move in their own soundworlds, like Odysseus and Fitzcarraldo, and they, too, can achieve the illusion of omnipotence through proximity and "connectedness." As one man I interviewed, Magnus, said of his Walkman use: "It enables me to sort of bring my own dreamworld. Because I have familiar sounds with my music that I know and sort of cut out people around me. So the music is familiar. There's nothing new happening. I can go into my perfect dreamworld where everything is as I want."

Walkman use reorganizes users' relations to space and place. Sound colonizes the listener but is also used to actively re-create and reconfigure the spaces of experience. Through the power of sound the world becomes intimate, known, and possessed. Sound enables users to manage and orchestrate their spaces of habitation in a manner that conforms to their desires. Walkman users construct their own privatized and intimate spaces of reception:

> It fills the space whilst you're walking. It also changes the atmosphere. If you listen to music you really like and you're feeling depressed, it can change the atmosphere around you. (Catherine)

> I think it creates a sense of kind of aura. Even though it's directly in your ears you feel it's all around your head. You're really aware it's just you. Only you can hear it. I'm really aware of my personal space. My own space anyway. I find it quite weird watching things that you normally associate certain sounds with. Like the sounds of walking up and down the stairs or tubes coming in and out, all of those things you hear. Like when you've got a Walkman on you don't hear any of those. You've got your own soundtrack. (Karin)

Walkman users also experience the world as a form of "we-ness" while on the move: "I don't necessarily feel that I'm there. Especially if I'm listening to the radio. I feel I'm there, where the radio is, because of the way, that is, he's talking to me and only me and no one else around me is listening to that. So I feel like, I know I'm really on the train, but I'm not really. . . . I like the fact that there's someone still there" (Mandy).

Yet Walkman users, in their colonization of space, are equally concerned with solipsistically transcending the urban. If indeed they aestheticize it, they do so, unlike the flaneurs of early-nineteenth-century Paris—by drawing it into themselves, making it conform to their wishes, in order to make it in their own image (Friedberg 1993; Jenks 1995). In this transformation of representational space, "personal space" is often defined in terms of a conceptual space. As geographical notions of personal space become harder to substantiate and negotiate in some urban environments, the construction of a privatized conceptual space becomes a common strategy for Walkman users: "Personal space. I think personal space is gone, in town anyway. Everyone's packed in. I think it's inverted. Because I think your personal space is inside, in the music. You can be in a crowd in town and everybody's crunching up. If you listen to the Walkman, it doesn't really matter that someone's pushing up behind you" (Paul).

In this aural solipsism, Walkman users often become indifferent to the presence of others: "When you've got your Walkman on, it's like a wall. Decoration. Surroundings. It's not anyone" (Ed). The simile of a wall aptly demonstrates the impenetrability of many users' states, or desired states, in relation to the geographical space of experience. Walkman users appear to achieve a subjective sense of public invisibility. They essentially disappear as interacting subjects, withdrawing into their chosen privatized and mobile states.

The world beyond their "Walkman sounds" becomes a function of the user's desire and is maintained through time, like Fitzcarraldo's world, through the act of listening. The world is brought into line, but only through a privatized yet mediated act of cognition. Users' sense of space is one in which the distinction between private mood or orientation and surroundings is often abolished. The world becomes one with the experience of the personal stereo user in a potentially perfect mimetic fantasy that denies the contingent nature of the user's relationship to the world beyond his or her chosen soundworld.

The Proximity of Sound Movement, Technologically Speaking

For Fitzcarraldo, his journey across the Amazon is both an adventure and a way in which he constructs his own narrative, to which the Amazon provides the backdrop. The music of Caruso, rather than giving him the desire to be elsewhere, makes the experience what it is. The Amazon and Fitzcarraldo's experience become one as he imposes himself on the space thus inhabited. Equally, Odysseus makes himself through the construction of his own private soundworld. These examples merely indicate a trajectory or moment in Western sound desire. The implications of this sound history have recently been commented upon by Philip Bohlman (2000: 188), who argues that "in order to invest itself with the power to control and maintain its external domination and its internal order, Europe has consistently employed music to imagine its selfness."

The sounds of Caruso enable Fitzcarraldo to exert order and control over himself. Odysseus, as we have seen, carries the internalized song of the Sirens within him as he travels, and Walkman users equally inhabit their own privatized spaces. They carry their culture with them in the form of mediated sounds wherever they go. Their response to the spaces they inhabit might be indifferent, aesthetic, or a strategy to exclude others:

> I have the warmth but I don't have all the crap around me. I can eliminate that and I can get much more out of what the ocean has to offer me. I can enjoy. I feel that listening to my music, I can really pull the sun's rays. Not being disturbed by screaming kids and all that shouting, which is not why I went there. I went to have harmony with the sea and sun. The plane journey, flying out and back, you listen to different music, but it just helps me to still my mind and to center myself, and I feel that by taking this tape with me I'm carrying that all day and I feel that I'm able to take more from the day and give more to the day. Whether that's right or wrong I don't know, but that's how I feel. (Jay)

The environment becomes reappropriated and experienced as part of the user's desire. By listening to "her" music, the listener gets more out of the environment, not by interacting with it, but precisely by not interacting with it. This indicates that Walkman use can make the environment "what it is" for users. The environment is received as a personal artifact via the Walkman. This is achieved by users' repossessing space as part of, or constitutive of, their desire and provides a clear example of the way Walkman users might colonize and appropriate the here-and-now as part of their "re-inscribing" of habitable space. They might be described as the privatized Fitzcarraldos of contemporary consumer culture or as sound consumers of a manufactured intimacy.

Walkman users increasingly live in a world of technologically mediated sounds and images in which states of "we-ness" are learned and embedded in communication consumption in the home and elsewhere through television, radio, and music reception. The intimacy of a world experienced through mediated and technologized sound becomes a taken-for-granted backdrop for Walkman users' daily experiences: "I can't go to sleep at night without my radio on. I'm one of those people. It's really strange. I find it very difficult. I don't like silence. I'm not that sort of person. I like hearing things around me. It's like hearing that there's a world going on sort of thing. I'm not a very alone person. I will always have something on. I don't mind being by myself as long as I have something on" (Mandy).

Walkman use creates both the experience of being "cocooned"—by separating the user from the world beyond—and, simultaneously, a different "space" whereby the user lives in the mediated space of the culture industry. Walkman users, rather like Kracauer's radio listeners, do not perceive themselves as being alone; theirs is an accompanied solitude. The mediated sounds of the culture industry transform the space of habitation for users. The "outside" world becomes a function of the desire of users and is maintained over time through continuous listening. The world is brought into line, but only through a privatized yet mediated act of cognition:

> Because when you have the Walkman it's like having company. You don't feel lonely. It's your own environment. It's like you're doing something pleasurable you can do by yourself and enjoy it. I think it creates a sense of kind of aura sort of like. Even though it's directly in your ears you feel like it's all around your head. You're really aware it's just you, only you can hear it. It makes you feel individual. Listening also constitutes "company." If there's the radio there's always somebody talking. There's always something happening. (Alice)

This sentiment is contrasted with the observation that nothing is happening if there is no musical accompaniment to experience. The aura that the user inhabits collapses. When the Walkman is switched off, accompanied solitude falls away, and the users' experience is diminished. Users need their Walkmans in everyday life, just as Fitzcarraldo needed the sounds of Caruso in the jungle to make and enhance its meaning for him.

Conclusion

Representational space becomes primarily an aural space for Walkman users. In the contemporary world of Walkman desire, like that of Kracauer's radio listeners, space is inhabited by the sounds of the culture industry coming directly into the users' ears. Like Odysseus's, their soundworld is constructed through the transmitting of sound from elsewhere. But in this instance, the Siren's voice is a domesticated and mechanically reproduced one. Unlike Odysseus, users suffer no penalties for listening. Equally, their own listening does not preclude others from listening. However, each listener, like Kracauer's radio user, must inhabit his or her own private and mediated soundworld. Contemporary Walkman users live in a more democratized consumer culture in which many are rather like Odysseus and fewer are "oarsmen." Walkman practices of aesthetic colonization appear to be both utopian—and hence transcendent in character—and located firmly in alienating and objectifying cultural predispositions that deny difference within culture (Sennett 1990). "The absence of encounters with different subjects is more restful, since it never puts our own identity into question" (Todorov 1993: 344). Equally for Adorno, according to Honneth (1993: 45), consumers "can stabilise their identity only through continual exclusion of all sense experience that threatens to impair the direct pursuit of the principle of control."

My brief analysis of Walkman users' construction of their aurally mediated experience suggests that users are both colonized and colonizing. They negate notions of difference in order to inhabit a transcendent and safe space of experience, a managed and controlled space that might be referred to as a sonorous envelope (Anzieu 1989). Sound and forms of "ontological security" appear to be closely related in the world of Walkman desires. If consumers are seeking ontological security through consumption, then the consumption of sound is highly successful in operationalizing this desire. States of "we-ness" are indeed states of ontological security.

Walkman users' sense of "being in the world" comes about through the re-inscription of the everyday through the technologies of the Walkman and reproduced sound. These strategies are neither merely emotional nor cognitive but both. Users are cognitively active in their construction of ontological security, which itself is the result of the construction of a virtual connection to, a "being-with," the products of the culture industry. Hence, Walkman users place great faith in the ability of their Walkmans actually to deliver what they want. Walkman use can produce a powerful sense of centeredness, of being in control, enabling users to manage their thoughts, emotions, and memories, together with their relationship to the world they inhabit. Just as Odysseus and Fitzcarraldo controlled their soundscapes, so the urban consumer might be seen, not so much as protecting the site of experience from others, but as creating, albeit ambiguously, a utopian space of habitation.

The fragility of this space is rendered more secure as the space becomes "occupied" by signifiers of an imaginary and reassuring presence in the form of chosen sound. The Sirens hold no fear for today's Walkman users, nor are users overtly concerned with impressing the "other" with the cultural status of the West, as Fitzcarraldo was. Today's Walkman user often experiences everyday life in a conceptual space somewhere between those of Odysseus and Fitzcarraldo. The sounds of "home" as experienced by Odysseus through knowledge become for Fitcarraldo the jungle re-inscribed through the voice of Caruso, whereas Walkman users habitually aestheticize their daily experience through sound in order to transcend their geographical space and manage their sense of presence in the world. Listening takes them away from the mundanity of their domestic place, their domestic thoughts and desires. The spaces of urban culture become both their jungle and a domesticated but effective siren song. It appears that as consumers become immersed in their mobile media sound bubbles, so those spaces habitually passed through in daily life increasingly lose significance and turn progressively into the "nonspaces" of daily life that users try, through those self-same technologies, to transcend. The need for proximity and for accompanied solitude expressed through the mediated sounds of the culture industry masks and furthers the trend of public isolation in the midst of privatized sound bubbles of a reconfigured representational space.

Notes

1. Murray Schafer, in *The Tuning of the World* (1977), used the term "soundscape" to describe the total experienced acoustic environment. This included all noises, musical, natural, and technological. Schafer, a composer by trade, was concerned to analyze the changing historical and cultural configuration of soundscapes, arguing that it was necessary to understand what effect the configuration of sounds in our environment has in shaping human behavior.

2. Kracauer (1995: 333) describes the transformation of space from individual to collective space through sound: "Even in the café, where one wants to roll up into a ball like a porcupine and become aware of one's insignificance, an imposing loudspeaker effaces every trace of private existence." For more on the history of the phonograph and its use and significance, see Gitelman 1999 and Kittler 1999.

3. Connor has recently commented on this routinization of technological innovations: "Although there were some who were intrigued and amazed by the new invention, in many ways, the contemporary reaction of the coming of the telephone seems to have been 'about time too.' The telephone had been in use only for months before users began wondering irritatedly why the sound

quality was so poor. . . . In periods like the late nineteenth century, and like our own, in which the technological imagination outruns technological development itself, new inventions have a way of seeming out of date, or used up, on their arrival, like a birthday present with which you have been secretly playing in advance" (Connor 2000b: 411). However, I wish to point to the attraction these routinized forms of consumption have in the successful management of experience.

4. Throughout this chapter, the reader will be aware that I use "music" and "sound" interchangeably. This is not to deny their distinctiveness. However, I wish to foreground the nature of sound's proximity to users and the power it gives them relationally, rather than discuss the distinctive role of music over the voice. For example, Kracauer's radio listeners are listening to the "voice," as are some of the Walkman users subsequently quoted.

5. The ethnographic material in this chapter comes from a study of Walkman users that I conducted between 1994 and 1996, to which I recently added in 2001. It consists primarily of in-depth, qualitative interviews with over one hundred personal stereo users living in and around London and, more recently, Cambridge and Brighton. The interviewees represented a cross section of users in terms of age, gender, ethnicity, and occupation. Walkman users proved to be particularly elusive subjects. By the very act of wearing a Walkman, they send out "do not disturb" messages. Younger users came from schools, colleges, and youth clubs. Others were contacted in their places of work through contacts and contacts of contacts. Perhaps the difficulty of contact is one explanation why, in the Open University text on the Sony Walkman (DuGay, Hall, and Mackay 1997), no attempt is made to interview Walkman users, despite a chapter's being given over to users' consumption practices. Here, I discuss Walkman practices through illustrative user accounts. For a fuller discussion of the methodology, see Bull 2000.

Wiring the World: Acoustical Engineers and the Empire of Sound in the Motion Picture Industry, 1927–1930

Emily Thompson

On 25 July 1930, the editors of the *New York Times* called attention to the fact that Americans were now "sound conscious" in a way they had never been before. The newspaper highlighted "the listening habit" as an important element of "modern life." The formation of this modern sound consciousness originated fifty years earlier, with the invention of the telephone and phonograph. Still, it was only at the close of the 1920s that auditors began to reflect self-consciously upon their new soundscape. A 1930 advertisement for Insulite Acoustile, a sound-absorbing building material, explained why this was so: "Especially since the advent of the 'talkies,'" the ad claimed, have people "become 'sound conscious.'" The technology of the talkies both culminated and celebrated the modern soundscape in ways that were impossible to ignore, for sound motion pictures gave voice, not just to the silent shadows on the silver screen, but to modernity itself (Branston 2000; Charney and Schwartz 1995; E. Thompson 2002).

This voice would ultimately reverberate around the world. Like the waves of sound broadcast from its loudspeakers, the new technology moved outward in all directions at once. From its technical origins circa 1926 in the American radio and telephone industries, the electro-acoustic machinery moved into the realm of motion picture production and exhibition, until, within a few years, virtually every studio and theater in the United States was wired for sound. The expanding wave

191

migrated far beyond its country of origin, and the expansion did not stop until a global empire of sound was constructed. From Fiji to Spain, rural New Zealand to the streets of Tokyo and Calcutta, the arrival of talkie technology was heralded with banners, signs, and parades.[1]

The American engineers who led those parades perceived themselves to be on a technological mission. Their goal was to get the world "in sync" with the modern United States, and they thought they could accomplish this through their synchronous sound technology. While the engineers deployed military and moral rhetorics of colonialism to understand their role in this ambitious enterprise, the models they drew upon were about to become outdated, for the proliferation of sound film technology proved to be a catalyst in moving the world away from earlier models of colonial imperialism and toward something that would become, by the close of the twentieth century, a tangled set of often contradictory relationships known today as globalism.

American engineers (as well as filmmakers) saw the worldwide expansion of sound film as a broadcast enterprise—one in which American technologies, commodities, and culture would disseminate throughout the world, standardize it, and thereby make it modern. Those at the receiving end of this broadcast, however, chose not simply to accept the machines and messages that were sent their way. Instead, they quickly learned to use the technology to talk back, and what they had to say was not necessarily what the American engineers expected to hear. Sound motion pictures provided a new forum in which nations, and colonies struggling to become nations, could transmit messages of their own. The messages they sent, while certainly influenced by what they had heard from the United States, simultaneously reflected the unique circumstances of each country and colony. Sound movies provided a powerful new means by which to articulate national agendas, and the end result was not a single, standardized and unified modern voice but a cacophony of competing signals and messages.

The essay that follows is a very preliminary exploration of this complicated and wide-ranging story. I am not primarily concerned with the actual sound of sound motion pictures (for more on this, see Crafton 1997; Lastra 2000; E. Thompson 2002); instead, I examine the cultural meaning of the new technology to those who deployed it. I open with a brief survey of the technological development of sound motion pictures and then consider the experiences of the engineers who wired America's theaters for sound. I close by sketching the global dimensions of this story and considering how the engineers' optimistic vision was defeated by a diversity of sounds.

A Brief History of the Development of Sound Motion Pictures

Thomas Edison's earliest ideas for moving pictures had been stimulated by his invention of the phonograph, and he intended from the start to synchronize his images with recorded sounds.[2] Turning this idea into a working technology proved difficult, however, and only after years of work, with considerable input from his assistant William Dickson and with the abandonment of synchronized sound, was Edison able to making his pictures move. In April 1894, the world's first Kinetoscope Parlor opened in a former shoe store in New York. Each peep-show device contained a twenty-second loop of film that customers viewed individually for a nickel a shot. Strongman Eugene Sandow flexed his muscles in one machine; in others appeared a barber shaving a bearded customer, the contortions of Madame Bartholdi, and a pair of fighting roosters. Edison's Kinetoscope was a tremendous success, and exhibitors were soon placing the machines in bars, amusement parks, and arcades across the nation. Rival devices also appeared, and the public developed a voracious appetite for moving images. A new industry was born as producers photographed virtually anything that moved to meet the seemingly incessant demand.

Within a year, however, the novelty had worn off. Edison attempted to reinvigorate the business by returning to his idea of pairing the picture with sound. With the Kinetophone, a customer peered through the standard viewfinder and listened to the sound of an accompanying phonograph through a set of ear tubes. No synchronization was attempted, the sound consisted of little more than background music, and the public, not surprisingly, failed to respond with enthusiasm to the new device. The nascent industry was nonetheless rejuvenated, not by sound, but by projection. Moving images projected onto a large screen and viewed in the company of others left a far greater impression upon an audience than did the tiny, individually experienced peep shows, and with projection, a new and permanent class of popular entertainment was established.

With projection, the challenge of providing synchronized sound became even greater. Now, there was not only the difficulty of maintaining synchronization between sound and image but also the problem of providing sound loud enough for everyone in a large theater to hear—a real challenge in an era in which the only source of recorded sound, the acoustical phonograph, was non-electric and non-amplified. Numerous inventors in Europe and North America confronted the dual challenges of synchronization and amplification, and a variety of sound motion picture systems appeared during the first two decades of the twentieth century. All suffered from a lack of sound volume and frequent loss of synchronization between sound and image, and none was commercially successful.

Edison himself tried one last time to marry his two inventions by tenuously linking a mechanically amplified, oversized phonograph to a projector via belts and pulleys. Although initially impressive, Edison's system ultimately proved as vulnerable as others to the loss of synchronization. At the Kinetophone's debut in February 1913, the audience was duly impressed, but subsequent screenings were far less successful. Synchronization came and went, the amplifier amplified the surface noise of the record as well as the voices recorded upon it, and within a month the Kinetophone had been branded a failure.

At this point, the motion picture industry basically gave up on the idea of synchronized sound. If Edison himself couldn't make the movies talk, who could? Besides, the public clamored for silent films; why change an already successful product? The impetus to continue experimenting now came, not from the industry itself, but from outsiders, electrical inventors and manufacturers who were not already benefiting from the success of silent films and who had not been discouraged by previous attempts to add sound to them. These men realized that vacuum-tube amplifiers and loudspeakers—innovations recently applied to the new electroacoustic technologies of long-distance telephony, radio, the electric phonograph, and public address systems—could also provide high-quality amplification of sound in a motion picture theater.

Even as Edison's Kinetophone was failing in 1913, the electrical inventor Lee de Forest, whose Audion vacuum tube was the basis for all forms of electroacoustic amplification, began experimenting with a means to record sound onto photographic film. The inventor Theodore Case improved upon de Forest's design and devised a method by which to reverse the process, thereby re-creating the sound that had originally been recorded on film. Case and de Forest ultimately created a system that provided synchronized and amplified sound, and the De Forest Phonofilm Corporation was formed in 1924, with Case as a partner. De Forest persuaded several dozen theater owners to install his equipment and to present the short sound films that Phonofilm produced. These films—typically musical numbers performed by vaudevillians—met with mixed reviews, but cranky critics were soon the least of the inventors' worries. De Forest pursued highly creative financial strategies to generate operating income for Phonofilm and soon ran afoul of the

United States Justice Department. Case left the organization, taking with him the patents for his own contributions to the system. Although de Forest's American company went bankrupt in 1926, he had licensed numerous international subsidiaries that continued to promote his system, and many moviegoers around the world experienced their first tantalizing taste of synchronized sound film in the late 1920s via Phonofilm installations.

Back in the United States, AT&T and General Electric shared legal access with de Forest to the technologies of vacuum-tube amplification and broadcast loudspeakers, and these companies simultaneously began to explore the development of sound pictures. GE researcher Charles Hoxie devised his own version of an optical sound recording system and euphoniously dubbed it the Pallophotophone. When the Radio Corporation of America was created in 1919 by merging the radio-related resources of GE and Westinghouse, the Pallophotophone was put to use recording music and speech for delayed radio broadcast. The company chose not to pursue its application to motion pictures.

Unlike RCA, the telephone company was interested in moving into the movie business. Experiments were made with both sound-on-film and sound-on-disc, but the engineers at Western Electric (the manufacturing subsidiary of AT&T) chose to focus on discs, taking advantage of the recording skills they had recently developed when they electrified the phonograph. A means of maintaining synchronization between camera, phonograph, and projector was devised, and by 1924, telephone salesmen were demonstrating the system to Hollywood's biggest players. Almost no one was interested. Virtually all of the industry's leaders had long since dismissed the viability of sound pictures, and the phone company was not about to change their minds. But while Paramount, MGM, and other first-tier studios all closed their ears to the new technology, a second-class outfit run by four brothers named Warner chose to listen.

In 1924, Warner Bros was a small but ambitious studio whose biggest asset was the canine action hero Rin Tin Tin. The studio had, however, recently initiated an aggressive campaign to become a dominant player in the production, distribution, and exhibition of films. Sam Warner was intrigued by the Western Electric sound film system and convinced his brothers that this was how their studio could make a name for itself: Warner Bros could use recorded sound to replace the live music heard in their theaters. Short films of Broadway's best vaudevillians could replace the less-than-stellar local fare offered in provincial theaters, and recorded orchestral scores for feature films could similarly replace the variable quality of musical accompaniment that was rendered in each individual house. By offering a standardized and high-quality musical program, the Warner brothers could transform every Warner theater—no matter how small or remote—into the equivalent of a "first run" house.

Warner Bros and Western Electric joined forces in 1925 to form the Vitaphone Corporation, and on 6 August 1926, Vitaphone presented its first program at the Warner Theatre in New York. The program opened with a filmed and recorded address by motion picture czar Will Hays, and a series of "high-class" musical shorts followed. The New York Philharmonic played Wagner's overture to *Tannhäuser*, and numerous other stars performed on screen and synchronized disc for the audience. Best received by far was tenor Giovanni Martinelli's dynamic rendition of the aria "Vesti la Giubba" from Ruggiero Leoncavallo's opera *Pagliacci*. The Vitaphone shorts were followed by the feature attraction, John Barrymore's *Don Juan*, a silent swashbuckler that was accompanied by a recorded, synchronized score of symphonic music with sound effects.

Musical shorts followed by a sync-scored feature also made up the second Vitaphone program a few months later, and this time the recorded performances of vaudevillians George Jessel and Al Jolson stole the show. Warner's competitors took note of the success of these films, but most producers remained convinced that Vitaphone was nothing more than a fad. Al Jolson's subsequent Vitaphone feature, *The Jazz Singer* (1927), would lead them to reevaluate this opinion.

In *The Jazz Singer*, musical shorts by Jolson himself were effectively inserted into a nontalking, sync-scored melodramatic feature. But when Jolson's character briefly conversed with his mother before bursting into song in one such segment, the possibilities of truly talking films became clear. As Richard Koszarski has shown, the fictional narrative of the film itself reinforced its technologically revolutionary impact. Jolson's character, Jack, is a modern, jazz-loving musician. His father, a tradition-bound cantor, disowns his sacrilegious son, and the climactic scene of the film occurs when Jack—now a star about to debut on Broadway—returns home to reconcile with his parents. In the famous talking sequence, his mother embraces his return and he woos her with snappy conversation and a jazzy melody. When the father encounters their revelry, however, he indignantly cries out, "Silence!" and the soundtrack goes silent for several long seconds before the old-fashioned background music returns. The reversion to intertitles for dialogue and the now-mute mimings of Jack on screen as he pleads with his father profoundly underscored the message that sound was the future and silence an affliction of those who would remain entrenched in the past (Koszarski 1989). This message was heard, loud and clear, by the film's audiences as well as by rival film producers.

By 1928, Hollywood fully realized that this new sound technology would not fade away like its predecessors. RCA now offered a sound-on-film system called Photophone to compete with Western's sound-on-disc, and the producer William Fox was turning out newsreels and features with Movietone sound provided by Theodore Case. Production of talking films increased dramatically during 1928 as studios raced to build sound stages, install sound equipment, and learn how to operate it. The number of theaters wired for sound grew, too, for exhibitors were now eager to present the new films. By 1932, only 2 percent of America's theaters remained silent (Hochheiser 1989).

Western Electric emphasized the connection between sound pictures and its older electroacoustic technologies by proclaiming the new system "a product of the Telephone." RCA similarly designated its sound films as "Radio Pictures" to highlight their acoustical pedigree. But the transition to sound in the movies was strikingly abrupt, and it focused consumers' attention in ways that these earlier technologies had not. The celebratory publicity and intense competition surrounding the different systems led listeners to listen more closely than ever before. As the *New York Times* noted, audiences became "sound conscious" as they critically consumed the new aural commodities that defined "modern life."

Sound Engineers and the Wiring of America's Theaters

It was an exciting time to be a sound engineer amid this acoustically self-conscious culture, and new job opportunities beckoned to acoustically inclined young men. Many were hired by ERPI, Electrical Research Products, Inc. (the subsidiary established by AT&T to handle its motion picture business), or by RCA to install and service sound systems in America's theaters, and many more clearly aspired to these positions. In 1929, ERPI received almost eight thousand applications. Only 432 of those who applied were offered employment, and while many of those hired came from within the Bell System, many others came from a wide range of backgrounds in radio, telephone, or electric power systems. The men were given three weeks of training before they were put to work in the field. They were taught the technical intricacies of the equipment as well as the basics of architectural acoustics. They were also taught to listen, and this "aural training," as it was called, enabled each engineer "to locate system troubles through his ability to recognize the lack of certain frequency ranges and to associate such disorders with equipment troubles which might cause them" (*Erpigram*, 1 May 1930, 5).

Upon completing his training and being sent into the field, the first thing an ERPI installation engineer did in converting a theater for sound reproduction was to perform an acoustical survey. He analyzed the auditorium's acoustical properties in order to recommend specific equipment for it and to suggest any architectural changes that might be required to ensure the quality of sound in the auditorium. The company newsletter, *Erpigram*, explained the procedure:

> In making the surveys, engineers are required to determine the exact volume and seating capacity, nature and thickness and amount of draping and decorating material used in the theatre, exact nature of all seats and furniture, etc. Also included is a noise survey and recommendations for eliminating all noises in the house. So complete is this survey, the report covers five pages and either accurate sketches or architects' drawings must be included in the survey reports. (15 December 1929, 3)

ERPI engineers were outfitted for this effort like big game hunters as they "went on the warpath with a full complement of weapons to banish the bogy Silence and his near relation, General Reverberation." "Each man," the *Erpigram* explained, "has been equipped with a large fibre knapsack in which to carry his equipment. Among other things, it contains a steel tape so that he may measure a house, and the structure with which he comes in contact will have to be analyzed for hidden horrors, such as 'plaster backed by brick.'" The kit also contained a cap pistol, to "hunt out Reverberation, and his Echoes, and banish him from the theater," so that the "T.I.," or Technical Inspector, could "leave the field a victor when the equipment is complete" (15 January 1930, 4). The ERPI engineers sent to inspect the Loew's Theatre in Canton, Ohio, might have felt as if they were truly on safari (20 July 1929, 5): the men heard a loud roar coming from the screen, and after "considerable time spent trying to trace the noise through the circuit" (as they had been trained), they discovered that it was coming from six caged lions that were being kept backstage!

By January 1929, more than 1,000 ERPI installations had been executed. At a rate of 250 more per month, the end of that year saw almost 4,000 total theater installations. The *Erpigram* noted, tongue-in-cheek, that the company was instituting a "humanitarian" policy of hiring only bachelors, in order to reduce the number of "ERPI widows." In fact, the majority of hires were young, single men, and the newsletter was filled with announcements of engagements, marriages, and births. The young men assigned to the Los Angeles area coveted the opportunity to work on private installations in the homes of movie stars like Douglas Fairbanks and Harold Lloyd, and they planned to hold a raffle to determine who would get the assignment if Clara Bow were to place an order for a system in her home (*Erpigram*, 20 March 1929, 2).

The work of the installation engineers was followed by that of the service engineers. Following the precedent of its handling of the telephone business, AT&T leased, rather than sold, its sound motion picture systems, and the follow-up service provided by the company was a strong selling point in the competitive market. Each service engineer was responsible for a geographic area and made regularly scheduled visits to each theater in his district, inspecting the equipment and correcting problems before they could interrupt a performance. William Schlasman covered the Albany–western Massachusetts–Connecticut district circa 1927–1928, and the care and enthusiasm with which he executed his work was remarkable. Although the historian steeped in twenty-first-century cynicism might tend to regard the hyperbolic rhetoric of a company organ like the *Erpigram* as little more than contrived corporate boosterism, Schlasman's papers indicate that such boosterism was, in fact, sincerely felt among the ranks of at least some ERPI engineers. It was clearly an exciting lifestyle for a young man—traveling constantly, staying in hotels, keeping in touch with headquarters through a stream of telegrams, and bringing the new technology to cities and towns that eagerly awaited its arrival. Schlasman telegraphed ahead to the manager of the Palace Theater in Fort Wayne, Indiana, prior to overseeing a Vitaphone opening there, with the announcement: "Will arrive Wednesday to help thrill invited guests with Vitaphone" (Schlasman, 12 April 1927).

Service engineers like Schlasman also handled technical emergencies, and the *Erpigram* is filled with dramatic stories of high-speed races and last-minute repairs to ensure that "The Show Might Go On." The ERPI men regularly suffered automobile accidents or were forced to talk their way out of speeding tickets with local police, and in special circumstances, parts and personnel were rushed in by boat, train, plane, or even dogsled, in the case of the engineer who covered the Alaska territory. The men were also responsible for following up on the instruction given to the projectionists who were in charge of operating the sound equipment, and Schlasman found that he often had to remind them of proper procedures—particularly with respect to the maintenance of the large array of batteries that powered the machinery. In some cases, the projectionists clearly resented being subject to this new authority. A Mr. Jarvis, for example, undertook a "heated and vigorous denunciation" of Schlasman when the engineer informed him that his batteries were poorly maintained. Theater managers sided with the ERPI engineers, however, and instructed their operators to defer to this outside authority in all technical matters (Schlasman, 9 November 1927).

The ERPI engineers' technical expertise endowed them with exceptional power, commanding respect and even gaining them entrée to places they otherwise would never have visited. In Montgomery, Alabama, for example, service engineer J. W. Borland was the only white person allowed to enter the "all-negro" Pekin Theatre. The theater manager, G. I. English, was a black vaudevillian who had once performed before royalty in England, and the establishment—although owned by a presumably white family named Seligman—was "'of, by, and for' negroes only." The exception made for Borland highlights the fact that there were no black ERPI engineers and it was thus necessary to admit a white engineer to inspect the sound equipment. But the *Erpigram*'s account presented Borland's access as if it were a privilege, accorded him as a result of his technical expertise (20 July 1929, 8).

The technical prestige enjoyed by the ERPI men turned easily to hubris, particularly when they described the reception given their new technology by people who—due to race or nationality—were perceived to be technologically unsophisticated. For example, the *Erpigram*'s account of opening night at the New Frolic Theatre in Jacksonville, Mississippi, noted: "It is doubtful whether the crowded audience of Negroes gave any thought to the hidden mechanical system that purveyed to them their entertainment,—nor could they have known that the installation of the equipment . . . was considered one of the most difficult ever made in the south" (20 February 1929, 6). Another account told of the frightened response by an audience of Native Americans at a theater in Yuma, Arizona, when an engineering test film consisting of high-frequency squeals and pops was accidentally projected in place of the opening reel of the scheduled feature (1 June 1930, 2).

This sense of superiority was only heightened when ERPI engineers traveled abroad. As early as December 1928, ERPI men were at work not only in Europe but also in Australia, India, the West Indies, and Brazil. The fanfare with which they were greeted and the adventures they experienced in these far-flung lands fueled their perception of their work as a technological mission. By wiring the world for sound, they believed they were installing a conduit to modernization that would soon enable these seemingly backward peoples to become more like themselves.

Wiring the World

The sound engineers' attitude toward their global mission was both captured and promulgated in the poem "Erpilog," by Baden Backhouse (*Erpigram*, 20 July 1929, 9):

> From Hollywood to Albuquerque,
> From Juneau to New York,
> Where movies flick across a screen
> No longer are they merely seen—
> For ERPI makes 'em talk!
>
> The cities of Australia
> All know the thrill of sound,
> While 'cross the pond in gay Paree
> They've introduced the word "talkee"—
> So ERPI's Europe-bound!
>
> The Chinaman neglects his joss,
> The Jap his hari-kari
> Mahomet's stocks are wearing thin
> For ERPI is established in
> The Lands of Rice and Curry!
>
> Quite soon among the Eskimos
> The fetish will be known,
> While mid-equator cannibals
> Leave cooking pots and Anabelles
> To hear the white sheet groan!
>
> Where nations lack a common bond
> And hate grows like a cancer,
> Who'll banish ignorance and strife
> And give the world new lease of life?
> Why, ERPI—is the answer!

Backhouse's poem describes a world of diverse peoples uniformly and enthusiastically abandoning their heritage and traditions in favor of the ERPI-enabled entertainments of "the white sheet," to the betterment of themselves and the world at large. The actual sending-off of the sound engineers to the four corners of the globe to complete this poetic modern mission was described more prosaically but in ways that explicitly evoked an earlier American endeavor to rescue world civilization—the deployment of American troops during the Great War. When the first group of ERPI engineers set sail for England in the summer of 1929, they were designated the "American Expeditionary Force." Four waves of "shock troops" were sent abroad, and news of the activities of this "flying squadron" of fifty "skilled engineers" appeared regularly in the *Erpigram* over the summer (20 June 1929, 1). The arrival of the engineers was equally newsworthy in the countries that received them. For example, when the "American experts" arrived in Sydney, Australia, they were greeted at the dock by a (silent) newsreel team. By August 1929, with an installation in a Cairo theater now under way, the newsletter could report that "Africa Falls Under ERPI's Advance," and with this installation the company claimed the last of all inhabited continents "in the course of penetration" (15 August 1929, 1). The northernmost ERPI-equipped theater was within sixty miles of the Arctic Circle, and the southernmost was located on the southern tip of the South Island of New Zealand. One single system, installed on an ocean liner, had circumnavigated the globe by May 1930.

The glamour of this global adventure affected even those who remained rooted in the United States. The workers in the shipping department at the Western Electric Hawthorne plant outside of Chicago, for example, experienced vicariously the excitement associated with the travels of the company's engineers. The department was, according to the *Erpigram*, "a scene of bustling activity":

> At the left of the room are some offices through the partitions of which escape music from the operas . . . and the latest jazz. Not bad to pack to the accompaniment of music! It adds fire to the imaginations already set off by the destinations marked on the boxes. That one over there goes to Geisha-land. These others are marked for mysterious India—lovely France—Sweden, the Land of the Midnight Sun—Egypt—Argentina—Canada.
>
> Special care has to be taken with these export shipments. Certain South American countries will not allow cases to enter that are packed with hay. Some governments require that cases be striped with blue paint and others

with gray paint. Dimensions and weights must be correct and there are other rules too numerous to mention. (1 April 1930, 2)

When the Western Electric equipment for Japan's first installation arrived on the docks in April 1929, a group of Japanese lawyers attempted to block its entry into the country. They argued to customs agents that the equipment violated patents held by a Japanese inventor, but their attempt to claim local technological sovereignty proved unsuccessful. ERPI engineer K. Kobayashi quickly and effectively disarmed their claims, and the equipment was soon on its way to an installation that would later be recognized by the emperor himself (*Erpigram*, 20 June 1929, 2).

The Japanese-born Kobayashi—the only non-Western ERPI engineer that I have encountered in the historical record—was clearly a valuable asset to the company. In most cases the company did not possess personnel with a native relationship to the destination country; instead, supervising engineers or agents who had at least some experience with the language or culture in each location were hired to assist the engineers. For example, ERPI engineer Pete Sheridan was accompanied on his trip to India by Colonel W. E. Dennis, who had previously spent several years there. Like Kobayashi, Dennis proved invaluable in moving the sound equipment through customs. Sheridan was also assisted in his technical and personal efforts by hired agents and by a personal servant named Sam (*Erpigram*, 20 December 1928, 1). It is also likely that the sound engineers worked with the agents for the various American film distribution companies that, by this time, had well-established foreign offices for arranging the exhibition of American films in theaters all over the world (Segrave 1997; K. Thompson 1985; Trumpbour 2002).

One can only assume that these agents and servants also served as translators, enabling the American engineers to instruct local electricians and carpenters how to install the equipment, as well as permitting them to teach local projectionists how to operate it. Sheridan learned at least how to swear in several Indian languages during his time abroad, but I have found no mention of any translation, by ERPI or Western Electric, of the English-language instruction manuals that were issued with the equipment. The goal was always to turn over all operations to the local theater staff as quickly as possible. In most cases, the Americans who were sent abroad spent no more than a week or so at any single location and returned to the United States after just a few months.

While away, however, these men wrote back with stories of the strange customs and habits of the people—theater workers and audiences—whom they met in their travels. Pete Sheridan, for example, noted the practice in India of "baptizing" the new equipment with coconut milk. This ceremony initially elicited his new vocabulary of Hindi profanities, but upon learning the intent of the ritual (and upon determining that the machinery was not damaged by it), he "fell thoroughly in love with the idea," because "it was meant to secure the propitious aid of the gods that the apparatus would operate properly" (*Erpigram*, 15 August 1929, 6).

The first showings of the new talking films were tremendously popular. Although the initial installations in many countries were generally made in theaters that catered, albeit not exclusively, to an expatriate European population, the crowds that gathered seeking admission on opening night proved far greater than this minority population alone would have generated. In Cali, Colombia, people were so eager to gain admission on opening night that a police force of thirty was unable to control them and they destroyed the theater's box office. "Such reception," noted the ERPI engineer who reported this story, "indicates that they like the talkies down here whether they can understand them or not" (*Erpigram*, 20 July 1929, 1). Though this sentiment proved true during the earliest days of sound motion pictures, it would not be long sustained. When audiences began to require from their talkies something more than the experience of an exciting new technology, the naïveté of the engineers' vision of one world, wired together in acoustical harmony and sociopolitical synchronization, was fully exposed. Indeed, before long, audiences around the world would be rioting against sound films, not for them.

For approximately the first year of global sound film, there were few alternatives to the American films that typically opened a newly wired house. The film industries in most European countries were still recovering from the devastations of the Great War, and most non-Western countries had yet to tool up for significant domestic film production. Many of these countries had exhibited primarily European films before the war. When hostilities shut down European production, American distributors took full advantage of the situation, enlisted the assistance of the federal government, and basically saturated the world market with the products of Hollywood (Jarvie 1992; Segrave 1997; K. Thompson 1985; Trumpbour 2002).

The emergence of sound film placed an additional financial burden upon European, Asian, and African producers struggling to compete, and so, during 1929–1930, the hegemony of Hollywood on the world's screens was only reinforced. India was serenaded with Universal's *Melody of Love;* Fiji came out for *Abie's Irish Rose*, and Shanghai showed *Love Parade, Rio Rita,* and *Hollywood Revue.* The preponderance of musicals during this period helped minimize the language problem, and westerns also played well, because they "concentrate on action, which is easily understandable to peoples of all lands" (*Movie Show Annual 1930* [India], 45). English-language musicals and westerns could captivate international audiences for only so long, however, and exhibitors soon began to devise creative methods for dealing with the language barrier newly imposed by the sound technology.

During the silent film era, the universal language of pantomime had ensured that motion pictures easily enjoyed an international market—indeed, American and European producers had depended upon this market to cover their costs and increase profits. Textual intertitles in English, French, Italian, or German were simply replaced with titles in the language native to the place the film was being shown. Japan integrated silent film into its distinct theatrical tradition by employing *katsuben* or *benshi*, live narrators who commented to theater audiences upon the action taking place onscreen. With the introduction of sound, this valued tradition was initially maintained, although, as one ERPI engineer reported, it turned some shows into a battle of "ERPI vs. Benshi," as the narrator struggled to be heard over the music and English dialogue pouring forth from the loudspeakers (*Erpigram*, 15 September 1929, 2; Anderson 1992; Kenji 1992). At the New Helen Theater in Shanghai, the manager constructed a booth in the auditorium in which he placed six Chinese performers who watched the film and carefully practiced simultaneous dialogue dubbing in their native language. During performances, they spoke, live, into microphones, and their voices were amplified and broadcast over the theater's sound system on top of the film's original soundtrack of music and non-Chinese language (*Erpigram*, 15 July 1930, 3).

American producers also began to experiment with releasing foreign versions of their films with integrated dubbed soundtracks, but the state of sound-editing technology circa 1930 rendered this process difficult and not very satisfactory. Dialogue subtitles were also explored, as in Egypt, where subtitles generated from a separate reel of film were run along the side of the screen. For English-language films, the subtitles were presented in French and Arabic; once French talking films became available, theaters provided subtitles in English and Arabic (*Erpigram*, 1 October 1930, 8). But audiences came to talking pictures expecting to listen, not to read, so subtitles—like dubbing—constituted a less than ideal solution to the language problem.

American producers—now fearful of the loss of their international market—briefly adopted the strategy of simultaneously producing multiple foreign-language versions of their feature films. Paramount dedicated a new studio at Joinville, France, to the production of these "multilinguals," and other studios brought French-, German-, and Spanish-speaking actors to Hollywood to re-create, scene for scene, the English-language features being produced there. These films, however, typically lacked the "star appeal" of the original productions, and they failed to generate the expected revenues abroad. By 1931, most studios had abandoned the practice as uneconomical (Durovicová 1992; Garncarz 1999; Vincendeau 1999). At this time, most European countries—and a few others, notably India—were able to offer their own domestic products to compete directly with the English-language American films.

In Europe, the sound film situation stimulated national governments to undertake action in support of the development of national film industries. Germany's courts successfully blocked both American sound systems and American sound films for over a year through the protection of rival sound-technology patents taken out by German engineers. Elsewhere, import quotas and taxes slowed the influx of American films, and laws were passed in France and Italy to protect both native workers and native speakers in the production of films within each country (Crafton 1997; Durovicová 1992; Gomery 1975; Higson and Maltby 1999; K. Thompson 1985).

Other countries now imported these films in addition to those from the United States, but they also began to produce their own. The film industry of India, in particular, began to flourish in the wake of the first Indian-produced talkie, *Alam Ara* (1931), and the production of this film was recalled with nationalistic pride upon its silver anniversary in 1956. "When I witnessed *Show Boat*," remembered director Shri Irani, "at the Excelsior [Theatre] in 1929, I was inspired to make a Talkie in India. . . . The project at first appeared too hazardous because in India we had absolutely no facilities, no equipment and no experience to start a sound film. But anyhow I decided to go ahead with the preparations as the temptation to make a picture in our own national language was simply irresistible" (*Indian Talkie 1931–1956*, 23).

Irani purchased a portable sound film recording setup, and he recalled that when this foreign equipment arrived at his Imperial Studios, "everyone felt that this was the dawn of a new age." Although he initially hired a foreign expert, Wilford Demming, to instruct him and his crew in the use of the sound system, by the time Irani was ready to shoot his film, Demming's expertise was no longer required, and *Alam Ara* was entirely and proudly the product of Indian labor. Its reception was tumultuous, and Indian film—particularly musicals like *Alam Ara*—was soon a vital and growing industry (Rajadhyaksha and Willemen 1999; Ramachandran 1985).

Within its boundaries, India reiterated the international language problem, because different populations spoke Hindi, Urdu, Telugu, and numerous other languages. Although sound films were produced in each of these many languages, one producer claimed that the growing prominence of Hindi films actually accomplished, within India, the ambitious international goal of unification that the ERPI engineers had projected. "The greatest achievement to the credit of our film industry," Shri Chandulal Shah claimed, "is the fact that the Talkie has been mainly responsible for spreading the Hindi language among the masses in every nook and corner of India. Provinces like Bengal and Madras were, literally speaking, taught Hindi through the Talkies" (*Indian Talkie 1931–1956*, 33–34).

Though I am not equipped to evaluate this claim, it is clear that talkie technology increasingly served the nationalistic agendas of numerous countries and colonies around the world over the course of the 1930s and beyond. Prem Chowdhry has characterized Indian cinema as a "nation space" that preceded the formation of the nation itself and has described how Indian films often explicitly challenged the views (and voices) of Indian colonials as presented in American and British films about "The Empire" (Chowdhry 1995: 11). In Greece, sound technology similarly proved a catalyst for the self-conscious creation of a definitively Greek cinema (Hess 2000). In Italy, Mussolini was one of the first to recognize the political usefulness of sound motion pictures, and the loudspeakers of Germany helped constitute National Socialism as they broadcast its messages to the German people. Non-Germans also reacted to the German voice as transmitted through sound picture technology. In Prague in 1930, German-language films instigated street demonstrations and the destruction of several theaters' interiors (Garncarz 1999: 255). French moviegoers reacted similarly against American English when the *Fox Movietone Follies of 1929* opened in Paris. There, too, displeasure at the sound of foreign dialogue filling a French theater precipitated protests that escalated into a mob riot and the destruction of the theater (Danan 1999: 230). Although the stars, stories, and songs of Hollywood—from Al Jolson and Gary Cooper to Humphrey Bogart and Shirley Temple—would ultimately survive this wave of protest and maintain a global presence through another great war and beyond, it is nonetheless clear that, with the introduction of sound, the internationalism of silent film was quickly replaced by a diversified market of national products.

By this time, however, the ERPI engineers were long gone. Experiencing only the euphoric initial reception of their technology by the many different peoples of the world, they failed to appreciate the complicated legacy that technology left in its wake. In his study of technology and colonialism in French Guiana, Peter Redfield charts the transformation, over the course of the twentieth century, of the modern "era of empire" into the postmodern "age of global connection" (Redfield 2000: xv). ERPI engineers operated within an age of empire. They understood their work through a thoroughly modern mentality, even as their work played a critical role in transforming the world into a postmodern network of global connections. For that brief moment when they traveled the globe, the engineers' dream that their sound technology would render harmony 'round the world seemed almost attainable. The new technology itself, as well as the flappers, gangsters, and jazzy melodies of the films it brought to life, embodied an idea of innovative modernity whose appeal was perceived to be universal. "You bet the world has changed," asserted the newsletter for the newly wired Capitol Theatre in Sydney, Australia, "and the Capitol is a 1929 example of the 'new' world—always there with the latest" (*Capitol News*, 19 May 1929, 3). The far reaches of the globe, it appeared, might be brought closer together through the machinations of Western—or, rather, Western Electric—technology.

Ultimately, this vision proved to be a chimera. While the new sound systems indeed provided a common materiality and stimulated technological progress in this sector around the world, they simultaneously enabled filmmakers in each country and colony to articulate—literally, to give voice to—their unique and often competing national characters. In striving for a transcendent international standard but also in falling short of that goal and instead reinforcing increasingly nationalistic tendencies, the "groans of the white sheet" were truly those of the modern condition.

Notes

1. See *Erpigram*, 20 July 1929, 2 (Tokyo), and 15 May 1930, 8 (Bundaberg), for representative photos of these parades.

2. This brief survey is a condensed version of that found in E. Thompson 2002: 235–248. See that work for citation of the numerous sources from which the survey is derived.

References

Abu-Samak, Mustafa Ahmed. 1995. *Al-madkhal li-dirasat al-khataba wa turuq al-tabligh fi al-Islam* [Introduction to the study of sermon delivery and the paths of proselytization in Islam]. Cairo: Dar al-Saba al-Muhamidiyya.

Ackerman, Diane. 1990. *A Natural History of the Senses.* New York: Random House.

Adorno, Theodor W. 1974. *Minima Moralia: Reflections on a Damaged Life.* London: New Left Books.

——. 1991 [1928]. "On the Fetish Character in Music and the Regression of Listening." In *The Culture Industry: Selected Essays on Mass Culture*, by Theodor W. Adorno. London: Routledge.

Anderson, J. L. 1992. "Spoken Silents in the Japanese Cinema, or, Talking to Pictures: Essaying the *Katsuben*, Contextualizing the Texts." In *Reframing Japanese Cinema: Authorship, Genre, History*, edited by Arthur Nolletti Jr. and David Desser, 259–310. Bloomington: Indiana University Press.

Anzieu, Didier. 1989. *The Skin Ego.* New Haven, CT: Yale University Press.

Aristotle. 1984. *On the Heavens (De Caelo)*, translated by J. L. Stocks. In *The Complete Works of Aristotle*, edited by Jonathan Barnes. Princeton, NJ: Princeton University Press.

Artaud, Antonin. 1993. *Le theatre et son double.* Paris: Gallimard.

Asad, Muhammed. 1980. *The Message of the Qur'an.* Gibraltar: Dar al Andalus.

Augustine, Saint. 1973. *An Augustine Reader.* Edited by John J. O'Meara. New York: Image Books.

Austern, Linda Phyllis. 1989. "'Sing Againe Syren'": The Female Musician and Sexual Enchantment in Elizabethan Life and Literature." *Renaissance Quarterly* 42: 420–448.

——. 2002. *Music, Sensation, and Sensuality.* New York: Routledge.

Bacon, Francis. 1626. *Sylva Sylvarum: Or, A Naturall Historie.* London: William Lee.

———. 2000 [1605]. *The Advancement of Learning.* Edited by Michael Kiernan. Oxford: Clarendon Press.

Badawi, Abdul Nazim. 1996. "Shurut al-intifa' bil-Qur'an" [Conditions for benefitting from the Qur'an]. *Al-Tauhid* 25 (4): 10–13.

Baggio, R. A. 1989. *The Shoe in My Cheese.* Melbourne: R. A. Baggio.

Barthes, Roland. 1985. "Listening." In *The Responsibility of Forms: Critical Essays on Music, Art, and Representation,* by Roland Barthes. Translated by Richard Howard. New York: Hill and Wang.

Barthes, Roland. 1991. *The Responsibility of Forms: Critical Essays on Music, Art, and Representation.* Translated by Richard Howard. Berkeley: University of California Press.

Baudrillard, Jean. 1993. *Symbolic Exchange and Death.* London: Sage.

Bauman, Zygmunt. 1993. *Postmodern Ethics.* Oxford: Blackwell.

Baumann, Max-Peter, and Linda Fujie, eds. 1999. "Hearing and Listening in Cultural Contexts." *The World of Music* 41, no. 1.

Beck, Guy L. 1995. *Sonic Theology: Hinduism and Sacred Sound.* Delhi: Motilal Banarsidass Publishers.

Beckett, Samuel. 1983. *Disjecta.* London: John Calder.

Beier, A. L., and Roger Finlay, eds. 1986. *London: The Making of the Metropolis 1500–1700.* London: Longman.

Benveniste, Emile. 1971. "Active and Middle Voice in the Verb." In *Problems in General Linguistics.* Translated by Mary Elizabeth Meek. Coral Gables, FL: University of Miami Press.

Berger, Anna Maria Busse. 1990. "Musical Proportions and Arithmetic in the Late Middle Ages and Renaissance." *Musica Disciplina* 44: 89–118.

Berger, John, and Jean Mohr. 1975. *A Seventh Man.* Harmondsworth: Penguin.

Bijsterveld, Karin. 2001. "The Diabolical Symphony of the Mechanical Age: Technology and Symbolism of Sound in European and North American Noise Abatement Campaigns, 1900–1940." *Social Studies of Science* 31 (1): 37–70.

Blacking, John. 1995. *Music, Culture, and Experience: Selected Papers of John Blacking.* Edited by Reginald Byron. Chicago: University of Chicago Press.

Blavatsky, H. P. 1971 [1888]. *The Secret Doctrine.* 6 vols. Adyar: Theosophical Publishing House.

Bloomfield-Moore, Clara. 1983. "Introduction." In *Keely and His Discoveries.* New York: Kegan Paul, Trench, Trübner.

Bohlman, Philip. 2000. "Composing the Cantorate: Westernizing Europe's Other Within." In *Western Music and Its Others: Difference,*

Representation, and Appropriation in Music, edited by Georgina Born and David Hesmondhalgh, 187–212. Berkeley: University of California Press.

Bolinger, Dwight. 1986. *Intonation and Its Parts: Melody in Spoken English.* Stanford: Stanford University Press.

Brakhage, Stan. 1982. "Interview with Richard Grossinger." In *Brakhage Scrapbook: Collected Writings,* edited by R. A. Haller, 190–200. New Paltz, NY: Documentext.

Branston, Gill. 2000. *Cinema and Cultural Modernity.* Buckingham: Open University Press.

Breathnach, C. S. 1998. "Richard Brocklesby FRS FRCP (1722–1797): Physician and Friend." *Journal of Medical Biography* 6 (3): 125–127.

Bregman, Albert S. 1990. *Auditory Scene Analysis: The Perceptual Organisation of Sound.* Cambridge, MA: MIT Press.

Brocklesby, Richard. 1749. *Reflections on Antient and Modern Musick, with the Application to the Cure of Diseases. To Which Is Subjoined, an Essay to Solve the Question Wherein Consisted the Difference of Antient Musick, from That of Modern Times.* London: Cooper.

Brodsky, Warren. 2002. "The Effects of Music Tempo on Simulated Driving Performance and Vehicular Control." In *Transportational Research Part F,* 219–241. New York: Pergamon Press.

Browne, Richard. 1729. *Medicina Musica: A Mechanical Essay on Singing, Music and Dancing. Containing Their Uses and Abuses, and Demonstrating by Clear and Evident Reasons, the Alterations They Produce in a Human Body.* London.

Bull, Michael. 2000. *Sounding Out the City: Personal Stereos and the Management of Everyday Life.* Oxford: Berg.

——. 2001. "Soundscapes of the Car: A Critical Ethnography of Automobile Habitation." In *Car Cultures,* edited by D. Miller, 185–202. Oxford: Berg.

Burch, Kerry, T. 2000. *Eros as the Educational Principle of Democracy.* New York: Peter Lang.

Burnett, Charles. 2000. "Spiritual Medicine: Music and Healing in Islam and Its Influence in Western Medicine." In *Musical Healing in Cultural Contexts,* edited by Penelope Gouk, 85–91. Guildford: Ashgate.

Burnett, Charles, Michael Fend, and Penelope Gouk, eds. 1991. *The Second Sense: Studies in Hearing and Musical Judgement from Antiquity to the Seventeenth Century.* London: Warburg Institute.

Burton, Robert. 1621. *The Anatomy of Melancholy.* Oxford.

Busoni, Ferruccio. 1962 [1907]. *Sketch of a New Aesthetic of Music.* In *Three Classics in the Aesthetic of Music.* New York: Dover.

Cage, John. 1961. *Silence.* Middletown, CT: Wesleyan University Press.

Cage, John, and Daniel Charles. 1981. *For the Birds.* Boston: Marion Boyars.

Calverly, Edwin. 1943. "Doctrines of the Soul (*Nafs* and *Ruh*) in Islam." *The Moslem World* 33 (4): 254–264.

Cantor, G. N., and M. J. S. Hodge, eds. 1981. *Conceptions of Ether: Studies in the History of Ether Theories, 1740–1900.* Cambridge: Cambridge University Press.

The Capitol News. Vol. 2, no. 7 (19 May 1929). Sydney, Australia. AMPAS Margaret Herrick Library, Beverly Hills, California.

Carter, Paul. 1992. *The Sound In-Between.* Sydney: New Endeavour/ University of New South Wales Press.

———. 1993. "The Native Informant." First broadcast on "The Listening Room," Australian Broadcasting Corporation FM-Radio, 29 July 1993. Citations from script (1–26) obtainable from author.

———. 1996. *The Lie of the Land.* London: Faber and Faber.

Chevrier, G. 1907. "Note sur les Gunas." *Transactions of the Second Annual Congress of the Federation of European Sections of the Theosophical Society, July 6–10, 1905,* 125–131. London: For the Council of the Federation.

Charney, Leo, and Vanessa Schwartz, eds. 1995. *Cinema and the Invention of Modern Life.* Berkeley: University of California Press.

Childs, G. Tucker. 1996. "Where Have All the Ideophones Gone? The Death of a Word Category in Zulu." *Toronto Working Papers in Linguistics* 15: 81–103.

Chittick, William C., ed. 1989. *The Sufi Path of Knowledge: Ibn al-'Arabi's Metaphysics of Imagination.* Albany: State University of New York Press.

Chou, Wen-Chung. 1971. "Asian Concepts and Twentieth-Century Composers." *Musical Quarterly* 53 (2): 211–229.

———. 1977. "Asian and Western Music: Influence or Confluence." *Asian Culture Quarterly* 5 (4): 60–66.

Chowdhry, Prem. 1995. *Colonial Cinema and the Making of Empire Cinema.* Manchester: Manchester University Press.

Christensen, Thomas. 1993. *Rameau and Musical Thought in the Enlightenment.* Cambridge: Cambridge University Press.

Classen, Constance. 1993. *Worlds of Sense: Exploring the Senses in History and across Cultures.* New York: Routledge.

———. 1997. "Foundation for an Anthropology of the Senses." *International Social Science Journal* 49: 401–412.

Clifford, James. 1986. "Introduction: Partial Truths." In *Writing Culture: The Poetics and Politics of Ethnography,* edited by James Clifford and George E. Marcus, 1–26. Berkeley: University of California Press.

Collingwood, R. G. 1976. *The Idea of* ␣ versity Press.

Columbus, Christopher. 1989. *The* Diario ␣ *Voyage to America, 1492–1493*. Translated ␣ Jr. Norman: University of Oklahoma Pres␣

Connor, Steven. 1997. "Feel the Noise: Excess, ␣ In *Emotion in Postmodernism*, edited by Gerha␣ Hornung, 147–162. Heidelberg: Universitätsv␣

——. 2000a. "Sounding Out Film." http://www.b␣ soundingout/

——. 2000b. *Dumbstruck: A Cultural History of Ventr␣* ␣. Oxford: Oxford University Press.

Copenhaver, Brian. 1988. "Astrology and Magic." In *The Cambridge History of Renaissance Philosophy*, edited by Charles B. Schmitt, Quentin Skinner, and Jill Kraye, 264–300. Cambridge: Cambridge University Press.

Cowart, Georgia, ed. 1989. *French Musical Thought*. Ann Arbor, MI: U.M.I. Research Press.

Cowell, Henry. 1969 [1929]. *New Musical Resources*. New York: Something Else Press.

Crafton, Donald. 1997. *The Talkies: American Cinema's Transition to Sound, 1926–1931*. New York: Charles Scribner's Sons.

Crary, Jonathan. 1999. *Suspensions of Attention: Attention, Spectacle, and Modern Culture*. Cambridge, MA: MIT Press.

Crooke, Helkiah. 1616. *Microcosmographia: A Description of the Body of Man*. London: Jaggard.

Crosby, Alfred W. 1998. *The Measure of Reality: Quantification and Western Society, 1250–1600*. Cambridge: Cambridge University Press.

Dahl, Oywind. 1999. *Meanings in Madagascar: Cases of Intercultural Communication*. Westport, CT: Bergin and Garvey.

Danan, Martine. 1999. "Hollywood's Hegemonic Strategies: Overcoming French Nationalism with the Advent of Sound." In *"Film Europe" and "Film America": Cinema, Commerce and Cultural Exchange, 1920– 1939*, edited by Andrew Higson and Richard Maltby, 225–248. Exeter: University of Exeter Press.

Danielson, Virginia. 1997. *The Voice of Egypt: Umm Kulthum, Arabic Song, and Egyptian Society in the Twentieth Century*. Chicago: University of Chicago Press.

Darrow, A. A., A. C. Gibbons, and G. N. Heller. 1985. "Music Therapy Past, Present, and Future." *American Music Teacher*, September– October: 18–20.

Debord, Guy. 1994. *Society of the Spectacle*. New York: Zone Books.

ᴋ. 1980. "Exegesis and Recitation: Their Development
̲̲al Forms of Qur'anic Piety." In *Transitions and Transforma-*
̲̲ *in the History of Religions*, edited by F. E. Reynolds and T. M.
Ludwig, 91–123. Leiden: E. J. Brill.

DeNora, Tia. 2000. *Music in Everyday Life*. Cambridge: Cambridge
University Press.

Denzin, Norman K. 1995. *The Cinematic Society*. London: Sage.

Derrida, Jacques. 1997. *Of Grammatology*. Baltimore, MD: Johns Hopkins
University Press.

Descola, Philippe. 1994. *In the Society of Nature: A Native Ecology in
Amazonia*. Cambridge: Cambridge University Press.

Drechsel, E. J. 1987. "Metacommunicative Functions of Mobilian
Jargon, an American Pidgin of the Lower Mississippi River Region."
In *Pidgin and Creole Languages*, edited by G. C. Gilbert, 433–444.
Honolulu: University of Hawaii Press.

DuGay, Paul, Stuart Hall, and Hugh Mackay. 1997. *Doing Cultural Studies:
The Story of the Sony Walkman*. London: Sage.

Dunn, Leslie C., and Nancy C. Jones, eds. 1994. *Embodied Voices:
Representing Female Vocality in Western Culture*. Cambridge: Cambridge
University Press.

During, Jean. 1997. "Hearing and Understanding in the Islamic Gnosis."
The World of Music 39 (2): 127–137.

Durovicová, Natasa. 1992. "Translating America: The Hollywood
Multilinguals, 1929–1933." In *Sound Theory/Sound Practice*, edited by
Rick Altman, 138–153. New York: Routledge.

Earle, Peter. 1989. *The Making of the English Middle Class: Business, Society
and Family Life in London, 1660–1730*. London: Methuen.

"Edison's Dream of a New Music." 1913. *Cosmopolitan* 54: 797–800.

Eliot, T. S. 1969. "The Family Reunion." In *The Complete Poems and Plays
of T. S. Eliot*. London: Faber and Faber.

Ellis, Catherine. 1964. *Aboriginal Music Making: A Study of Central
Australian Music*. Adelaide: Libraries Board of South Australia.

Erpigram. 1928–1932. Corporate newsletter of Electrical Research
Products, Inc. AT&T Archives, Warren, NJ.

Fabian, Johannes. 1990. *Power and Performance: Ethnographic Explorations
through Proverbial Wisdom and Theater in Shaba, Zaïre*. Madison:
University of Wisconsin Press.

Feld, Steven. 1990. *Sound and Sentiment: Birds, Weeping, Poetics, and Song
in Kaluli Expression*. Chicago: University of Chicago Press.

——. 1991. *Voices of the Rainforest* (compact disc). Rykodisc.

——. 1996. "Waterfalls of Song: An Acoustemology of Place Resounding
in Bosavi, Papua New Guinea." In *Senses of Place*, edited by Steven

Feld and Keith H. Basso, 91–135. Santa Fe: School of American Research Press.

——. 2000. "The Poetics and Politics of Pygmy Pop." In *Western Music and Its Others: Difference, Representation, and Appropriation in Music*, edited by Georgina Born and David Hesmondhalgh, 254–279. Berkeley: University of California Press.

Fenlon, Iain, ed. 1989. *The Renaissance: From the 1470s to the End of the Sixteenth Century. Man and Music.* London: Macmillan.

Ficino, Marsilio. 1989. *Marsilio Ficino: Three Books on Life.* Edited by Carol V. Kaske and John R. Clark. Binghamton, NY: Medieval and Renaissance Texts and Studies.

Fiumara, Gemma Corradi. 1990. *The Other Side of Language: A Philosophy of Listening.* Translated by Charles Lambert. London: Routledge.

Flichy, Patrice. 1995. *Dynamics of Modern Communication: The Shaping and Impact of New Communication Technologies.* London: Sage.

Foucault, Michel. 1972 [1969]. *The Archaeology of Knowledge.* Translated by A. M. Sheridan-Smith. New York: Pantheon.

——. 1994. *The Order of Things.* New York: Vintage Books.

Fox, Adam. 2000. *Oral and Literature Culture in England 1500–1700.* Oxford: Clarendon Press.

Franklin, C. H. H. 1907. "Vibratory Capacity, the Key of Personality." *Transactions of the Second Annual Congress of the Federation of European Sections of the Theosophical Society, July 6–10, 1905*, 329–343. London: For the Council of the Federation.

Friedberg, Anne. 1993. *Window Shopping.* Berkeley: University of California Press.

Friedrich, Paul. 1991. "Polytropy." In *Beyond Metaphor: The Theory of Tropes in Anthropology*, edited by J. W. Fernandez, 17–55. Stanford, CA: Stanford University Press.

Friedson, Steven M. 1996. *Dancing Prophets: Musical Experience in Tumbuka Healing.* Chicago: University of Chicago Press.

Fubini, Enrico, ed. 1994. *Music and Culture in Eighteenth-Century Europe: A Source Book.* Chicago: University of Chicago Press.

Gaffney, Patrick D. 1991. "The Changing Voices of Islam: The Emergence of Professional Preachers in Contemporary Egypt." *The Muslim World* 81 (1): 27–47.

Garncarz, Joseph. 1999. "Made in Germany: Multiple-Language Versions and the Early German Sound Cinema." In *"Film Europe" and "Film America": Cinema, Commerce and Cultural Exchange, 1920–1939*, edited by Andrew Higson and Richard Maltby, 249–273. Exeter: University of Exeter Press.

Geurts, Kathryn Linn. 2002. *Culture and the Senses: Bodily Ways of Knowing in an African Community.* Berkeley: University of California Press.

Girard, René. 1976. *Deceit, Desire, and the Novel: Self and Other in Literary Structure.* Baltimore, MD: Johns Hopkins University Press.

Gitelman, Lisa. 1999. *Scripts, Grooves, and Writing Machines: Representing Technology in the Edison Era.* Stanford, CA: Stanford University Press.

Goffman, Erving. 1981. "Footing." In *Forms of Talk,* by Erving Goffman, 124–159. Philadelphia: University of Pennsylvania Press.

Gomery, Douglas. 1975. "The Coming of Sound to the American Cinema: A History of the Transformation of an Industry." Ph.D. dissertation, University of Wisconsin, Madison.

Gomi, Taro. 1989. *An Illustrated Dictionary of Japanese Onomatopoeic Expressions.* Translated by J. Turrent. Tokyo: Japan Times.

Gouk, Penelope. 1991. "Some English Theories of Hearing in the Seventeenth Century: Before and After Descartes." In *The Second Sense: Studies in Hearing and Musical Judgement from Antiquity to the Seventeenth Century,* edited by Charles Burnett, Michael Fend, and Penelope Gouk, 95–113. London: Warburg Institute.

——. 1999. *Music, Science, and Natural Magic in Seventeenth-Century England.* New Haven, CT: Yale University Press.

——. 2000a. "Sister Disciplines? Music and Medicine in Historical Perspective." In *Musical Healing in Cultural Contexts,* edited by Penelope Gouk, 171–196. Guildford: Ashgate.

——. 2000b. "Music, Melancholy and Medical Spirits in Early Modern Thought." In *Music as Medicine: The History of Music Therapy since Antiquity,* edited by Peregrine Horden, 173–194. Guildford: Ashgate.

——. 2000c. "Beyond Rationality? The Paradox of Writing about Non-Verbal Ways of Knowing." *Intellectual News* 8: 44–57.

Graham, William A. 1987. *Beyond the Written Word: Oral Aspects of Scripture in the History of Religion.* Cambridge: Cambridge University Press.

Greenblatt, Stephen. 1991. *Marvelous Possessions.* Chicago: University of Chicago Press.

Guerrini, Anita. 2000. *Obesity and Depression in the Enlightenment: The Life and Times of George Cheyne.* Norman: University of Oklahoma Press.

Hass, Robert. 1994. *The Essential Haiku: Versions of Basho, Buson, and Issa.* Hopewell, NJ: Ecco Press.

Heath, Shirley Brice. 1983. *Ways with Words.* New York: Cambridge University Press.

Henry, John. 1997. *The Scientific Revolution and the Origins of Modern Science.* London: Macmillan.

Hess, Franklin L. 2000. "Sound and the Nation: Rethinking the History of Early Greek Film Production." *Journal of Modern Greek Studies* 18: 13–36.

Heyd, Michael. 1984. "Robert Burton's Sources on Enthusiasm and Melancholy: From a Medical Tradition to Religious Controversy." *History of European Ideas* 5: 17–44.

Higson, Andrew, and Richard Maltby, eds. 1999. *"Film Europe" and "Film America": Cinema, Commerce and Cultural Exchange, 1920–1939.* Exeter: University of Exeter Press.

Hinde, Julia. 2001. "Big Man versus Big Bang Theory." *Times Higher Education Supplement,* 15 June, 20–21.

Hirschkind, Charles. 1995. "Heresy or Hermeneutics: The Case of Nasr Hamid Abu Zayd." *Stanford Humanities Review* 5 (1): 35–49.

——. 2001a. "The Ethics of Listening: Cassette-Sermon Audition in Contemporary Egypt." *American Ethnologist* 28 (3): 623–649.

——. 2001b. "Civic Virtue and Religious Reasoning: An Islamic Counter Public." *Cultural Anthropology* 16 (2): 3–34.

Hochheiser, Sheldon. 1989. "AT&T and the Development of Sound Motion-Picture Technology." In *The Dawn of Sound,* edited by Mary Lea Bandy, 23–33. New York: Museum of Modern Art.

Hollingshead, John. 1895. *My Lifetime.* 2 vols. London: Sampson, Low, Marston.

Honneth, Axel. 1993. *The Critique of Power.* Cambridge, MA: MIT Press.

——. 1995. *The Fragmented World of the Social: Essays in Social and Political Philosophy.* Albany: State University of New York Press.

Horden, Peregrine, ed. 2000. *Music as Medicine: The History of Music Therapy since Antiquity.* Guildford: Ashgate.

Horkheimer, Max, and Theodor W. Adorno. 1973. *The Dialectic of Enlightenment.* London: Penguin.

Howes, David. 2003. *Sensual Relations: Engaging the Senses in Culture and Social Theory.* Ann Arbor: University of Michigan Press.

Howes, David, ed. 1991. *The Varieties of Sense Experience: A Sourcebook in the Anthropology of the Senses.* Toronto: University of Toronto Press.

Hull, A. Eaglefield. 1916. "A Survey of the Pianoforte Works of Scriabin." *Musical Quarterly* 2: 601–614.

Ibn Khaldun. 1958. *The Muqaddimah.* Translated by F. Rosenthal. New York: Pantheon.

Indian Talkie 1931–1956: Silver Jubilee Program. 1956. Bombay: Film Federation of India. AMPAS Margaret Herrick Library, Beverly Hills, CA.

Inoue, Miyako. 2003. "The Listening Subject of Japanese Modernity and His Auditory Double: Citing, Sighting, and Siting the Modern Japanese Woman." *Cultural Anthropology* 18 (2): 156–193.

Isakower, Otto. 1939. "On the Exceptional Position of the Auditory Sphere." *International Journal of Psycho-Analysis* 20: 340–348.

Israel, Paul. 1998. *Edison: A Life of Invention.* Chichester: Wiley.

James, Jamie. 1993. *The Music of the Spheres: Music, Science and the Natural Order of the Universe.* London: Little, Brown.

James, William. 1974. *The Varieties of Mystical Experience.* New York: Collins.

Janzen, John. 2000. "Theories of Music in African *Ngoma* Healing." In *Musical Healing in Cultural Contexts,* edited by Penelope Gouk, 46–66. Guildford: Ashgate.

Jarvie, Ian. 1992. *Hollywood's Overseas Campaign: The North Atlantic Movie Trade, 1920–1950.* Cambridge: Cambridge University Press.

Jenks, C., ed. 1995. *Visual Culture.* London: Routledge.

Jóhanneson, Alexander. 1958. *How Did Homo Sapiens Express the Idea of Flat?* Reykjavik: Fylgirit Arbókar Háskólans.

Johnson, Mark. 1987. *The Body in the Mind: The Bodily Basis of Meaning, Imagination, and Reason.* Chicago: University of Chicago Press.

Kahn, Douglas. 1992. "Histories of Sound Once Removed." In *Wireless Imagination: Sound, Radio, and the Avant-Garde,* edited by Douglas Kahn and Gregory Whitehead. Cambridge, Mass.: MIT Press.

——. 1999. *Noise, Water, Meat: A History of Sound in the Arts.* Cambridge, MA: MIT Press.

Kahn, Douglas, and Gregory Whitehead, eds. 1992. *Wireless Imagination: Sound, Radio, and the Avant-Garde.* Cambridge, MA: MIT Press.

Kant, Immanuel. 1974. *Anthropology from a Pragmatic Point of View.* Translated by Mary J. Gregor. The Hague: Martinus Nijhoff.

Kantor, Tadeusz. 1993. *A Journey through Other Spaces: Essays and Manifestos, 1944–1990.* Edited and translated by M. Kobialka. Berkeley: University of California Press.

Kassabian, Anahid. 2001. *Hearing Film: Tracking Identifications in Contemporary Hollywood Film Music.* New York: Routledge.

Kassler, Jamie C. 1995. *Inner Music: Hobbes, Hooke and North on Internal Character.* London: Athlone Press.

Katz, James, and Mark Aakhus, eds. 2002. *Perpetual Contact: Mobile Communication, Private Talk, Public Performance.* Cambridge: Cambridge University Press.

Kefala, Antigone. 1984. *Alexia: A Tale of Two Cultures.* Sydney: John Ferguson.

Keifenheim, Barbara. 2000. *Wege der Sinne: Wahrnehmung und Kunst bei den Kashinawa-Indianern Amazoniens.* Frankfurt: Campus.

Kenji, Iwamoto. 1992. "Sound in the Early Japanese Talkies." In *Reframing Japanese Cinema: Authorship, Genre, History,* edited by Arthur

Nolletti Jr. and David Desser, 311–327. Bloomington: Indiana University Press.

Kilian-Hatz, Christa. 2001. "Universality and Diversity: Ideophones from Baka and Kxoe." In *Ideophones,* edited by F. K. E. Voeltz and C. Kilian-Hatz, 155–163. Amsterdam: John Benjamins.

Kircher, Athanasius. 1650. *Musurgia universalis, sive ars magna consoni et dissone, in decem libros digesta.* 2 vols. Rome.

Kita, Sotaro. 1997. "Two-Dimensional Semantic Analysis of Japanese Mimetics." *Linguistics* 35: 379–415.

Kittler, Frederik. 1999. *Gramophone, Film, Typewriter.* Stanford, CA: Stanford University Press.

Koszarski, Richard. 1989. "On the Record: Seeing and Hearing the Vitaphone." In *The Dawn of Sound,* edited by Mary Lea Bandy, 15–22. New York: Museum of Modern Art.

Kozulin, Alex. 1986. "Vygotsky in Context." In *Thought and Language,* by Lev Vygotsky, xi–lxi. Cambridge, MA: MIT Press.

Kracauer, Siegfried. 1995. *The Mass Ornament: Weimar Essays.* Cambridge, MA: Harvard University Press.

Kumi, Shami Abdul-Aziz al-. 1992. *Al-sahafa al-Islamiyya fi Masr fi qarn al-tasi'a 'ashar* [Islamic journalism in Egypt in the nineteenth century]. Cairo: Dar al-Wafa'.

Kümmel, W. F. 1977. *Musik und Medizin: Ihre Wechselbeziehungen in Theorie und Praxis von 800 bis 1800.* Freiburg/München: Karl Alber.

Kunene, Daniel. 2001. "Speaking the Act: The Ideophone as a Linguistic Rebel." In *Ideophones,* edited by F. K. E. Voeltz and C. Kilian-Hatz, 183–191. Amsterdam: John Benjamins.

Lactantius. 1871. *The Works of Lactantius.* 2 vols. Ante-Nicene Christian Library, vols. 21 and 22. Translated by W. Fletcher. Edinburgh: T. and T. Clark.

Lakoff, George, and Mark Johnson. 1980. *Metaphors We Live By.* Chicago: University of Chicago Press.

Lane, E. W. 1984 [1863]. *Arabic-English Lexicon,* vols. 1 and 2. Cambridge: Islamic Texts Society.

Lastra, James. 2000. *Sound Technology and the American Cinema: Perception, Representation, Modernity.* New York: Columbia University Press.

Lawrence, Amy. 1991. *Echo and Nacissus: Women's Voices in Classical Hollywood Cinema.* Berkeley: University of California Press.

Lecourt, Edith. 1990. "The Musical Envelope." In *Psychic Envelopes,* edited by Didier Anzieu, translated by Daphne Briggs, 211–235. London: Karnac.

Levin, David Michael. 1993. *Modernity and the Hegemony of Vision.* Berkeley: University of California Press.

Lewin, Bertram D. 1946. "Sleep, the Mouth, and the Dream Screen." *Psychoanalytic Quarterly* 15: 419–434.

Linge, David E. 1977. "Editor's Introduction." In *Philosophical Hermeneutics,* by Hans-Georg Gadamer, xi–lviii. Berkeley: University of California Press.

Livingstone, Sonia M. 2002. *Young People and New Media: Childhood and the Changing Media Environment.* London: Sage.

Lockhart, James. 1994. "Sightings: Initial Nahua Reactions to Spanish Culture." In *Implicit Understandings: Observing, Reporting, and Reflecting on the Encounters between Europeans and Other Peoples in the Early Modern Era,* edited by S. B. Schwarz, 218–248. Cambridge: Cambridge University Press.

Lodge, Sir Oliver. 1909. *The Ether of Space.* New York: Harper and Brothers.

Lowe, Donald M. 1982. *The History of Bourgeois Perception.* Chicago: University of Chicago Press.

Lubet, Alex J. 1999. "Indeterminate Origins: A Cultural Theory of American Experimental Music." In *Perspectives on American Music since 1950,* edited by James R. Heintze, 95–140. New York: Garland.

Lull, James. 1990. *Inside Family Viewing.* London: Routledge.

MacDowell, Edward. 1912. *Critical and Historical Essays: Lectures Delivered at Columbia University.* Edited by W. J. Baltzell. Boston: Arthur P. Schmidt.

MacGaffey, Wyatt. 1994. "Dialogues of the Deaf: Europeans on the Atlantic Coast of Africa." In *Implicit Understandings: Observing, Reporting, and Reflecting on the Encounters between Europeans and Other Peoples in the Early Modern Era,* edited by S. B. Schwarz, 249–267. Cambridge: Cambridge University Press.

Madi, Jamal. 1995. *Al-da'wa al-mu'athira* [Effective preaching]. Mansura: Maktabat al-Wafa'.

Madigan, Daniel. 1995. Reflections on Some Current Directions in Qur'anic Studies. *The Muslim World* 85 (3–4): 345–362.

Madsen, Virginia. 1999. "The Call of the Wild." *In Uncertain Ground: Essays between Art and Nature,* edited by Martin Thomas, 29–49. Sydney: Art Gallery of New South Wales.

Mahfouz, Ali. 1979 [1952]. *Hidayat al-murshidin* [The guidance of the rightly guided]. Cairo: Dar al-A'itisam.

Majumdar, Barada Kanta. 1880. "Tantric Philosophy." *The Theosophist* 1 (7): 173–174.

Mannoni, O. 1956. *Prospero and Caliban: The Psychology of Colonisation.* Translated by P. Powesland. London: Methuen.

Mason, Herbert. 1986. *A Legend of Alexander* and *The Merchant and the Parrot*. Notre Dame, IN: University of Notre Dame Press.

McCarthy, Anna. 2001. *Ambient Television: Visual Culture and Public Space*. Durham, NC: Duke University Press.

McClary, Susan. 1995. "Music, the Pythagoreans, and the Body." In *Choreographing History*, edited by Susan Leigh Foster, 82–104. Bloomington: Indiana University Press.

McLuhan, Marshall. 1962. *The Gutenberg Galaxy.* Toronto: University of Toronto Press.

Merleau-Ponty, Maurice. 1962 [1945]. *The Phenomenology of Perception*. Translated by Colin Smith. London: Routledge.

Meyer-Baer, Kathi. 1984. *Music of the Spheres and the Dance of Death: Studies in Musical Iconology.* New York: Da Capo Press.

Meyer-Kalkus, Reinhart. 2000. *Stimme und Sprechkünste im 20. Jahrhundert.* Berlin: Akademie Verlag.

Moores, Shaun. 1993. *Interpreting Audiences: The Ethnography of Media Consumption.* London: Sage.

Morley, George. c. 1630. *MS Commonplace Book.* Westminster Abbey MS Dean and Chapter 41.

Movie Show Annual 1930. "India's National Guide to Motion Pictures." Vol. 2, no. 12 (April 1930). AMPAS Margaret Herrick Library, Beverly Hills, CA.

Mrazek, Rudolf. 2002. *Engineers of Happy Land: Technology and Nationalism in a Colony.* Princeton, NJ: Princeton University Press

Muhammed, Ali Rif'ai. 1972. *Kaifa takun khatib* [How to become a preacher]. Cairo: Maktabat wa Matbu'at Muhammed Ali.

Munrow, David. 1976. *Instruments of the Middle Ages and Renaissance.* Oxford: Oxford University Press.

Murdoch, Iris. 1977. *The Fire and the Sun: Why Plato Banished the Artists.* Oxford: Clarendon Press.

Niederland, William G. 1958. "Early Auditory Experiences, Beating Fantasies, and Primal Scene." *Psychoanalytic Study of the Child* 13: 471–504.

Noss, Phillip. 2001. "Ideas, Phones and Gbaya Verbal Art." In *Ideophones,* edited by F. K. E. Voeltz and C. Kilian-Hatz, 259–270. Amsterdam: John Benjamins.

Novaes, Sylvia Caiuby. 1997. *The Play of Mirrors: The Representation of Self as Mirrored in the Other.* Translated by I. M. Burbridge. Austin: University of Texas Press.

Nuckolls, Janis. 1993. "The Semantics of Certainty in Quechua and Its Implications for a Cultural Epistemology." *Language in Society* 22: 235–255.

——. 1995. "Quechua Texts of Perception." *Semiotica* 103 (1–2).

——. 1996. *Sounds Like Life: Sound-Symbolic Grammar, Performance, and Cognition in Pastaza Quechua.* New York: Oxford University Press.

——. 1999. "The Case for Sound Symbolism." *Annual Review of Anthropology* 28: 225–252.

——. 2001. "Ideophones in Pastaza Quechua." In *Ideophones,* edited by F. K. E. Voeltz and C. Kilian-Hatz, 271–285. Amsterdam: John Benjamins.

Oja, Carole J. 2000. *Making Music Modern: New York in the 1920s.* Oxford: Oxford University Press.

Ong, Walter J. 1958. *Ramus, Method, and the Decay of Dialogue.* Cambridge, MA: Harvard University Press.

——. 1965. "Oral Residue in Tudor Prose Style." *PMLA* 80 (3): 145–154.

——. 1970. *The Presence of the Word.* New York: Simon and Schuster.

——. 1981. *The Presence of the Word: Some Prolegomena for Religious and Cultural History.* Minneapolis: University of Minnesota Press.

Oresme, Nicole. 1968. *Le Livre du ciel et du monde.* Edited by Albert D. Menut and Alexander J. Denomy. Madison: University of Wisconsin Press.

Palisca, Claude V. 1985a. *Humanism in Italian Renaissance Musical Thought.* New Haven, CT: Yale University Press.

——. 1985b. "The Science of Sound and Musical Practice." In *Science and the Arts in the Renaissance,* edited by John W. Shirley and F. David Hoeniger, 59–73. Washington, DC: Folger Books.

——. 2000. "Moving the Affections through Music: Pre-Cartesian Psycho-Physiological Theories." In *Number to Sound: The Musical Way to the Scientific Revolution,* edited by Paolo Gozza, 289–308. Dordrecht: Kluwer.

Poole, Deborah. 1997. *Vision, Race, and Modernity: A Visual Economy of the Andean Image World.* Princeton, NJ: Princeton University Press.

Porush, David. 1993. "Voyage to Eudoxia: The Emergence of a Post-Rational Epistemology in Literature and Science." *SubStance* 22 (2–3): 38–49.

Prasad, Rama. 1894 [1889]. *Nature's Finer Forces: The Science of Breath and the Philosophy of the Tattvas.* Kila, MT: Kessinger Publishing.

Putnam, Robert. 2000. *Bowling Alone: The Collapse and Revival of American Community.* New York: Simon and Schuster.

"Quaere." 1866. "The Philosophy of Caning." *Notes and Queries* (3d series) 9 (April 14): 296.

Racy, Ali Jihad. 1998. "Improvisation, Ecstasy, and Performance Dynamics in Arabic Music." In *In the Course of Performance: Studies in the*

World of Musical Improvisation, edited by B. Nettl and M. Russell, 95–112. Chicago: University of Chicago Press.

Rahman, Fazlur. 1979 [1966]. *Islam.* Chicago: University of Chicago Press.

Rajadhyaksha, Asish, and Paul Willemen. 1999. *Encyclopedia of Indian Cinema.* London: Fitzroy Dearborn Publishers.

Ramachandran, T. M., ed. 1985. *Seventy Years of Indian Cinema (1913–1983).* Bombay: Cinema India-International.

Rasmussen, David M. 1971. *Mythic-Symbolic Language and Philosophical Anthropology.* The Hague: Martinus Nijhoff.

Raylor, Timothy. 1993. *Cavaliers, Clubs, and Literary Culture.* Newark: University of Delaware Press.

Redfield, Peter. 2000. *Space in the Tropics: From Convicts to Rockets in French Guiana.* Berkeley: University of California Press.

Rée, Jonathan. 1999. *I See a Voice: Language, Deafness and the Senses. A Philosophical History.* London: HarperCollins

Ricoeur, Paul. 1969. *The Symbolism of Evil.* Boston: Beacon Press.

Riskin, Jessica. 2002. *Science in the Age of Sensibility: The Sentimental Empiricists of the French Enlightenment.* Chicago: University of Chicago Press.

Roseman, Marina. 1993. *Healing Sounds from the Malaysian Rainforest: Teimar Music and Medicine.* Berkeley: University of California Press.

Rudhyar, Dane (Chenncvièc, Rudhyar D.). 1919. "The Two Trends of Modern Music in Stravinsky's Works." *Musical Quarterly* 5: 169–174.

——. 1922. "The Relativity of Our Musical Conceptions." *Musical Quarterly* 8 (January): 108–118.

——. 1930. "The Mystic's Living Tone." *Modern Music* 7 (3): 32–36.

——. 1931. *Liberation through Sound.* Brookline, MA: Hamsa Publications.

——. 1979 [1928]. *The Rebirth of Hindu Music.* New York: Samuel Weiser.

Russolo, Luigi. 1916. *L'Arte dei rumori.* Milan: Edizioni futuriste di "Poesia."

——. 1986 [1913]. "The Art of Noises Futurist Manifesto." In *The Art of Noises,* translated by Barclay Brown. New York: Pendragon Press.

Said, Edward. 1993. *Culture and Imperialism.* New York: Alfred A. Knopf.

Sandys, George. 1632. *Ovid's Metamorphosis Englished, Mythologized, and Represented in Figures.* Oxford: J. Lichfield.

Sawyer, Suzanne. 1997. "The 1992 Indian Mobilization in Lowland Ecuador." *Latin American Perspectives* 24 (3): 65–82.

Schafer, R. Murray. 1977. *The Tuning of the World.* New York: Knopf.

——. 1993. *The Soundscape: Our Sonic Environment and the Tuning of the World.* Rochester, VT: Inner Traditions International.

Schiesari, Juliana. 1992. *The Gendering of Melancholia: Feminism, Psycho-analysis, and the Symbolics of Loss in Renaissance Literature.* Ithaca, NY: Cornell University Press.

Schlasman, William H. 12 April 1927. Telegram. AT&T Archives, Warren, N.J., Western Electric Collection, Box 430, Location 100–09–01, Folder 3.

Schlasman, William H. 9 November 1927. Letter to R. M. Hatfield. AT&T Archives, Warren, N.J., Western Electric Collection, Box 430, Location 100–09–01, Folder 1.

Schmidt, Leigh Eric. 2000. *Hearing Things: Religion, Illusion, and the American Enlightenment.* Cambridge, MA: Harvard University Press.

Seeger, Anthony. 1981. *Nature and Society in Central Brazil: The Suyá Indians of Mato Grosso.* Cambridge, MA: Harvard University Press.

——. 2002. "Sounds, Social Organization, and Cosmology among the Suyá Indians of Mato Grosso, Brazil." Paper presented at the Wenner-Gren International Symposium "Hearing Culture: New Directions in the Anthropology of Sound."

Segrave, Kerry. 1997. *American Films Abroad: Hollywood's Domination of the World's Movie Screens from the 1890s to the Present.* Jefferson, NC: McFarland.

Sennett, Richard. 1990. *The Conscience of the Eye.* London: Faber.

Seremetakis, C. N. 1994. *The Senses Still: Memory and Perception as Material Culture in Modernity.* Chicago: University of Chicago Press.

Serres, Michel. 1997. *The Troubadour of Knowledge.* Translated by Sheila Faria Glaser with William Paulson. Ann Arbor: University of Michigan Press.

——. 1999. *Les cinq sens.* Paris: Hachette.

Al-Sha'b. 1995. "Mu'jazat al-Qur'an: Lafziyya aydan!" [The miracle of the Qur'an: Literal also!]. 21 February.

Shakespeare, William. 1988. *The Complete Works.* Edited by Stanley Wells and Gary Taylor. Oxford: Clarendon Press.

Shiloah, Amnon. 1963. *Characteristiques de l'art vocale arabe au moyen age.* Tel Aviv: Israeli Music Institute.

Silverstone, Roger. 1999. *Why Study the Media?* London: Sage.

Simmel, George. 1997. *Simmel on Culture.* London: Sage.

Siraisi, Nancy G. 1990. *Medieval and Early Renaissance Medicine: An Introduction to Knowledge and Practice.* Chicago: University of Chicago Press.

Sluga, Glenda. 1985. "Bonegilla Reception and Training Centre, 1947–1971." M.A. thesis, University of Melbourne.

Smart, Mary Ann, ed. 2000. *Siren Songs: Representations of Gender and Sexuality in Opera.* Princeton, NJ: Princeton University Press.

Smith, Bruce R. 1999. *The Acoustic World of Early Modern England: Attending to the O-Factor.* Chicago: University of Chicago Press.

Spitz, René. 1955. "The Primal Cavity: A Contribution to the Genesis of Perception." *Psychoanalytic Study of the Child* 10: 215–240.

Sterne, Jonathan. 2003. *The Audible Past: Cultural Origins of Sound Reproduction.* Durham, NC: Duke University Press.

Stobart, Henry. 2000. "Bodies of Sound and Landscapes of Music: A View from the Bolivian Andes." In *Musical Healing in Cultural Contexts,* edited by Penelope Gouk, 26–45. Guildford: Ashgate.

Stock, Brian. 1983. *The Implications of Literacy: Written Language and Models of Interpretation in the Eleventh and Twelfth Centuries.* Princeton, NJ: Princeton University Press.

Stoller, Paul. 1989. *The Taste of Ethnographic Things: The Senses in Anthropology.* Philadelphia: University of Pennsylvania Press.

Sutton, R. Anderson. 1996. "Interpreting Electronic Sound Technology in the Contemporary Javanese Soundscape." *Ethnomusicology* 40 (2): 249–268.

Szendy, Peter. 2001. *Écoute: Une histoire de nos oreilles.* Paris: Minuit.

Tatian. 1982. *Oratio ad Graecos* and *Fragments.* Edited and translated by Molly Whittaker. Oxford: Clarendon Press.

Taussig, Michael. 1993. *Mimesis and Alterity: A Particular History of the Senses.* New York: Routledge.

Thirsk, Joan. 1984. *The Rural Economy of England.* London: Hambledon.

Thomas, Keith. 1986. "The Meaning of Literacy in Early Modern England." In *The Written Word: Literacy in Transition.* Edited by Gerd Baumann. Oxford: Clarendon Press.

Thompson, Emily. 2002. *The Soundscape of Modernity: Architectural Acoustics and the Culture of Listening in America, 1900–1933.* Cambridge, MA: MIT Press.

Thompson, Kristin. 1985. *Exporting Entertainment: America in the World Film Market, 1907–1934.* London: BFI.

Todorov, Tzvetan. 1982. *Theories of the Symbol.* Translated by Catherine Porter. Ithaca, NY: Cornell University Press.

——. 1993. *On Human Diversity: Nationalism, Racism, and Exoticism in French Thought.* Cambridge, MA: Harvard University Press.

Tomas, David. 1990. "Collapsing Walls or Puffing, Smoking Sea Monsters? Ambient Sonic Spaces, Aural Cultures, Marginal Histories." *Public* 4–5: 125–140.

——. 1996. *Transcultural Space and Transcultural Beings.* Boulder, Col: Westview Press.

Tomlinson, Gary. 1993. *Music in Renaissance Magic: Toward a Historiography of Others.* Chicago: University of Chicago Press.

Trimbuk, Bulwant. 1879. "Hindu Music." *The Theosophist,* November, 46–50.

Truax, Barry. 1984. *Acoustic Communication.* Norwood, NJ: Ablex.

——. 1992. "Electroacoustic Music and the Soundscape: The Inner and Outer World." *In Companion to Contemporary Musical Thought,* vol. 2, edited by J. Paynter, R. Orton, P. Seymour, and T. Howell, 374–398. London: Routledge.

Trumpbour, John. 2002. *Selling Hollywood to the World: U.S. and European Struggles for Mastery of the Global Film Industry, 1920–1950.* Cambridge: Cambridge University Press.

Urry, John. 2000. *Sociology beyond Societies: Mobilities for the Twenty-first Century.* London: Routledge.

Vasse, Denis. 1974. *La Voix et l'ombilique.* Paris: Editions du Seuil.

Vincendeau, Ginette. 1999. "Hollywood Babel: The Coming of Sound and the Multiple-Language Version." In *"Film Europe" and "Film America": Cinema, Commerce and Cultural Exchange, 1920–1939,* edited by Andrew Higson and Richard Maltby, 207–224. Exeter: University of Exeter Press.

Viveiros de Castro, Eduardo. 1998. "Cosmological Deixis and Amerindian Perspectivism." *Journal of the Royal Anthropological Institute* (new series) 4: 469–488.

Voeltz, F. K. Erhard, and Christa Kilian-Hatz, eds. 2001. *Ideophones.* Typological Studies in Language 44. Amsterdam: John Benjamins.

Voss, Angela. 2000. "Marsilio Ficino, the second Orpheus." In *Music as Medicine: The History of Music Therapy since Antiquity,* edited by Peregrine Horden, 154–172. Guildford: Ashgate.

Wagner, Roy. 2001. *An Anthropology of the Subject: Holographic Worldview in New Guinea and Its Meaning and Significance for the World of Anthropology.* Berkeley: University of California Press.

Walker, D. P. 1⁰⁻ *Spiritual and Demonic Magic from Ficino to Campanella.* Lor⁻   ʼg Institute.

        ʼent Theology: Studies in Christian Platonism from the
        ʼteenth Century.* London: Duckworth.

        Spirits in Philosophy and Theology from Ficino
        du spectacle et histoire des ideés, 287–300. Tours:
        rieures de la Renaissance.

        ʼom Paracelsus to Newton: Magic and the Making
        ʼridge: Cambridge University Press.

        Music as Heard." *Musical Quarterly* (special

——. 1998b. ""Das Musikalische Hören" in the Middle Ages and Renaissance: Perspectives from Pre-War Germany." *Musical Quarterly* (special issue) 82 (3–4): 434–454.

Wehr, Hans. 1980. *A Dictionary of Modern Written Arabic.* Beirut: Libraire du Liban.

Welsch, Wolfgang. 1997. *Undoing Aesthetics.* London: Routledge.

Wenzel, Horst. 1995. *Hören und Sehen, Schrift und Bild: Kultur und Gedächtnis im Mittelalter.* Munich: Beck.

Whalen, D. H. 1981. "The Native Speaker and Indeterminacy." In *A Festschrift for Native Speaker,* edited by F. Coulmas, 263–278. The Hague: Mouton.

Williams, Alfred. 1984. *Life in a Railway Factory.* Gloucester: Alan Sutton.

Williams, Raymond. 2003 [1977]. *Television: Technology and Cultural Form.* New York: Routledge.

Winternitz, Emmanuel. 1979. *Musical Instruments and Their Symbolism in Western Art: Studies in Musical Iconology.* 2d ed. New Haven, CT: Yale University Press.

Woodroffe, Sir John (Arthur Avalon). 1969 [1922]. *Garland of Letters.* Madras: Ganesh.

——. 1995 [1918]. *The Serpent Power.* Madras: Ganesh.

Wright, Thomas. 1604. *The Passions of the Minde in Generall, Corrected, Enlarged, and with Sundry New Discourse Augmented.* London.

——. 1986 [1604]. *The Passions of the Mind in General.* Edited by W. Webster Newbold. New York: Garland.

Zumthor, Paul. 1990. *Oral Poetry: An Introduction.* Minneapolis: University of Minnesota Press.

Contributors

Michael Bull is a lecturer in media studies at the University of Sussex. He is the author of *Sounding Out the City: Personal Stereos and the Management of Everyday Life* (Berg, 2000) and the co-editor of *The Auditory Culture Reader* (Berg, 2003). He is presently writing a monograph on a range of mobile sound technologies entitled *Mobilising the Social: Technology and the Sounds of Urban Experience.*

Paul Carter is a writer and artist. He recently wrote *Repressed Spaces: The Poetics of Agoraphobia* (Reaktion Books, 2002), and his newest title is *Material Thinking: Local Invention and Creative Culture* (Melbourne University Publishing, 2004). He is currently writing an imaginary history of parrots. His public artwork *Nearamnew,* a plaza ground pattern with inscribed texts, opened at Federation Square, Melbourne, in 2002. In 2004 he co-directed a four-language stage adaptation of his radio work "What Is Your Name," with Prompt! Berlin. He is a research professor in the faculty of Architecture, Building and Planning at the University of Melbourne.

Steven Connor is a professor of modern literature and theory at Birbeck College, London. He is a writer and broadcaster for radio and the author of books on Dickens, Beckett, Joyce, and postwar British fiction, as well as of *Postmodernist Culture* (Blackwell, 1989), *Theory and Cultural Value* (Blackwell, 1992), *Dumbstruck: A Cultural History of Ventriloquism* (Oxford University Press, 2000), and *The Book of Skin* (Reaktion Books, 2003).

Veit Erlmann teaches ethnomusicology and anthropology at the University of Texas at Austin. He is the author of several books on South African music, the latest being *Music, Modernity, and the Global Imagination: South Africa and the West* (Oxford University Press, 1999). He is currently working on a book on the cultural history of the ear.

231

Penelope Gouk is a Senior Wellcome Researcher in the History of Medicine at the University of Manchester. She is currently writing about changing medical explanations for music's effects on human nature between the Renaissance and the Enlightenment. Her publications include *Musical Healing in Cultural Contexts* (Ashgate, 2000), *Music, Science and Natural Magic in Seventeenth-Century England* (Yale University Press, 1999), and *The Ivory Sundials of Nuremberg, 1500–1700* (Whipple Museum, Cambridge, 1988).

Charles Hirschkind teaches anthropology at the University of California, Berkeley. His work addresses issues of politics, language, media, and the cultural organization of sensory experience within contemporary Islam in Egypt. He is currently completing a book entitled *The Ethics of Listening: Cassette-Sermons and Islamic Revival in Contemporary Egypt*.

Douglas Kahn is director of Technocultural Studies at the University of California at Davis. He is the author of *Noise, Water, Meat: A History of Sound in the Arts* (MIT Press, 1999) and co-editor of *Wireless Imagination: Sound, Radio, and the Avant-garde* (MIT Press, 1992).

Janis B. Nuckolls is a linguistic anthropologist with a broad interest in poetic forms and processes of all kinds. Her linguistic work has focused upon a dialect of Quechua spoken in Amazonian Ecuador. She has also conducted fieldwork in India and Japan. Her particular interest in ideophones has motivated much of her published work. Her next book will explore ideophones as a sociocultural phenomenon and will grapple with issues revolving around the language and nature debates and with the matter of sound symbolism generally.

Bruce R. Smith, a professor of English at the University of Southern California, is the author of *The Acoustic World of Early Modern England* (1999). A Guggenheim Fellow in 2001–2002, he is completing a book on passionate perception in early modern culture. The color green forms the focus of the study.

Emily Thompson is a historian whose work focuses on sound technology and cultures of listening. She is the author of *The Soundscape of Modernity: Architectural Acoustics and the Culture of Listening in America, 1900–1933* (MIT Press, 2002) and is currently writing a book about the transition to sound in the American motion-picture industry.

Index